Black Female Sexualities

Black Female Sexualities

EDITED BY
TRIMIKO MELANCON
AND
JOANNE M. BRAXTON

Foreword by
Melissa Harris-Perry

RUTGERS UNIVERSITY PRESS
NEW BRUNSWICK, NEW JERSEY, AND LONDON

Library of Congress Cataloging-in-Publication Data

Black female sexualities / edited by Trimiko Melancon, Joanne M. Braxton ; foreword by Melissa Harris-Perry.

     pages cm

  Includes bibliographical references and index.

    ISBN 978–0-8135–7174–4 (hardback)—ISBN 978–0-8135–7173–7 (pbk.)—ISBN 978–0-8135–7175–1 (e-book)

    1. African American women—Sexual behavior. 2. African American women—Social conditions. 3. Sex role. 4. Identity (Psychology) 5. Feminism. I. Melancon, Trimiko, editor of compilation. II. Braxton, Joanne M., editor of compilation.

HQ29.B557 2015

305.48'896073—dc23

2014017499

A British Cataloging-in-Publication record for this book is available from the British Library.

Visit our website: http://rutgerspress.rutgers.edu

Manufactured in the United States of America

Contents

Foreword

Melissa Harris-Perry

At the turn of the twentieth century, W. E. B. Du Bois captured the soul-splitting experience of reconciling blackness with American identity by describing double consciousness as "this sense of always looking at one's self through the eyes of others, of measuring one's soul by the tape of a world that looks on in amused contempt and pity."[1] While Du Bois delineated this spiritual striving of the black self to find wholeness, particularly in light of a malevolent racial gaze, he did not fully imagine the particular forms of psychological, physical, and sexual threats confronting black women and their bodies by racist, sexist, and imperialist eyes and, indeed, practices.

Black Female Sexualities addresses, in the spirit of the long history of feminist traditions, conceptualizations and consequences of the power of the racial gaze. It does so by bringing together the work of scholars who interrogate both the power of looking—the act of spectatorship—and the experiences of being looked at for African American women. Kimberly Juanita Brown prefaces her chapter for this volume, "Entering through the Body's Frame," by quoting bell hooks's observation that "there is power in looking."[2] This idea of the power in looking and the experience of powerlessness that so many black women experience when being looked at—especially as these relate to sexual politics, race, and the sociosexual—is central to this volume.

For many, the treatment of Saartjie Baartman, the so-called Hottentot Venus, stands as a warning of the exploitive possibilities inherent in being looked upon by those who find black women's bodies to be savage oddities or sexual commodities worthy of both visual and physical dissection. Baartman was a Khoikhoi woman from South Africa who became a canonized exhibit at London's Piccadilly Circus as a result of her supposedly abnormal sexual organs. Her large buttocks and elongated labia subjected her to exhibition and public ridicule. After her death, French anthropologist Georges Cuvier dissected her and crafted body casts of her sexual organs in an attempt to garner evidence for theories of essentialized racial (and by extension sexual) difference. As a result of Cuvier's work, Baartman's remains were on display for public view in a French museum until the mid-1970s. More than a century after her death, Baartman was still exposed to dehumanizing patriarchal and racist observation.

In the same decade that Baartman's remains were finally removed from public display and returned to South Africa for burial, American writer Toni Morrison published her first novel, *The Bluest Eye* (1970), which illuminates the dangers to black girls of the gaze of sinister others. Morrison shows us the destructive capacity of a white racist gaze that changes a tender, consensual first sexual encounter into a violent rape rendered open to spectatorship. Morrison describes an adolescent Cholly Breedlove and his girl Darlene exploring one another's bodies with affectionate and privately intimate gentleness when they are happened upon by two white men who demand that Cholly "get on wid it. An' make it good, nigger."[3] Through their abusive looking and threats at gunpoint, the men make Cholly the instrument of rape—of their own desire for sexualized violence against young Darlene vicariously through Cholly. Their gaze turns innocence, Cholly and Darlene's organic sensual intimacy and desire, into violence.

Morrison forces readers to ride the spiral of violence all the way to Cholly Breedlove's later rape—one that begins with his look, a seemingly innocent stare at his eleven-year-old daughter Pecola as she hunches over the sink washing dishes. The rape is initiated when Cholly observes Pecola scratching the back of her calf with her toe, a gesture he saw Pecola's mother make when he first met her. Observing Pecola's physical posture simultaneously shames and seduces Cholly and culminates in his doing the unthinkable: dragging the girl to the floor, raping her, and ultimately impregnating her in a sinister act he considers love. For Pecola, it is far from safe to be seen, to be merely looked upon, even by her own father, even in her own home.

These stories represent the vulnerability and the violence, sexual and otherwise, that so frequently punctuate black women's experiences of being seen. Du Bois worried about the amused contempt and pity of the onlooking world; bell hooks acknowledged the power of both looking and the oppositional gaze; and other black women have documented the malice and brutality that accompanies the visual engagement, the ocular assaults, and the gaze of others. As Kimberly Juanita Brown writes in her chapter for this book, "People are too comfortable with black women in various states of sexual violence and unrest, too comfortable with their dismemberment and their utter corporeal destruction." The 2014 Hollywood awards season produced an example of this comfort with black women's "utter corporeal destruction." In 2014, the film adaptation of Solomon Northup's memoir, *12 Years a Slave,* was a standout of the film awards season. At the heart of this powerful cinematic achievement was the grotesque psychological, sexual, and physical abuse of an enslaved black woman played by

the extraordinary actor Lupita Nyong'o. Although Nyong'o's on-screen endur-
ance of unfathomable cruelty earned her a well-deserved Academy Award and
much critical praise, these accolades telegraphed the ongoing message that the
viewing public is most interested in seeing black women's bodies when they are
subjected to ferocious terror.

But the experiences of black women's bodies are not exclusively those of
destructive assault or morbid fascination. To be an embodied black woman is
also to know joy, subjectivity, pleasure, and the latent capacity to enjoy being
seen: to, in a sense, transcend invisibility and to resist erasure. Even, then, as
viewers were given opportunities to wallow in black women's suffering in 2013,
and such cinematic enactments were awarded in 2014, a strikingly complex,
discordant representation of black women's experiences with controlling and
"disengaging the gaze" was occasioned in the surprise release of the self-titled
visual album by megasuperstar Beyoncé Knowles on December 13, 2013. Beyoncé's fifth album is notable in large part because each of the fourteen musical
tracks includes an accompanying video: a gesture with which Beyoncé insists
that she be not only heard but, equally important, also be seen.

The videos invite a breathtaking, almost uncomfortable level of intimate
spectatorship. In "Pretty Hurts," for instance, Beyoncé addresses the pain, at once
physical and visceral, women experience when their value is connected solely
and superficially to looks and aesthetics, to meeting the beauty status quo and
standards about women's body image. More importantly, this track explores
what is at stake in pleasing those who want to look at them and, in so doing,
inflict pain.[4] In the track "Blue," titled for her daughter, Beyoncé allows viewers
to participate in the visible manifestations of her maternal adoration and her
own complex embodiment of womanhood. It provides a glimpse, on the one
hand, of the reproductive aspects of her sexuality (her daughter) and her role
as mother, coupled with a sensuality that resists simplistic conceptualizations
of black women's sexualities.[5] More critically, she uses the video to present a
micro-ethnography of Afro-Diaspora dance traditions that reframe the body:
celebrating the gyrating, booty-shaking, and twerking in movements that highlight the ample backsides of black women that we see in so many popular music
videos, including Beyoncé's own work. By forcing viewers to encounter these
actions in the innocent, joyful, street dance of Afro-Brazilian children, "Blue"
strips ass-shaking of the lewd sexual implications and skewed misreading that
the American and larger Western gaze imposes. Through the almost jarring pair-
ing, then, of the maternal ballad with swift posterior gyrations, the movements
suddenly resonate as joyful, playful, and indeed sociocultural rather than as a
myopic indication of untamed, illicit sexuality. The inversion is achieved only in
the visual portrayal of the song, in the very power that accompanies looking, that
otherwise does not occur when the music is encountered sonically. This lesson
requires looking.

Nowhere does Beyoncé's album more fully demand black female autonomy in defining the terms of spectatorship—the oppositional gaze, if you will—than in "Partition."[6] The track opens with a dolled-up Beyoncé, an image that alludes to and transforms the notion that "pretty hurts," sitting at the end of a long table laden with breakfast. Her love interest is hidden behind a newspaper, oblivious to her red lips, curled hair, and provocatively draped robe. The viewer is sucked into a powerful, almost pornographic and titillating series of lyrics and images as a scantily clad Beyoncé dances for and arouses her man, all the while available for public consumption. The video seems to be an open invitation to fully view her sexuality, but the lyrics, and the title "partition" itself, offer an important boundary and caveat. In the first line Beyoncé demands that her driver put the "partition" up "please," in order to prevent "you [from] seeing" her "on her knees." Replete with sexual innuendo, the lyric both reveals what is to happen behind the partition and demands a right to act with some measure of privacy. It is a reminder that we are allowed to look, but only on her terms and only through a lens of her design. Like the partition itself, she acts as the entity that controls and even guards: defining her sexuality while simultaneously exercising ownership of its boundaries and accessibility. "Partition" is electric, not only in its embrace of sexuality but also in its suspense: it is entirely fantasy, a performance that takes place in thought, not action. As the video ends, Beyoncé is still sitting at the end of the table. Her love interest is still reading the paper. What we have seen is her sexual reverie. She exposes the intimacy of her thoughts and desires while also elucidating the ways in which the gaze is not reliable: it is fallible and susceptible to error (as in the misreading of gyrating black bodies). Also, it does not always capture the essence or reality of its own ocular fixation. Even, then, as her performance for her man and for us has unfolded in her mind, occurring behind a partition that she controls, she invites, mediates, and encourages spectatorship of her sexuality as she deems fit. What can feel on first view like a reproduction of a troubling "Hottentot Venus" act—with black female sexuality on display in ways that seemingly reaffirm myths of black female hypersexuality—is a more nuanced representation of the body, since the locus of control remains with Beyoncé herself.

Beyoncé's fifth album is complicated, especially in its problematization of hegemonic expressions of sexuality, race, and gender. It is a pop culture intervention worth pausing to consider, as it challenges, as do the engaging chapters of this book, the almost universal cultural notion of black women's bodies as mired inevitably in violence and sexual dehumanization that compromise their sexual agency, subjectivity, and control. Beyoncé counters the narratives that black women who are seen must be broken, that they are unequivocal victims of the gaze, or that they do not possess ownership of their intimate desires and sexual pleasures. Instead, with her self-titled album, *Beyoncé*, she not only privileges an actualized and sexualized self (hence the eponymous title) but also evidences that black women can invite watching, even ogling, and maintain a space for pleasure and autonomy across a spectrum of possibilities.

These reflections, ranging from Saartjie Baartman to a contemporary pop icon, barely break the surface of the rich terrain and intellectual coverage that constitute the remainder of this volume. These authors interrogate the multiple spaces black women occupy: from popular culture and college classrooms to the pages of novels and cultural discourses in ways that also illuminate their complex sexual identities, choices, and gender presentations. They question how black girls can grow into women under the weight, literally—see Courtney J. Patterson's chapter on body size—of cultures that seem to despise while also challenging us to redefine freedom and sexual citizenship from the perspective of black women. For when "we prioritize, foreground, and place black women at the center of cultural discourse, popular culture, and in both public and private arenas," to evoke Trimiko Melancon's introduction, we honor the spirit, complexities, and totality of black women instead of diminishing them or the range of their unique experiences and desires. The scholars represented in this book demand accountability for sexual violence committed against black women while insisting on black women's right to enjoy and explore the fullness of their sexualities. This book is not simple. It is not easy. It is not uncomplicated. But how could it be? It is about black women's bodies.

NOTES

1. W. E. B. Du Bois, *The Souls of Black Folk* (Chicago: McClurg, 1903), 3.
2. bell hooks, *Black Looks: Race and Representation* (Boston: South End Press, 1992), 115.
3. Toni Morrison, *The Bluest Eye* (New York: Plume, 1970), 148.
4. Beyoncé Knowles, *Pretty Hurts,* Columbia Records, 2013.
5. Beyoncé Knowles, *Blue,* Columbia Records, 2013.
6. Beyoncé Knowles, *Partition,* Columbia Records, 2013.

"somebody almost walked off wid alla my stuff"*

BLACK FEMALE SEXUALITIES AND BLACK FEMINIST INTERVENTION

Trimiko Melancon

Definitions belong to the definers, not the defined.

—*Toni Morrison*

I still remember with unobstructed vividness screening Lee Daniels's 2009 film *Precious: Based on the Novel Push by Sapphire*. It was a Saturday matinee in New York City's Union Square with two of my dearest black women friends. As we navigated the long ticket line, we noticed an audience as diverse in terms of demographics as it was in its responses to the myriad scenes in the film: at times silence and tears, at others applause and laughter. Even more indelible is the incredibly unsettling feelings my friends and I experienced as we shifted out of the theatre at the film's closing. The heaviness, that visceral feeling, was not simply a reflection of the gravity of the movie's content and its simultaneous tragic, graphic, and quasi-triumphant scenes. Rather, it was the kind of inundation of spirit that accompanied the reality that we had witnessed a narrative, an adaptation of a feminist text—a rendition of Sapphire's novel and black women's sexualities—in the hands, interpretations, and mediation of a male director. What was absent, in other words, was the narrative presented from the authentic perspective and cinematic vantage point of the very subjects, the protagonists, of the film (and the novel itself): black women. Coming to terms with the cinematic adaptation of black women's experiences and sexualities, forced access and

---

* Ntozake Shange

journey to subjectivity, through the (black) male imagination felt like a double tragedy, a multiple violation of sorts that necessitated that we, upon leaving the theater, not only debrief but do so over alcohol.

By contrast, I recall very little in terms of my screening nearly a year later of Tyler Perry's *For Colored Girls*, which in its opening weekend in November 2010 grossed nearly $21 million. My lack of recollection of the specificity of the experience is, as I ruminate in hindsight, a kind of willed and strategic disengagement, a result of my skepticism about Perry's capacity to replicate—to do justice to the eloquence, poeticism, feminist politics, artistic genius, and complexities of black women's lives and sexualities in—Ntozake Shange's groundbreaking 1975 choreopoem *For Colored Girls Who Have Considered Suicide When the Rainbow Is Enuf.* As I watched the film, my sense of disengagement transmuted into indignation as my reservations concretized and were proven by Perry's cinematic treatment of Shange's work. How was it that a piece as rich, vibrant, and complex as Shange's in its presentation of the dynamics governing black women's lives, experiences, and sexualities, which ranged from the tragic to the liberatory, could be so compromised and misrepresented—even defiled? Where was the depth and range? And why, in Perry's rendition, were all expressions of black female desire and sexual intimacies met invariably with castigation? Accompanied, that is, not by complexity, agency, empowerment, or pleasure but rather by punitive measures not reflective of the authenticity or the unfolding of Shange's choreopoem. In Perry's adaptation, when the women on the screen—the ladies of color, literally and figuratively (whose names spanned the color palate from "Lady in Yellow" to "Lady in Purple"), engaged in sex, they confronted everything from unwanted pregnancy (and a near-death back-alley abortion), rape, and exposure to a sexually transmitted disease that later compromised fertility to sexual dehumanization and, far worse, the contraction of HIV. Regardless of Tyler Perry's directorial intentions or his ideological convictions, his cinematic adaptation of *For Colored Girls* is rife with a masculinist construction and interpretation of black women's sexualities that not only mediate but, far more deleterious, define black women's sexual politics and erotics of desire. That is, his treatment, whether consciously or inadvertently, imputes a fundamentalist-like, misogynist, and heteronormative sensibility that punishes black women who operate in the sociosexual realm.

Little did I know that my screenings of *For Colored Girls* and *Precious* would be the instances, the temporal moments that would mark the genesis of this collection. *Black Female Sexualities* is the product of those catalyzing moments reflective of a particular exigency, the very need for black feminist intervention in the routine, inauthentic (mis)representations of black women's sexualities by men and others. Moreover, it underscores the need for the telling of black women's narratives, sexual especially and otherwise, by black women so that our stories reflect the range and totality of our sexualities, our agency and subjectivity in defining the terms of our experiences as sexual citizens, and in shaping and problematizing representations of our intimate lives and sexual identities. For as the opening epigraph emphasizes, "Definitions belong to the definers, not the defined." It is this sensibility that encapsulates the spirit of this collection, which could not be more pressing than in this current moment, as the American political right resurges, with its extremist policies and uber-conservative politics that seek to turn back time regarding women's rights, to co-opt and dictate women's bodies, police women's reproductive rights, and govern female sexuality. This collection, this exercise in self-definition that is at once political and personal, could not be more necessary or timely.

Black Female Sexualities is a rich intellectual tapestry that foregrounds a number of guiding questions: How do black women's sexualities operate? In what ways are black women's sexualities represented in the literary, visual, and cultural imagination and in society at large? How do black women negotiate their intimate experiences, the politics of their pleasure, and the particularities of their sexualities? And, equally consequential, how do we prioritize, foreground, and place black women at the center of cultural discourse, popular culture, and in both public and private arenas in ways that do not reify or reinscribe mandates and stereotypes of performative sexual behavior? Given the degree to which black female sexuality has historically been mediated by politics of respectability or silence and has been both hindered by and constructed in opposition to Western paradigms of womanhood and "normative" female sexuality, this book consists of contributions that address and illuminate black female sexual desires marked by both agency and empowerment and pleasure and pain in order to elucidate the ways black women regulate their sexual lives.

Contributing essays not only examine twentieth- and twenty-first-century representations and black sexual politics, particularly after the sexual revolution, but they also engage and challenge earlier constructions and paradigms governing intimacy and the politics of black female desire. Instead of characterizing black sexuality as marked by silence or hypersexuality in ways that polarize or obfuscate, this collection presents the complexities of black female sexualities along a complex continuum. Drawing upon critical frameworks informed by feminist theories, theoretical discourses in gender and sexualities studies, and theories in critical race, cultural, literary, visual and performance studies and sociology (among other fields), the essays constituting *Black Female Sexualities* address the ways black women, via their sexualities, experience and express sensation with feeling that is not characterized invariably by violence, marked by suffering or punitive measures, regulated by men or the state, pathologized, or encumbered by restrictive practices or models.

As a critical study, *Black Female Sexualities* is part of a vibrant and growing body of scholarship on black women's sexualities, sexual politics, and critical race feminist studies. In honoring and underscoring the ways black women have long theorized their sexual lives and in charting the politics and experiences governing their sexual expressions, this collection acknowledges the rich history of black female sexuality. It is indebted to pioneering black feminist sexuality studies scholars Barbara Smith, Cheryl Clarke, Jewelle Gomez, and Ann Allen Shockley particularly, who theorized early on about sexuality to challenge homophobia and heteronormativity. Audre Lorde and June Jordan explicated the politics of the erotic as liberatory and empowering while charting a "new politics of sexuality." And, Pat Parker, the Combahee River Collective, and others elucidated the complexities of identities through their own simultaneous embodiment as undeniably and inextricably black, female, and lesbian in ways that were consequential precursors to Kimberlé Crenshaw's conceptualization of "intersectionality."

Black Female Sexualities is an intergenerational endeavor—a collaborative effort that speaks across generations, silences, knowledge, discourses, and traditions about sexuality that far too often are not fully engaged, passed down, or contemplated trans-generationally. This collection seeks to inspire diversity and cross-generational dialogue, while also recognizing the growth and dynamism that has developed in black women's sexuality studies—over generations—since its inception. Black feminist scholar-intellectuals, including but not limited to M. Jacqui Alexander, Evelynn Hammonds, Mae Henderson (along with E. Patrick Johnson), Tricia Rose, and Hortense Spillers have charted new "geometries" and "pedagogies" of black female sexual desire, challenged the regulatory practices and inauthentic heteronormativity imposed by modernity, and verbalized and sought to dismantle the power structures that threaten to obscure intersecting identities that shape and form the foundations of black (queer) (female) sexualities and studies.

Other black feminist interlocutors—Jennifer Brody, Cathy Cohen, Sharon Holland, Michelle M. Wright, Mireille Miller-Young, L. H. Stallings, and Jennifer Nash, to name a few—have further mapped the field with new ideological energy and theoretical insight. Their work compels us to reconsider what constitutes normativity where pleasure and pain, sexual deviance and/as resistance, pornography, and the intersections of race and eroticism are related to black women's sexualities and to fluid gender and sexual identities in the United States and the African diaspora. *Black Female Sexualities* builds upon and augments these "generations" of scholarship in black women's sexuality studies and further explores and illuminates how black women define their sexualities, exercise their sexual citizenship, assert their racialized/gendered/sexualized embodiment, and exert agency with pleasure even as they at times contend with danger, violence, or pain.

This collection has three parts and consists of twelve essays. Its innovation and intellectual vibrancy reside, in part, in its scope, as evidenced by the chapters that engage and analyze black women's sexualities in history, literary studies, education (through pedagogical explorations of black lesbian embodiment), performance studies, visual culture, film and cinematic studies, media and popular culture studies, rhetoric and hip-hop studies, sociology, African American and black/diaspora studies, women's and gender studies, black queer studies, and the relatively newer arena of "fat (black) studies." While the essays span various ideological, thematic, conceptual, and disciplinary boundaries, they speak, individually and collectively, to the dynamic breadth and continuum of intellectual thought on contemporary black women's sexualities.

Part I, "Sexual Embod(y)ment: Framing the Body," examines how black women's sexualities are embodied. It illuminates the extent to which black women's bodies engage the sexual through examinations of how their corporeal and bodily presences operate in varied sociocultural contexts and manifest, more specifically, in movie posters, speculative fiction and literature, language and rhetoric governing body size, and the college classroom. In "Entering through the Body's Frame: *Precious* and the Subjective Delineations of the Movie Poster," Kimberly Juanita Brown examines the nexus of black women's bodies, racialized sexuality, sexual trauma, and representation as they manifest not only in Lee Daniels's *Precious* and Sapphire's novel *Push* but also, provocatively, in the visual through movie posters. Brown's essay examines *Precious* through the film posters that viewers encountered in the theaters and on the Internet in order to explore the graphic display of the body, the sexual access and availability of the protagonist Precious, and the visual affect the viewers must negotiate. It argues that the multiple acts of violence Precious endures on screen are foreshadowed by the film posters and that the viewer's (ocular) understanding of how to situate the visual as an acceptance of the protagonist's (sexual) bodily degradation is one of the film's mandates. Contrasting Sapphire's novel *Push* with the film adaptation, Brown explores the "corpus of the film's corpus," arguing that it is a reinforcement of a racialized, gendered, and corporeal politics of disgust in that redemption is visualized as a possibility only after the subject has suffered an almost incalculable degree of sexual, psychological, physical, and intellectual destruction.

Courtney J. Patterson explores the phonic and literal appropriation and reclamation of fat (to phat) as it relates to the stigma surrounding black females and their sexual desirability in "Is It Just Baby F(Ph)at? Black Female Teenagers, Body Size, and Sexuality." Drawing on feminist and sexual scripting theories, literary readings, and qualitative sociological data, she examines adolescent sexual development, body image, and teenage sexuality in ways that shift the focus of baby fat/phat back onto fat black female teenagers to explore how that group uses black feminism to subversively script its own sexuality. In so doing, this essay not only illuminates how cultural and sexual scripts both relate and contribute to stereotypes about overweight young black women, but it also demonstrates that understanding fat black female teenage sexuality is crucial to understanding black female sexuality overall.

In "Corporeal Presence: Engaging the Black Lesbian Pedagogical Body in Feminist Classrooms and College Communities," Mel Michelle Lewis examines black lesbian pedagogical bodies, modes of corporeal embodiment in the classroom, and particularly how black lesbian feminist professors/pedagogues harness their "otherness"—teaching the "'other' as the self"—while engaging their creative pedagogical power through embodiment and performance. For pedagogues whose "embodied text" (their very bodies) highlights the intersections of race, gender, and sexuality, identity informs and constructs the classroom. As Lewis argues, these intersections can be disruptive and shape the broader pedagogical project. These interlocking identities also influence the expectations of students and colleagues regarding the emotional and intellectual labor of professors whose roles are defined by female, black, and lesbian identities. The essay offers excerpts from valuable interviews and discursive materials that privilege black feminist lesbian-identified professors/pedagogues instead of marginalizing their voices and experiences.

In "Untangling Pathology: Sex, Social Responsibility, and the Black Female Youth in Octavia Butler's *Fledgling*," Esther L. Jones examines sex, social responsibility, and representation as they intersect with frameworks and tropes of pathology in Butler's vampire novel. Historicizing the text in the context of major welfare reform legislation in the United States and discourses on black pathology, this essay argues that the protagonist embodies anxieties about adolescent sexuality and its undesirable consequences: reproduction of more undesirable bodies that threaten the body politic and the state, which will go to extremes to contain that sexuality. Jones explores why black girls' sexual behaviors are targeted for social control and how *Fledgling* challenges the ethical logic that justifies oppressive state practices. Moreover, she illuminates how mythologies and social policies that are predicated on black pathology inform Butler's text and society at large.

Part II, "Disengaging the Gaze," examines representations of black women's sexualities in media such as Web series, urban fiction, and popular culture through the lyrical and lived experiences of black women and looks at sexual identities in the age of hip-hop. In what ways, it asks, do black women disengage the gaze and mediate racialized sexualities in complex and at times complicated ways? How are their sexualities treated in cyberspaces and in real lives, and how do they operate in the contexts of rhetoric, lyricism, and performance? Collectively, the essays in this section elucidate the complexities of black women's sexualities and politics of the intimate in twentieth- and twenty-first-century contexts and discourses. Ariane Cruz's "(Mis)Playing Blackness: Rendering Black Female Sexuality in *The Misadventures of Awkward Black Girl*" examines how black women's sexualities are complicated and, at times, authenticated through the trope of awkwardness in new media, thereby challenging dominant codes of black female sexuality anchored in a foundation of pathology, respectability, and patriarchal heteronormativity. Cruz argues that awkwardness serves to mediate performances of black female racial, sexual authenticity on the show, while "black female sexuality becomes authenticated in and through its ontological failure and nonbelonging, however comic." Moreover, as the essay illustrates, representations of black female sexuality in *ABG*—in the contemporary landscape of black female sexuality and cybersexualities—facilitate alternative performances of racialized sexualities and technologically inspired rearticulations of popular black female sexuality.

In "Why Don't We Love These Hoes? Black Women, Popular Culture, and the Contemporary Hoe Archetype," Mahaliah Ayana Little argues that the cavalier and frequent use of the word "hoe" in current cultural parlance contributes to the counterfactual, monolithic, and stereotypical labeling of black women. Using various rap and hip-hop song lyrics, data, and observation, she illuminates how the deployment of the rhetoric "hoe" by black women represents an act of unacknowledged insult and sadomasochism in that black women who are labeled as such suffer irreversible damage to their personhood and the public perception of their humanity. As such, when deployed by black women, the rhetoric "hoe" poses just as much of a threat to black women's subjectivity and sexual identity as misogynistic rap lyrics or their male counterparts.

K. T. Ewing's "What Kind of Woman? Alberta Hunter and Expressions of Black Female Sexuality in the Twentieth Century" examines the life of singer Alberta Hunter, an internationally known blues and cabaret singer, complicating her life experiences, black women's sexualities, and early twentieth-century paradigms governing black womanhood. Ewing problematizes the two-pronged approach to analyzing models of black womanhood while challenging the putative tension between middle-class respectability and a working-class blues aesthetic. To this end, this essay elucidates the ways African American women accepted, challenged, and manipulated conventional gender roles throughout much of the twentieth century while illuminating the complexities governing black women's lives and sexualities in the twentieth century and beyond.

In "The P-Word Exchange: Representing Black Female Sexuality in Contemporary Urban Fiction," Cherise A. Pollard posits that aside from street violence and the romanticization of drug culture, one of the most compelling elements of urban fiction is the depiction of black female sexuality in the context of hip-hop culture's misogynistic sexual economy. Novels by Sister Souljah and Sapphire have captured the popular cultural imagination, Pollard argues, precisely because of their unflinching descriptions of young black female sexuality and, more specifically, because of their uncensored and strategic use of explicit language and graphic descriptions of sex and violence. In this essay, Pollard examines how black female sexuality is figured in contemporary urban fiction through the depiction of black female characters' articulation of their relationship to and/or their deployment of their genitalia, or what she refers to as "the p-word exchange." In the context of contemporary black urban fiction, the "p-word," she argues, resonates on multiple levels. This essay uses the word strategically, then, to critique the contemporary sexual politics of hip-hop culture.

Part III, "Resisting Erasure," examines cultural issues such as virginity testing, sexual assault, and same-sex desire, as well as complex sexual identities and politics alongside racialized-gendered discourses on respectability and redemption. Collectively, the essays in this section elucidate how black women resist, take ownership over their sexualities, and operate in domestic and global landscapes in black U.S. and diasporic contexts. In "'*Ou libéré?*' Sexual Abuse and Resistance in Edwidge Danticat's *Breath, Eyes, Memory*," Sandra C. Duvivier examines how Haitian women have emerged and galvanized themselves to challenge sexual violence, sanctioned efforts to (re)build the nation, and have extricated themselves from abuse and its ramifications while challenging patriarchal and gendered practices that marginalize girls and women. In alignment with the practices of Haitian women activist-feminists, whose work demonstrates their steadfast refusal to passively acquiesce to female victimization, this essay uses Danticat's novel to examine sexual politics, state-sanctioned violations of women and girls, virginity testing, and sexual redemption, as well as looks at portrayals of sexualized violence and Haitian women's responses to it. In so doing, Duvivier reveals the complexities surrounding the sexual lives of Haitian women, who are not entirely victimized or revolutionarily subversive, to chart modes of resistance and agency in both U.S. and transnational black diasporic contexts.

Erin D. Chapman's "Rape Fantasies and Other Assaults: Black Women's Sexuality and Racial Redemption on Film" analyzes interracial sexual engagements and the ways that male characters, through black women and their sexual(ized) bodies, facilitate racial redemption for both male characters and America. This essay illuminates the extent to which white male characters also putatively overcome racism or, at the very least, certain manifestations of it, if even only momentarily. Developing a new theoretical frame, "the rape fantasy," Chapman argues that the films *Crash* and *Monster's Ball* function to minimize black women characters' abuse and oppression and ultimately attempt to obscure their subjectivity. Although these films have been lauded as novel representations of progressive, twenty-first-century post-racial politics, they rely on racial/sexual mythologies and stereotypes entrenched in our culture regarding the vexed and complex dynamics governing interracial sexual congress.

Johanna X. K. Garvey's "'Embrace the Narrative of the Whole': Complicating Black Female Sexuality in Contemporary Fiction" analyzes representations of female sexualities, particularly same-sex desire and fluid gender and sexualities, in contemporary black women's fiction. Exploring literary representations of black female sexualities, Garvey argues that while none of the texts depicts queer and/or lesbian communities for their black female characters, these fictive narratives illuminate the multiplicity of experiences that govern black women's sexualities and lived experiences. This essay explores not only the complexities of the continuum of sexual politics among black women in literary characterizations but also how these texts provide paradigms of sexuality, family, and belonging that challenge (hetero)normative models of citizenship and female gender/sexual identities.

Ayana K. Weekley explores down-low discourses, representations, and treatments of black women's sexualities in film and examines the intersections of middle-class black women and down-low discourses in "Saving Me through Erasure? Black Women, HIV/AIDS, and Respectability." Shifting attention to black heterosexual women as the specters that animate and validate these discourses, Weekley argues that a punitive standard of respectability and black womanhood is at work in down-low discourses that shapes who constitutes—are meant to be considered—deserving or undeserving "victims." Like similar discourses of the down-low, Bill Duke's 2007 film *Cover* provides little space to consider the (sexual) agency, desires, and needs of the women in these discourses. This essay highlights the challenges these discourses pose for black women with regard to gender and sexuality generally, while also raising questions and gender-specific awareness regarding the HIV/AIDS epidemic.

Black Female Sexualities offers discourses, examinations, analyses, and discussions of black women's sexual politics across several disciplines and media and along varied intellectual, theoretical, and cultural platforms. Even as it seeks comprehensiveness—to reflect the fullness and totality of black women's sexualities—it also recognizes that such an attempt in any single volume is futile. No single collection could do justice to the complexities, profundity, and depth of black women's sexual expressions and politics of the intimate. What the essays in this collection speak to collectively is the necessity for black feminist intervention to orchestrate the terms of our sexualities, provide the space for transgenerational dialogues and discourses regarding our selves, and maintain ownership of our sexualities—and characterizations of them. For, as this introduction's title in the words of Shange's "Lady in Green" proclaims, "somebody almost walked off wid alla my stuff." This collection not only seeks to rectify but to inspire, as it is deplorable for any "somebody," male or other, to appropriate—to cinematically or intellectually "pimp"—black women's narratives at any time, let alone in the twenty-first century.

PART I

SEXUAL EMBOD(Y)MENT

Framing the Body

CHAPTER 1

Entering through the Body's Frame

PRECIOUS AND THE SUBJECTIVE DELINEATIONS OF THE MOVIE POSTER

Kimberly Juanita Brown

There is power in looking.

—*bell hooks*

BODY IMPOSSIBLE

Before *Precious* was nominated for four and won two Academy Awards, there was the all-important Sundance Grand Jury Prize, which the movie won in a triumphant display of limited cinematic and restricted envisioning of black women's lives and sexual experiences.[1] Voted into the "oblivion of hypervisibility," viewers and voters were determined to make their mark on that ubiquitously overburdened text: the black female body.[2] They have done this before and do this still, but with *Precious* the stakes were higher. The transformation of the protagonist's fictional body into a visual text provided space for a feigned engagement—what I like to call the "head tilt of sympathy"—in which a performance of engagement takes place repeatedly but only within the space of ineffable and unimaginable sexual trauma. This is where black women are offered up in pieces: as broken, bruised, fragmented pseudo-subjects seeking redemption through white empathetic renderings of collective suffering.[3] Sexuality is rendered here as a violated corpus: a grand jury prize for a body impossible. This essay looks at the origin point of this interaction—the marketing space of the movie poster—and explores the currency of print imagery in the reiteration and reinforcement of the viewer's hegemonic incline through the black female subject's racialized and gendered decline.

The Derivative Riff of Poster Imagery

Consciously engaging the artistic sensibilities of early motion picture poster production, the initial (and probably most recognizable) graphic image for the film is an homage (if we can call it that) to Saul Bass, specifically the image he produced for Otto Preminger's 1959 film *Anatomy of a Murder*. Striking and provocative, the Bass image features a body displayed in vertical silhouette against a burnt-orange background. The body is severed at the waist, arms, and neck; it is decapitated and in a state of dissection (see figure 1.1). The title of the film is written on the body's torso and thighs, and the "anatomy" taking place begins with the poster's marketing of the courtroom drama starring James Stewart and Lee Remick.

Saul Bass's ability to trouble the line between artistic production and consumer marketing made him a sought-after and prolific illustrator (he created the posters for *Vertigo* and *The Godfather*).[4] Art Sims's image for Spike Lee's film *Clockers* (1995) is a relational duplication of the Bass graphic style.[5] One of the movie posters for *Precious* followed the poster for *Anatomy of a Murder* stylistically (more so than *Clockers*), but it diverges from the original in very important ways. These distinctions offer us a more layered context through which to read the film, its presumed audience, and the often-unacknowledged interplay of black female subjectivity and representational imagery. They are a way into the concept of the racial imaginary and a useful place to begin.

Movie posters originated as advertisements for traveling circuses, according to Gary D. Rhodes. "It is very clear," he writes, "that the early film industry believed that the circus poster had led to the creation of the moving picture poster."[6] As a given in our image-thick visual environment, movie posters have lost some of their wonder amidst the static expectation of their arrival. We expect to see them. Nevertheless, whether viewed on the Internet or on a moving billboard in Times Square, they still have an immediate and visceral impact. The initial teaser poster for *Precious* aimed for that impact and achieved it by participating in the long and egregious visual history of objectifying black women's bodies. "If media are middles," W. J. T. Mitchell writes, "they are ever-elastic middles that expand to include what look at first like their outer boundaries. The medium does not lie between sender and receiver; it includes and constitutes them."[7] Film posters are often the first point of visual contact between the film and the viewer. They can layer expectations with their static imagery, allowing the viewer to parse out the particularities of their investment one unbridled visual infraction at a time. This is especially so with movie posters, and films like *Precious*, that showcase black women's bodies and in turn provide occasions for viewers to both witness and visually enact violence against black women's bodies through spectatorship.

The first of four promotional images for the film *Precious*, generated by the Los Angeles graphic design company IgnitionPrint, featured a large-bodied female in silhouette. Her whole body is cracked and fragmented (figure 1.2). The

Figure 1.1. Detail of Saul Bass's poster for *Anatomy of a Murder*, 1959.

origin of the fragmentation is a large left handprint strategically placed on the figure's vagina, while diagonal lines emanate from the hand. There are two main points of divergence from the Bass image, and both of them are connected to a 1987 graphic poster by Lanny Sommese. In Sommese's famous graphic of social commentary (the poster advertised a rape hot line), the torso, thighs, and upper arms of a woman's body (which is cut off at the neck) are shown in a state of vulnerable display (see figure 1.3). It is not clear whether the figure is lying down or standing, but the placement of the arms (spread out) seems to indicate a prostrate position of forced submission; it is depicted as a body under violent sexual attack might be visually portrayed.

The film poster differs in two very specific ways from this poster: the figure in the *Precious* poster is fragmented beyond and across the lines produced by the

Figure 1.2. Teaser poster for *Precious,* Lionsgate Films, 2009.

foreign hand, and despite this extensive fracturing she is still standing. It is even possible that she is in a process of moving, walking forward even though her body is literally in pieces. In Sommese's image, the proximity to the body refuses the viewer's desire for voyeuristic distancing and thus the intimation is that the viewer is *this close* to sexual violence. As a victim? A perpetrator? A witness? However the viewer encounters this image, they cannot escape the violation on display. They cannot step back from it, as is possible with the *Precious* poster, since the distance and the assumed fragility of the woman is literally standing in the way of the viewer's capacity to encase the image with its totalizing effect. With the *Precious* poster there is no *this close,* no intimate proximity of viewer and voyeur. The hand seems superhuman—it is larger than the scale of the hands on the woman's body—and contributes to the concept of distancing. Sommese's

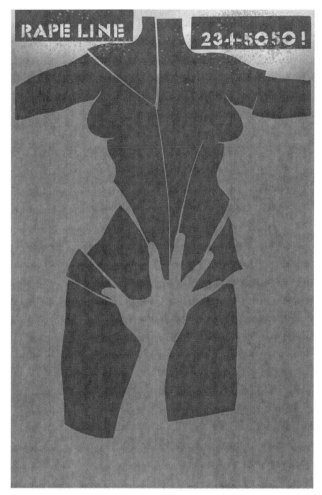

Figure 1.3. Lanny Sommese's Rape Line poster, 1987. Courtesy of the artist.

handprint belongs to a figure emerging from below, its origin either exposed or obscured by the body parts that do not appear in the poster (lower legs, feet). In the movie poster for *Precious*, the larger-than-scale hand also comes up from below, but this below is different. Reminiscent of the hand of that ubiquitous movie villain Freddie Krueger, this alien hand is climbing out of the ground below.

With horizontal as well as vertical severing, the figure assembles and reassembles the form of visual engagement (a spreading apart and a coming together) so that the fullest measure of violation on display is muted. She seems to be at the juncture of an invisible mechanical apparatus that has just recently quartered (or sixteenthed) her corpus with the assistance of the otherworldly hand emerging from the ground. For the viewer to negotiate the bifurcated homage (or violated homage), they would have to be equally engaged in both the arts/graphic universe of Saul Bass's cinematic advertisements and the social/political interventions Lanny Sommese's work created. Without these very specific reference points, the viewer is left with a sense (via the enlarged hand) of concealed corporeal horror alongside the triumphantly capable survival of this gendered body (and who is more buoyant than black women in the national imaginary?).

Thus, the clear victimization of the scene Sommese's illustration portrays is betrayed here, since it is not an image of dissection (as in Preminger's film) and it is also not a clear social commentary on the evils of sexual violence. Instead it lodges itself between the spectral currency of the circus poster and the utter ridiculousness of an autopsy performed on a living person. This is the spectacle of a multilayered cultural production: an anonymous silhouetted black woman's body, portioned and possessed by an alien hand, is presented to the viewer as an offering that does not indict him.[8] The poster functions as a commentary on black female sexual subjectivity that does not take that subjectivity seriously. Instead, it plays on those familiar tropes of race and gender, further producing the handprint of hegemony on an already fragmented surface. The handprint is therefore part of the riddle. Is the woman's body broken or triumphant? Are we looking at a cartoon or currency? We will never know. And as long as we do not know for sure, we do not know at all. The crowded metahistory of black women's representational subjection is well documented. It is important, though, that we look at *Precious* as the intended analog to a fraught and contentious politics of representation. As Peggy Phelan writes, "Seeing the other is a social form of self-reproduction, for in looking at/for the other, we seek to represent ourselves to ourselves. As a social relation the exchange of gazes marks the failure of the subject to maintain the illusionary plentitude of the Imaginary."[9] The Precious poster thus not only enables the viewer to "see the Other" but also presents him with a potent modality of race and gender through the imagery of a fractured black female body. How do you feign interest in a throwaway body and a throwaway gender? You shred it to pieces and see if that has the desired effect.

The burnt-orange *Precious* poster shatters, it literally fractures and shreds to pieces, black women's long-fought battles to reclaim their bodies. Turning the delineation of traumatic physical and sexual violence into a maddening display of the carnivalesque, the graphic opens out into a world where black women's corporeal vulnerabilities are as illegible as the face on the silhouette. The poster offers a free-for-all for the eye—a gaze unencumbered by questions of subjectivity, by requirements of empathetic engagement. The distanced centering of the body affords the viewer this double positioning: the viewer remains invisible to the subject and can gaze at (or visually assail) the available body at will, while feigning concern about black women's sexual and literal lives. Because the image lacks corporeal specificity, the viewer engages with a form that implies a body in pieces but never encounters Precious. And so this irony splinters the scene: a chopped and fragmented figure, ingloriously broken, has the name that indicates a loved possession and the integrity of familial protection. The definition of the adjective (valuable, beloved, adored) does not fit the figure in the image. Here the viewer gets to participate in ironic subjectivity: a dead walking body that is also a valued and loved human being. Since the graphic borders on the ridiculous (and we can return here to the earlier allusion to the carnival), its cartoonishness distances the viewer. In other words, it is a refusal of engagement.

Writ Large: Broad Brush Strokes and the Faceless Form of Supplication

Another poster for Precious is different in several significant ways. Instead of a silhouette, it presents a mock painting illustrating a close-up of a faceless figure that is obese and darkened to the point of pitch-blackness (see figure 1.4). The figure is cut off right below the waist and is created out of broad and loose brush strokes, so the viewer encounters form but no face and is therefore unable to engage with the personhood of the figure. There is literally no *there* there—no one with which to concern oneself. In bell hooks's analysis of spectatorship of the black female body in films, she notes the strategies black women have used to ameliorate the violence of what is taking place on the screen. "Conventional representations of black women have done violence to the image," she writes. "Responding to this assault, many black women spectators shut out the image, looked the other way, accorded cinema no importance in their lives."[10] Unfortunately, black women's criticism of the film industry has not been met with a serious attempt to represent their lives and dimensions on the silver screen. Precious joins a mélange of recent movies that have placed black women (and the many types of violations of black women) at the center of the performance of social-cultural engagement. Consistent only in their misapprehension, these representations seem to ignore black feminist criticism and concern that has attempted to draw attention to the issue of who gets to tell a black woman's story.[11] Black women in films are seen as always already sexual beings, and they are seen through the vehicle of a visual medium that shreds, diminishes, and mutes them.[12]

In this second poster for Precious, the pattern of misapprehension gathers in the center of the image, where the title of the film and its protagonist are featured on a nameplate necklace draped around the neck of the figure (see figure 1.4). This figure's existence has been smudged out. There is no face, no eyes, and thus nothing to elicit concern or connection. The frame of her body extends nearly beyond the edge of the left and right sides of the frame. The proximity and anonymity here mute the explicit violence of the silhouette. Since there is no *there* there, it is of proximal but not specific concern.

The figure reinforces this concept with her corporeal stance. Her fingerless hands are crossed in front of her in a gesture that is half-protective, half-supplicant. Are the palms of her hands facing out or facing in? Is she clasping

Figure 1.4. Teaser poster for *Precious*, Lionsgate Films, 2009.

her hands in a gesture of self-soothing and comfort or are the generalized strokes
meant to intimate the absence of even that ability? The swirling brush movements
manage to dab out all references to shape, form, and individualized humanity.
If this portrayal is offered as a critique of representations of black female sexuality, it is what it claims to interrogate: an empty void visualized through the black
female body, which the gaze can enter, puncture, or eviscerate. The choice and
specificity of the colors (red, white, black, gray) illustrate the convergence of symbols that layer the discourses of race, nation, and corporeality. Outlined by shades
of gray (in fact, framed by them), whiteness pushes in from the outer edges of
the frame, effectively narrowing the figure's ability to claim space. The space the
figure inhabits is as untenable as her face is illegible and is draped in a kind of

nonspecific blanketed blackness that is either narrowed by vertical whiteness or expanded by rebellious corporeal blackness. And that is where her sexual existence adheres to the mores of invisibility. In the middle there is a swath of red pouring down from the shoulder to the upper thigh that is either an intimation of violence or an intimation of religious sacrificial martyrdom. The figure seems (without facial specificity) to be presenting herself to a higher power. That higher power is the viewer. She presents this form to the viewer as a named nonentity, smudged and formless, hands clasped in supplication, waiting for (visual) deliverance. Unlike the fragmented figure, this one is closer to the eye of the viewer. Yet in the subjective delineation of the objectifying gaze, this proximity is mediated by the total absence of facial features. "When it comes to seeing," James Elkins writes, "objects and observers alter one another, and meaning goes in both directions."[13] What could that meaning mean? "Although the eyes of the viewer are fairly free to scan a work of art in a way that confirms or disturbs the composition's intrinsic structure," Rudolph Arnheim explains, "the mechanism of vision itself does not operate entirely without constraints."[14] When we consider the movie poster as a purposeful gesturing toward the painterly arts and as being in dialogue with a generalized aesthetic of ambiguity, these "constraints" facilitate a distanced projection of martyrdom through which the viewer can imagine, with the best of that twisted liberal intentionality, "I am Precious." In fact, the many ways "I am not Precious" informs the face-to-faceless interaction. In the second *Precious* poster, the impetus is to draw the eye to the center of the image, but broad paintbrush strokes not only trouble the confrontation but also manage to efface, and by extension disembody, a body that is not fully present.

There is the sense here that through the lack of specificity, what this image hopes to portray is that the protagonist of the film is not yet finished—that she is to draw herself into being with some future sexual self-possession produced through her personal traumas. When Precious herself is wearing the actual outfit in the film, it is at a moment of pride, accomplishment, and personal confidence.[15] Yet for a figure who is raped and impregnated twice by her father, beaten and sexually exploited by her mother, infected with HIV, illiterate, and force-fed to the point of dangerous obesity, the poster is an effacement that manages to reinforce Precious's unformed and aesthetic, painted-on visuality. This is the body impossible made cinematic.

Butterflies?

Butterflies. The third image in our trilogy is photographically specific, but with an added fantastical dimension that is, at best, problematically rendered. This poster presents us with our first visual of the actress who portrays Precious, Gabourey Sidibe, with large butterfly wings careening out of her back like some fortunate saving grace ensuring that her feet never have to touch the unsettled and untrustworthy ground. Yet she is firmly on the ground (no confusing

silhouette here); indeed, she is actually in the process of walking with the flut-
tering movement of wings from an unknown origin (see figure 1.5).[16] The wings
are a problem, as is the choice of background color—a maddening white that
nearly renders Sidibe's complexion ashen and unreadable. The point here (and
the central position of the actress in the middle of the image gives us a clue) is
that she has little or no knowledge of her regal nature (the crown above her head)
and her transformative abilities (butterfly wings). Her sexuality is a nonpresence;
she seems contained within the mandates of some far-flung asexuality. Again the
viewer gets to harass with the eye; yet Sidibe is figured so far back in the frame
that even if she is able to return the gaze, it will be impossible to see.

The backpack she has strapped about her provides a possible origin point for
the wings, but this does not seem to be the case. In fact, it appears that the visual

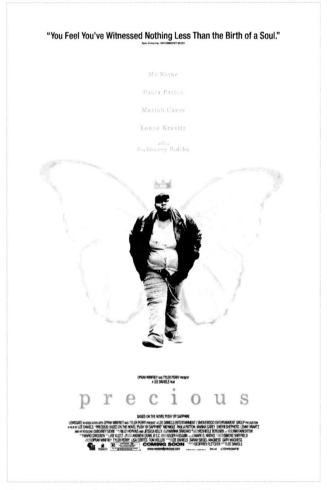

Figure 1.5. Poster for *Precious*, Lionsgate Films, 2009.

possibility lingers somewhere more sinister. As burden (and as a layered demar-
cation of this burden), the backpack symbolizes an imagistic heaviness that her
body extends. Her body seems to have been cut out of another photograph, and
quite precisely, so that she could be placed in the middle of this fractured display
of real (photograph) and imaginary (butterfly wings) distanced visibility. What
is being muted here and what exaggerated? According to Madhu Dubey, in Sapphire's novel *Push,* "Precious's critical take on the spuriously universal promise
of modern print culture speaks for itself, yet it is through the print medium
that Precious believes she can most effectively conduct her critique."[17] The print
medium that Precious comes to privilege is literature, and her engagement with
creative writing in the novel is how she engages with herself, her world, her
desires, and her self-possession. "Song playing in my head now," Precious writes:

> Not TV colors flashing funny noise pictures in on me, scratching and itching
> in my brain at the same time. I see a color I don't know the name for, maybe
> one like only another kind of animal that not human can see. Like butterflies?
> I ask Ms. Rain tomorrow do butterflies see colors. Song caught on me like how
> plastic bags on tree branches. . . . Where my *Color Purple*? Where my god most
> high? Where my king? Where my black love? Where my man love? Woman
> love? Any kinda love? Why me? I don't deserve this. I not crack addict. Why I
> get Mama for a mama? Why I not born a light-skin dream? Why? Why? It's a
> movie, splashing like swimming pool at Y in my head.[18]

Precious's use of metaphor is particularly powerful ("song caught on me like
plastic bags on tree branches"), and the text highlights the vibrancy of her constant engagement, literary evolution and developing feminist sensibilities. In
other words, Precious comes into being through her words. However, the image
of her in the posters for the movie betrays this engagement. Visually she is a
text acted upon, an object further objectified.[19] The film posters reproduce this
without allowing her the space that her erotic self-conscious coming to being
requests. "I see a color I don't know the name for," she writes, pushing her imagination into the realm of suspenseful creation. "Like butterflies?" she wonders.
In an attempt to literalize her emergent writerly sensibilities, she presents the
reader with the imagistic organization of her subjective concerns. Fully present,
though victimized, her body is the marker of the many ways she is encased in
her surroundings but wants something more and better for herself. The series
of questions she poses here begin with a literary engagement: "Where my *Color
Purple*? Where my god most high? Where my king? Where my black love? Where
my man love? Woman love? Any kinda love?"

A great deal of gendered damage takes place in the film, and it has only a
smattering of relational connection to the novel. As Madhu Dubey maintains,
Sapphire's novel "gains mimetic authority from the fact that it is written in
the first person voice of Precious, a member of this so-called underclass" of

Harlem teenagers and young women navigating a system that did not make room for them. In the novel, the failure of the nation-state is precisely its blind reproduction—indeed, its incestuous production—of the domestic space as safe, nurturing, and able to produce generations of grateful citizens. The film plays down precisely these novelistic interventions, instead preferring to highlight an overwrought rendering of these failures, using Precious's body as the reductive (and reproductive) price of acquiescing to the state apparatus.

More than the other two posters, this one depends on the viewer's knowledge of the novel, though the title of the novel is an open secret placed at the very bottom of the poster in tiny letters. Other than her declaration in the film that her favorite color is yellow, the butterfly imagery is tethered to the novel. In this way it functions as quite the anomaly and is part of the visual carnival the movie has already promised via the graphic images used to publicize its imminent release.

THE DAYMARE

Daymares blanket Lee Daniels's filmic rendering of Sapphire's novel with its unyielding attention to the assaults Precious is forced to sustain. Ending in an urban swirl of maternal redemption and not the marked temporal intentions and unfoldings of the novel (the final words are "tick/tock"), the visual offering of the film, like the visual offering of the film poster, places a black teenage girl in the harmful direction of the gaze without a lens of self-conscious engagement with and through her own body. There is no safe space for her. Beginning in the auditory and stark dark and light of New York City, the opening scene deploys both the imagery of lynching and the heightened isolation of a post–Civil Rights urban existence. A scarlet red scarf hangs hauntingly from a streetlamp (instead of a southern tree), intimating the willful and racialized lynchings of mostly (but not exclusively) black males. The red scarf (which one can imagine draped around the neck as either a gesture of comfort or one of violence) then falls, presumably into the nothingness of urban detritus and gritty surroundings—a different kind of willful lynching. Though Daniels has never met a shade of red he could not corrupt for his films, this initial introduction has more than a measure of intrigue.

The intrigue does not last long. After a resplendent Susan Taylor offers the protagonist a red scarf of her own, that fantasy is cut quickly, and we enter Precious's real and surreal life. The sequence of sexual violence begins at minute 6 and is as graphically violent as was possible under an R motion picture rating. Spliced with Precious's lively fantasy of being famous and desired (draped again in red), this layering offers the viewer a visual escape the novel does not offer and therefore appeases the sensibilities of a viewing audience that does not expect to receive this kind of imagery without a place to put it. This happens repeatedly in the film each time Precious's body is being violated in some way. So the head tilt lingers and loiters, while it appears that people only care enough to award the very best (Grand Jury Prize, Audience Award) when black women are literally and metaphorically sliced to pieces. And they only care when the woman (or teenage girl) they see on the screen is not real.

People are too comfortable with black women in various states of sexual violence and unrest, too comfortable with their dismemberment and their utter corporeal destruction. *Precious* is a film that presupposes an intimate, proximate, and violent relationship with the viewer, supposedly for the sake of the subject, then heightens and exploits it. All with the permission of the viewer. The multiple publicity posters produced for the film counted on a previous engagement of exposure, torture, rape, and psychological degradation, leaving little space for the protagonist's sexual redemption. Viewers witnessed all of this in the film and the posters advertising it and then called it a gritty fantasy. There is nothing wrong with a daydream. But if the only way black women can be rendered visible is through violent acts of sexual expression, someone ought to be more concerned with their waking lives.

Notes

1. The movie also won the Sundance Audience Award (Dramatic), while Mo'Nique won the Special Jury Prize for Acting. Mo'Nique went on to win the Academy Award for Best Supporting Actress.

2. My use of the "oblivion of hypervisibility" refers precisely to the oxymoronic notion that Black women are everywhere in the popular imaginary but they are always also obliterated within the space of visibility. This is an interplay that the movie highlights to graphic effect. With "make their mark," I refer to Hortense Spillers' famous "Mama's Baby, Papa's Maybe" essay, which opens with "Let's face it. I am a marked woman." Spillers goes on to use a series of nicknames and black female stereotypes ("peaches," "brown sugar," "sapphire," etc.) that mark black female representations. Thus, while she understands that she enters this framework "already marked," she investigates the theoretical and historical sutures that continue to mark black women against themselves.

3. Cinematic renditions of black women as pseudo-subjects include films across a range, from John Stahl's (1934) and Douglass Sirk's (1959) versions of *Imitation of Life* to Steven Spielberg's *The Color Purple* (1985), Joel Schumacher's *A Time to Kill* (1996) and Marc Forster's *Monster's Ball* (2001).

4. According to Emily King, "When developing identities for films, in each case Bass attempted to find a strong graphic symbol that would act as the summary of the plot." Emily King, *A Century of Movie Posters: From Silent to Art House* (Hauppauge, N.Y.: Barron's Educational Series, 2003), 54.

5. Saul Bass reportedly attempted to sue Lee for plagiarism but died in 1996 before the case progressed.

6. Gary D. Rhodes, "The Origin and Development of the American Moving Picture Poster," *Film History* 19, no. 3 (1997): 229.

7. W. J. T. Mitchell, *What Do Pictures Want? The Lives and Loves of Images* (Chicago: University of Chicago Press, 2006), 204.

8. Here I am positioning the gaze of the viewer, in Laura Mulvey's parlance, as male.

9. Peggy Phelan, *Unmarked: The Politics of Performance* (New York: Routledge Press, 1993), 21.

10. bell hooks, "The Oppositional Gaze: Black Female Spectators," in *The Feminism and Visual Culture Reader,* ed. Amelia Jones (London: Routledge, 2003), 97.

11. Significant for this discussion is the director Lee Daniels, whose directorial debut, *Shadowboxer,* was awash with dead black bodies, incest narratives, and gratuitous violence. He also produced *Monster's Ball* (2001) and *The Woodsman* (2004).

12. Significantly for this film, Precious barely speaks, often mumbles, and mostly scowls.

13. James Elkins, *The Object Stares Back: On the Nature of Seeing* (New York: Mariner Books, 2007), 43.

14. Rudolph Arnheim, *The Power of the Center: A Study of Composition in the Visual Arts* (Berkeley: University of California Press, 1988), 47.

15. Since the poster here clearly draws on the film itself, this is yet another place where a possible engagement with the viewer and the protagonist is lost in a swirling refusal of visibility.

16. Emerging quite graphically out of nowhere like some Kafkaesque accepted anomaly, the butterfly wings are a near-florescent yellow against a stark white background.

17. Madhu Dubey, *Signs and Cities: Black Literary Postmodernism* (Chicago: University of Chicago Press, 2003), 56. Dubey writes that the novel rejects "organic and folk notions of community, insisting instead on the need to forge contingent associations among strangers" (81).

18. Sapphire, *Push* (New York: Vintage Books, 1996), 87.

19. Aliyyah Abdur-Rahman calls Precious Jones "an almost absurd character," highlighting the layered burdens her characterization must contain. Aliyyah Abdur-Rahman, *Against the Closet: Black Political Longing and the Erotics of Race* (Durham, N.C.: Duke University Press, 2012), 133.

CHAPTER 2

Is It Just Baby F(Ph)at?

BLACK FEMALE TEENAGERS, BODY SIZE, AND SEXUALITY

Courtney J. Patterson

When popular hip-hop group De La Soul debuted its single "Baby Phat" in 2001, it tapped into some of the intricacies present in the intersections of black women's body size, age, and sexuality. Although the group raps about adult women, their usage of the term "baby fat" reminded me not only of its typical use to refer to the pudgy appearance of young children transitioning into adulthood but also about what I used to hear some of my relatives say when my mother would voice her concern over my ever-increasing weight: "Don't worry, it's only baby fat."[1] In retrospect, I do not believe my mother was worried about my weight as much as she was about the way society would view me and the attention that men were giving my quickly developing body. From the age of ten, I remember schoolboys teasing me about my baby fat, but I also remember grown men heckling me because of the places where some of my baby fat was located. During her *Who Is Jill Scott?* tour stop in Philadelphia, soul artist Jill Scott performed an original piece entitled "The Thickness" about a fourteen-year-old girl with a mature, developed body. Scott describes the young girl as a "big chick" who has "big ol' legs, big ol' thighs, big ol' hips, big ol' ass, big ol' tits," and from the behavior of male onlookers, Scott gathers that the older men read the fourteen-year-old's body as a site of intense objectification.

Many women know about this gaze, regardless of their body size, but the male gaze—and sexually suggestive lyrics directed toward larger bodies—complicates how we view body size and sexuality. For the men who do this gazing, the enlarged (or arguably fat) sexualized organs of these young women suggest an enlarged sexuality. These are all components of sexual scripts that have marked the fat black female body as immoral, excessive, and deviant, thus stripping it of its humanity and making it susceptible to violence.[2] However, De La Soul's use of the term baby phat disrupts these scripts.

Although implicitly and explicitly sexist and paternalistic in its views of black female sexuality, De La Soul's song transforms "baby fat" into "baby phat," showing that young black women can step out of their marginalized positions, making fat black female bodies operate as sites rife with possibilities. The idea of baby phat reconstitutes what it means to live inside black, female, and fat/phat bodies in ways that complicate black female embodiment and corporeality. Drawing upon black feminist thought and theories of sexual scripting, this essay pools qualitative data from sociological studies and uses literary analysis of texts to examine adolescent sexual development, body image, and teenage sexuality in an interdisciplinary context. Shifting the focus of baby phat onto black female teenagers, I argue that these subjects subvert scripts about black female sexuality and demonstrate that understanding black fat female teenage sexuality is critical to understanding black female sexuality more generally.

WHY FAT? WHY PHAT? WHY NOT OBESITY?

When De La Soul invoked the words baby phat in their song, they did so purposefully and for a multiplicity of reasons. First, baby fat could be considered a cultural reference to a type of fatness that is acceptable, meaning that it occurs naturally and is, as such, void of the stigma that derives from obesity epidemic politics that associate fatness with personal responsibility narratives, such as laziness and poor food choices. Moreover, "phat" has replaced, if not displaced, "fat" as a positive connotation for bigger women's bodies in the world of hip-hop. (It is used to connote abundance, as in a phat record deal or a phat house, or something or someone that is aesthetically pleasing, as in describing Halle Berry as phat.) By depicting a variety of (mostly) black women as large and telling their listeners that it is "just a little baby phat," De La Soul reassures us that baby phat is nothing to stigmatize, although a certain type of "phatness" or fatness is more acceptable. However, the clash of meaning in these similar phonic terms illustrates how the ability to redefine such terms is a demonstration of power. Although De La Soul may have expanded the acceptance of baby phat, they still subjected these bigger black female bodies to sexist objectification. What would happen if the women themselves reclaimed fat and used it for their own understanding of their bodies and their sexualities?

The collision of past and present meanings of fatness becomes fertile ground for exploring the nexus of sexuality and developing black female bodies. If we use "fat" instead of "overweight," "curvy," or "voluptuous," might we uncover or eliminate biases and prejudices associated with big black bodies and, in turn, assert verbal power in the process? Medical conversations about fat and fatness, under the guise of terms such as "obese" and "morbidly obese," tend to demonize both women of color and poor people, situating them as deviant and thus deserving of the myriad chronic illnesses perceived to be linked to obesity. Using phat to refer to fat black women has both racial and cultural implications for black women's bodies and black female identity in popular culture (in hip-hop or in films, such as *Phat Girls,* where the actors reveal that phat is an acronym for "Pretty Hot And Thick"). Juxtaposing both terms asks us to consider how baby fat and baby phat can give us insight into how fat black female teenagers view and make decisions about their sexualities. What choices, if any, are available to them, and how do fat black female teenagers—and those with whom they engage in sexual activity—act upon those choices?

I combine both terms into "baby f(ph)at," then, to situate fat black female teenagers at the center of an intersectional analysis of race, body size, gender, age, and sexuality. Drawing upon Kimberlé Crenshaw's concept of intersectionality in this particular nexus of marginalized identities (black, fat, female, and teenager can all be oppressed identities in the context of social relations, socioeconomic policy, access to power, knowledge, and socioeconomic resources), I argue that f(ph)at black female teenagers occupy a particular social location that not only urges them to confront sexuality much earlier and more precariously than their (white) counterparts but also ties their adolescent sexual decisions to their overall identity.

Cultural Scenarios and Sexual Scripts

Power and sexuality are intrinsically woven into a predetermined societal fabric. In fact, societies often attempt to regulate sex and sexuality by defining the terms and setting boundaries for human (sexual) behavior.[3] By constantly employing regulatory strategies, however, these same societies only encourage people to find different ways of representing their sexual desires.[4] Such strategies are what William Simon and John Gagnon would call cultural scenarios: cultural scripts that act as "instructional guides" to determine how people should behave. People are often taught to reenact and reinforce cultural scenarios with other society members, yet cultural scenarios are not always indicative of actual behavior, and people often become "scriptwriters" and "actors."[5] For instance, people write interpersonal scripts (which show how people can collaborate to change dominant scripts) and intrapsychic scripts (internal dialogues and personal behaviors that affect individual development) to rewrite cultural scripts with each other and within their own psyche.[6]

Although intrapsychic scripts are internal by nature, Simon and Gagnon believe they are the foundation of social existence and ultimately carry meaning for all people. Individual desires are connected to the social world, but when people engage in what Simon and Gagnon call "the process of the creation of the self," that process brings transformative possibilities for behavior and identity.

Because of this, intrapsychic scripts are highly influential in the creation of sexual scripts, those that give meaning to sexual activities and naturalize these meanings through people, or actors, who engage in sexual activities.[7] A person makes sexual choices and establishes a sexual identity because an inward pressure drives her to do so, balancing her decision between desire and expected behavior.[8] Although intrapsychic scripts change slowly, they have a significant impact "during moments of crisis, disjuncture, or transition."[9] When examining how f(ph)at black female teenagers script their own sexuality, it is imperative to look into intrapsychic scripts, especially during moments of crisis, disjuncture, and transition, to explain how they translate their intersectional experiences with race, gender, body size, and age using their sexuality. The group faces hypervisibility because of their darker skin and bigger bodies, but they also encounter a form of invisibility rooted in Western beauty ideals that label them unattractive and unworthy of attention.[10] Intrapsychic and sexual scripts allow them a way not only to negotiate their baby f(ph)at against previously determined meanings of sex and sexual behavior but also to become scriptwriters of new cultural scenarios.

BLACK FEMINIST THOUGHT AND BABY F(PH)AT

As scriptwriters, f(ph)at black female teenagers are part of a long history of black women's rewriting cultural scenarios. Black feminist scholars and activists have published a significant body of work that theorize the position of black women at various intersections of identities, including race, class, gender, and sexuality. As an ideology that theorizes and acknowledges systems of power, privilege, and oppression in the lives and experiences of individuals at the intersections of complex identities, black feminist thought offers frameworks to analyze black women's positionalities and how they are affected by interlocking systems of oppression: patriarchy, racism, and sexism. Black women's postitions at these intersections require a particular type of study that interrogates race, class, or gender simultaneously, not additively, and reveals how communities inside and outside the academy have denied black women complex personhood(s).[11]

One way black feminists take the academy to task is by addressing "controlling images" that separate black women into several categories that are both fixed and contemporarily nuanced, such as the "mammy," emasculating "matriarch," "welfare mother," and "jezebel."[12] Although we should recognize the power in all of these images, a closer look at mammy and jezebel reveals that many black feminists discuss these images in a very particular way. Derived during slavery, both of these images are cultural scripts that attempt to regulate black women's sexuality. Mammy's asexuality and jezebel's hypersexuality are representative of both black female productive and reproductive labor: mammy as caretaker of the slaveholding family and jezebel as the birth giver of future slaves regardless of paternity.[13] However, black feminists often associate these images with adults, when, especially in the context of slavery, many of these enslaved women were actually teenagers.[14] These adolescent and young adult women were scripted by society to birth a labor force and take care of all children. Is there space in black feminism for us to bring mammy and jezebel up to date with f(ph)atness? Are the controlling images still meaningful for our f(ph)at teenagers? If so, do they acknowledge these scripts before making sexual choices, and, if not, how do they reject or negotiate them? Would society label the young woman that Jill Scott discusses in "The Thickness" a jezebel, mammy, or a hybrid of those images in an attempt to regulate her identity? I argue that while the images of mammy and jezebel have been the channels through which black feminists have critiqued society's definition of black female body size and sexuality, we must turn to f(ph)at black female teenagers to explain their relationship to mammy and jezebel in order to get a better understanding of what it means to live at their identity intersections.

Fat/Black/Female/Teenage Bodies and Sexuality Research

It is important to consider the role body size plays when fat black female teenagers make their sexual choices. While some work regarding black women has circulated moderately through academia, very little scholarship concerns fat black female teenagers' bodies and sexualities. Most sociological and medical research about fat, black, female, and teenage bodies focuses on eating disorders; compares the body images of black and white teenagers; discusses attractiveness as frequently (but not always) based on European beauty ideals; links fatness to the obesity epidemic and chronic illness; or shows how pubertal development or transitions affect sexual debut. In the work that reflects the dominant discourses on fatness and sexuality, scholars typically discuss fatness in medical frames and sexuality by looking at the sexual expression and sexual health of primarily whites and/or adults. Research about sexual behavior among teenagers focuses on teen pregnancy and disease control with a focus on teenage parenthood, HIV, and how black teenagers are disproportionately experiencing earlier sexual debuts because of earlier onsets of puberty.[15] While this work is immensely important for challenging medical definitions of fat and fatness, reversing sexual oppression, and unearthing sexual health issues of teenagers, it neglects fat black female teenagers in ways that render them invisible.

Sometimes this invisibility leads to a particular silencing that suggests that the personal experiences of this group are inconsequential. First Lady Michelle Obama's "Let's Move" campaign to tackle childhood obesity as defined by Body Mass Index (BMI) data was, I believe, an earnest and honest effort to address our children's physical well-being. However, a closer look at the initiative reveals that the First Lady may be addressing our nation's fixation with excess as the cause of obesity, particularly among poor women of color disproportionately affected by the "obesity epidemic."[16] Scholars have informed us for years that the concept of BMI has been biased against communities of color and other marginalized groups.[17] Instead of basing the "Let's Move" campaign on so-called normal and abnormal BMI ranges, why not critically examine environmental racism, limited access to health care, and how we negatively perceive poor and/or unhealthy people around the world? Celebrating our First Lady as a black woman with "fit arms" and a "small waist" attempts to resist some cultural scripts about black women and excess by implying that black women can be fit, too. However, this celebration may also proliferate the notion that being black and fat is still unwanted and unacceptable, so those without these physically fit characteristics remain deviant and inadequate. This could surely affect how our fat black female teenagers develop their sense of body image and body confidence. I argue that advocating for healthy living for our children, while necessary, can be quite relative and that instead of solely focusing on maintaining a "healthy" weight, we might shift our focus to simultaneously change cultural and societal norms of what we view as "healthy"—thereby rewriting cultural scripts.

One way to rewrite these scripts is to assess how teenage girls view themselves in the context of their peers, families, and communities. In 1995, Sheila Parker and her colleagues completed a study with approximately 300 high school girls (forty-six of whom were African American) on their concerns about dieting, smoking, and body image. The initial findings indicate that both African American and white girls were attempting to lose weight. However, conflicting data emerged in small group sessions that revealed that the African American girls, unlike their white female counterparts, were generally more satisfied with their weight and separated their beauty ideals from a white or mainstream image of beauty.[18] This could be a form of resistance, by which young African American girls refuse to subscribe to European beauty standards that mandate that they change their hair, skin color, and/or bodies (including size) to fit into an aesthetic model of beauty that would otherwise exclude them.

This resistance is vital to black women's existence, especially since scripts of black women's purported lack of beauty have dominated media outlets and other public discourses. While Parker and her colleagues show that this particular group of African American girls are complicit in subscribing to what their male counterparts define as attractive (i.e., "a big butt"), they are still engaged in a complex analysis and rewriting of a dominant script that defines attractiveness. I argue that if this practice were used for f(ph)at black female teenagers, we would see firsthand how the group accepts, rejects, and rewrites cultural and sexual scripts—and how vital their experiences are in constructing a black female sexual identity.

What Does Literature Do for F(Ph)at Black Female Teenagers?

Just as Simon and Gagnon assert that the cultural scenario is simply a guide, and although many people may follow it, individual players at the intrapsychic level have the power to incrementally change the script. Still, according to Parker and colleagues, no one in their study described the ideal girl as fat. Does a space exist for women and girls who prefer to live at the intersection of black and fat? Some writers think so. Zora Neale Hurston's 1926 short story "Sweat" teases out how Sykes, who abuses his wife Delia, prefers the sexual company of fat women, particularly one character named Bertha. While a nod to "big fat momma[s] wit de meat on huh bones" (a line from a blues song that describes some men's preference for fat women over skinny women), the idea of Sykes committing adultery with a fat woman is a complicated one. On one hand, Bertha's body exists in the text solely for Sykes' consumption: he uses her for an ostentatious display of his wealth and sexuality. On the other hand, while it may be that Bertha is at the financial mercy of Sykes, she shows agency in their affair by appearing with him in public and confronting him at the married couple's home. However, we never get to hear from Bertha directly. I believe her intrapsychic scripts might tell us that a marriage between two women and a man had its benefits, that being big would not lead to an asexual or lonely life, and that having sex as a big woman with a man of your choosing who financially supports you—yet to whom you have no legal ties—is the ultimate expression of a fat sexual freedom or enterprise. These possible intrapsychic scripts show a departure from dominant cultural established norms and would have been a great contribution to f(ph)at black women's literature.

Like Hurston, Alice Walker's *The Color Purple,* Lucille Clifton's "What the Mirror Said" and "Ode to My Hips," and Grace Nichols's *The Fat Black Woman's Poems* foreground fat black women's resistance to cultural norms. By showing fat black women resisting sexual violence, poor body image, and European ideals of beauty, these writers not only celebrate large black women's bodies as they are but also offer them as sites of resistance. In *The Embodiment of Disobedience: Fat Black Women's Unruly Political Bodies,* Andrea Shaw analyzes some of these literary works to show that fat black female bodies are in direct opposition to dominant cultural norms. She argues that since black women's bodies have been subject to subordination, their mere existence registers their bodies as sites of resistance. In addition, Tamara Beauboeuf-Lafontant tackles deviance and body size by asserting that black women overeat compulsively under a cloak of invisibility created by social, cultural, and environmental stimuli.[19] I argue that while some may overeat under a cloak of invisibility, others may overeat as an act of empowerment that increases black women's visibility.

Perhaps black women overeat to appear sexually attractive. This could stem from the standard of beauty that makes some thin women feel as though they do not have the hourglass silhouette that some men and same-sex-loving women prefer or from another standard that induces big women to eat to maintain the silhouettes their partners prefer. I also argue that some women enjoy their fat bodies and do not see thin bodies as attractive/healthy or as more attractive/healthy than fat ones. Even though fat black women's bodies are labeled deviant, they can and do oppose scripts that label thinness as healthy and black and fat as unattractive. They also complicate scripts that consider black and female as weak but black and fat as invincible. Their bodies are essential to the rewriting of identity scripts and show that black women can embody some, all, or none of these characteristics.[20] Although Hurston, Walker, Clifton, and Nichols have portrayed adult characters in their works, teenage readers who happen to read these literary works might witness the power of literature to not only portray the dynamism of black fat female identity but also showcase its resilience to a society that has historically rendered it invisible.

Fat Black Female Teenage Sexual Realities, Voices, and Choices

Because fat black female teenagers are considered a vulnerable group to institutional review boards (IRBs) across the country, conducting research that focuses on their bodies can often be a challenging task.[21] However, it is a necessary one. This section illuminates how literature and sociological study can carve a space for f(ph)at black female teenagers to tell their own stories about sexuality and prove, in the same way that black feminists before them have, that their stories are worthy of attention.

In *Dilemmas of Desire: Teenage Girls Talk about Sexuality,* Deborah Tolman constructs teenage sexuality as an extension of a dominant "sexed and gendered" sexuality that influences girls to yearn for "love, relationships, and romance" while it encourages boys to pursue sexual relationships with as many girls as possible (and applauds them for doing so). Tolman conveys to readers that girls who do not play their part in the script of chastity "instigate what has been called a moral panic, or a societal nervous breakdown of sorts."[22] This "moral panic" or "societal nervous breakdown" has been well documented in studies of teenage pregnancy, early parenting, and sexually transmitted diseases and infections. In cultural scenarios of parenting, marriage, and sex, women are to be married before engaging in sexual intercourse and having children.[23] The sexual scripts that "boys have healthy sexual desire" and "girls who have healthy sexual desires are dangerous" mean that unwed pregnant female teenagers carry a greater burden and shame about having a child out of wedlock than their male counterparts. This places black female teenagers and their baby f(ph)at at a very peculiar precipice: their black femaleness disrupts the "chaste" script, while their black fatness makes them the supreme caregiver. Do they think about burden and shame in the same way that their white peers do? If so, how does society view their sexual choices (and the potential consequences such as teenage pregnancy and sexually transmitted infections) with regard to these scripts and their identities?

As discussed earlier, cultural scenarios operate to dehumanize and repress women's sexuality, controlling women and female sexuality by objectifying them, downplaying female sexual pleasure, tolerating and even promoting sexual violence, and erasing lesbian contributions to history and culture.[24] In recognition that this repression of female sexuality begins during the formative years, Tolman interviewed a group of girls (fifteen to eighteen years old) to demonstrate that although teenage girls lack the language to speak directly about their sexuality, they still demonstrate their desire for pleasure through their experiences. After sifting through the girls' preliminary fear of (and conservativeness about) talking about sexuality, she found that many of them had desires but were restrained from acting on them by sociocultural boundaries. During their interviews, the teenagers told Tolman what their desires were by recounting stories of sexual encounters, discussing their sexual preferences, and talking about how they negotiate what they want versus what their families expect of them.

Of the thirty-one girls Tolman interviewed, seven teenagers were black (and heterosexual), and the parents of a majority of this subgroup were immigrants. Only one respondent, Rochelle, was a "full-figured" black girl whose body contrasted with her "small, sweet voice."[25] Throughout her interview, Rochelle spoke about sexual intercourse (in terms of whether or not she wanted to have it), success in formal education, and respect. She linked the act of sex with very real consequences, such as an unwanted pregnancy that could delay schooling or bring on unwanted attention. She also discussed how an assault by a past boyfriend and fear of being considered "immoral" caused her to really think about how her (lack of) desire for sexual activities affects her relationships. Tolman showed that Rochelle accepted the challenge of configuring her own sexual identity by showing her awareness of societal standards and her internal, intrapsychic scripts. At one particular point in the text, Rochelle spoke specifically about how her desire for sex increases:

> There are certain times when I really, really, really enjoy it, but then, that's like, not the majority of the times, it's only sometimes, once in a while. . . . If I was to have sex once a month, then I would enjoy it. . . . If I like go a long period of time without havin' it, then it's really good to me, 'cause it's like I haven't had something for a long time and I miss it. It's like, say I don't eat cake a lot, but say, like every two months, I had some cake, then it would be real good to me, so that's like the same thing . . . if you have sex moderately, then you have more desire.[26]

Putting Rochelle's cake-sex metaphor and its implications for fat black teenagers and dieting aside, it is important to note that she used her own language to formulate an example of desire. Here, her own body's longing, not her partner's, is what drove her desire for sex. Through notions of "lacking" and "longing," she takes ownership over her desire and legitimizes why and when it is pleasurable. She further demonstrated this ownership by admitting that she disconnected her consciousness from her body when she engaged in intercourse in which she had no desire to participate. Her intrapsychic script complicated her ideas about how teenagers should enjoy intercourse, how often they should participate in it, and with whom they enjoy and engage in sexual activities.

Voices such as Rochelle's are difficult to discover in the academy and in other venues of mainstream society. So much so that many f(ph)at teenage girls, although recognizable within their own communities, have to be constructed and packaged in alternative ways. Lee Daniels's adaptation of Sapphire's *Push: A Novel* into the critically acclaimed film *Precious* lost much of Precious' intrapsychic dialogue about fatness, beauty, and sexuality in the novel, further signifying the disinterest for such a discourse in a public arena. Claireece "Precious" Jones is a 200-pound, illiterate, sixteen-year-old mother of two who has suffered sexual abuse at the hands of both parents: her father not only fathered both of her children but, equally egregious, transmitted HIV to her. Precious's sexuality is defined for her, converting her into both mammy and jezebel. She is confined in a dilapidated urban landscape of an existence, a place where many girls like Precious live at the intersection of race, poverty, and sexual violence. It is within this landscape, however, that f(ph)at black teenagers are the most visible. While some are ignored, teased, or attacked by community members, teenagers like Precious are visible to their communities and become resistant and resilient to the negative scripts that label them deviant in their own neighborhoods.[27]

While tapping into this visibility, Sapphire unveils sexual abuse within black communities and unravels a sexualized subjectivity that makes critical interventions in current sexual discourse. When Precious is prompted by her counselor to recall her relationship with her father, she says:

> I tell counselor I can't talk about Daddy now. My clit swell up I think Daddy. Daddy sick me, *disgust* me, but still he sex me up. I nawshus in my stomach but hot tight in my twat and I think I want it back, the smell of the bedroom, the hurt . . . [he] call me names, pump my pussy in out in out in awww I come. . . . [he] Orgasm in me, his body shaking, grab me, call me Fat Mama, Big Hole! You LOVE it! Say you love it! I wanna say I DON'T. I wanna say I'm a chile. But my pussy popping like grease in frying pan.[28]

Precious's intrapsychic script, aligned with what many rape survivors have experienced, has complicated the scripted response to rape: her consciousness reprimands her father for sexually violating her body, but a pleasurable bodily reaction from the act of sexual intercourse causes her to orgasm. Here, her intrapsychic script is not only at work rewriting the mammy and jezebel images by navigating her sexuality through rape, abuse, fatness, and poverty but is also showing how legal institutions need to reconsider how rape and sexual violence affect women on personal and individual levels.

Precious's internal dialogue might cause negative legal and social implications if she were to share them, but she, like other victims of rape, had no control over her assailant or her body's reaction during the assault. For f(ph)at black female teenagers who have experienced or are considered to be at risk for sexual violence, the idea of exercising desire during an assault seems to be linked to the notion that any female desire at all is taboo. Tolman would certainly object to the sexual assault committed against Precious, but she might consider Precious's grasp of her sexual desires as an important step in establishing sexual subjectivity instead of being completely objectified. She writes:

> *Not* feeling sexual desire may put girls in danger and "at risk." When a girl does not know what her own feelings are, when she disconnects the apprehending psychic part of herself from what is happening in her own body, she then becomes especially vulnerable to the power of others' feelings as well as to what others say she does and does not want to feel.[29]

The separation of mind and body can be more disastrous for teenagers such as Precious, whose fatness, blackness, gender, and socioeconomic status may cause them to struggle to establish their personhood in the face of so many oppressive identities, especially during adolescence.

In their study of the sexuality of black youth, Marcus Hunter, Marissa Guerrero, and Cathy Cohen assert that "healthy sexual development encompasses development of self-esteem and self-efficacy to foster safe-sex behaviors, attitudes, and decision making both in adolescence and throughout the life course."[30] Tolman's depiction of Rochelle illuminates the importance of this development. Power struggles resulting from gender and age difference are prevalent in many sexual relationships, but it leaves fat black female teenagers particularly vulnerable. As one of the most socially and economically disenfranchised groups in the United States, they are less likely to be empowered to use contraceptives during intercourse (for fear of suggesting their infidelity to their partners) or to voice their desires.[31] Many of these young women have older partners, and, because their respective ages assign them different gradients of power, their difficulty to "say no" to their partners could place them at risk for unwanted pregnancies, domestic violence, and HIV infection.[32] Empowering black youths to explore their sexuality and conveying that the exploration itself is a vital part of becoming one's true self will prevent many of the sexual health problems that medical and sociological researchers are currently examining. Furthermore, investing in how black youths, especially f(ph)at black female teenagers, develop their sense of self, self-esteem, and the ability to make choices through a lens of baby f(ph)at will undoubtedly affect their transitions into adulthood.

CONCLUSION

When Jill Scott concluded her performance of "The Thickness," she stated repeatedly, "She's so big," while gesturing toward her mind and heart, implying that female bodies, particularly those of black teenagers, are a complex combination of mind, body, and spirit. Her references to these physical and metaphysical parts affirm that more than just baby f(ph)at is at work in establishing this fat black female's physicality. Intricate systems of identity, socialization, and oppression also give fat black female teenagers a unique social position that is very different from those of their white, male, or thin counterparts. Complex identities lie at the intersections of race, class, gender, age, sexuality, and body size, and while each identity marker is critical in shaping a person's life experiences, they cannot be studied separately, in isolation, or as disparate entities. Doing so risks excluding some groups, making some individuals invisible, and stunting identity formation. While sexual scripting outlines how sexuality is sexed, classed, and gendered, black feminist theory shows that race is also sexed, classed, and gendered.

Interrogating baby f(ph)at illuminates the extent to which fat black female teenagers employ tenets of black feminism in constructing their identities. More research about body size, body image, and fat black girls and teenagers will uncover critical linkages between body size, sexuality, and sexual choices. Young black women are interpreting cultural scripts and (re)writing intrapsychic scripts in order to (re)construct their identities. They make connections between their social and subjective realities in ways that further cultivate their own subjectivity. This means that their sexuality and sexual choices have serious implications for the growth, development, and physical and sexual health of black women. While the discussion of black women's health positions both young and older members of the group at the center of analysis, this does not mean that transgender people should be excluded from the conversation. As my preliminary explorations have shown, black fat teenagers are all sorting out their respective sexualities, sometimes in direct opposition to heteronormative scripts. Further research must include studies about lesbian, gay, bisexual, transgender, queer, questioning, and intersex youth and/or fat black boys in order to compile a more comprehensive study of the intersections between body size, body image, sexual choices, and sexuality.

NOTES

1. Here "baby fat" is used in the sense that Stanley M. Garn and Joan A. Haskell use it in "Fat Changes during Adolescence," *Science* 129, no. 3363 (1959): 1615.

2. Patricia Hill Collins, *Black Feminist Thought: Knowledge, Consciousness, and the Politics of Empowerment,* 2nd ed. (New York: Routledge, 2000), 73–74; Tracy Royce, "The Shape of Abuse: Fat Oppression as a Form of Violence against Women," in *The Fat Studies Reader,* ed. Esther Rothblum and Sondra Solovay (New York: New York University Press, 2009), 151–152.

3. Michel Foucault, *The History of Sexuality, Volume 1: An Introduction* (1978; repr., New York: Vintage Books, 1990), 3. Foucault explains how societies' attempts to regulate sexuality only create subversive spaces for people to explore their sexualities.

4. Ibid., 47, 106.

5. This is similar to Foucault's discussion of what occurs in the subversive spaces.

6. William Simon and John H. Gagnon, "Sexual Scripts: Permanence and Change," *Archives of Sexual Behavior* 15 (1986): 99–100. Simon and Gagnon explore how people

act as agents in recreating new scripts for their behaviors. They assert that while both interpersonal and intrapsychic scripts are important, it is the latter that holds the most transformative power for society and societal roles.

7. Ibid., 109–111.

8. Ibid., 108–109.

9. Ibid., 118. While I am deeply invested in intrapsychic scripts, I do acknowledge the difficulties in acquiring said scripts. Will respondents tell the truth? Will we ever know what someone is truly thinking? While personal behaviors may be more accessible, internal dialogues, as critical as they are, may not be as easily uncovered. This is also why I chose literature and film to discuss intrapsychic scripts because of the direct access to the character's consciousness.

10. Audre Lorde's theory that silence must be transformed into action highlights the invisibility black lesbian women experience. I use her notion of invisibility to tap into the discrimination that f(ph)at black female teenagers also experience.

11. This non-additive approach is described in Kimberlé W. Crenshaw, "Demarginalizing the Intersection of Race and Sex: A Black Feminist Critique of Antidiscrimination Doctrine, Feminist Theory and Antiracist Politics," *University of Chicago Legal Forum* (1989): 140.

12. Collins, *Black Feminist Thought*, 284–285.

13. Ibid., 78; Jennifer L. Morgan, *Laboring Women: Reproduction and Gender in New World Slavery* (Philadelphia: University of Pennsylvania Press, 2004), 92.

14. Thavolia Glymph, *Out of the House of Bondage: The Transformation of the Plantation Household* (Cambridge: Cambridge University Press, 2008), 194.

15. Marcus Anthony Hunter, Marissa Guerrero, and Cathy J. Cohen, "Black Youth Sexuality: Established Paradigms and New Approaches," in *Black Sexualities: Probing Powers, Passions, Practices, and Policies,* ed. Juan Battles and Sandra Barnes (New Brunswick, N.J.: Rutgers University Press, 2010), 377–400.

16. Cynthia L. Ogden, Molly M. Lamb, Margaret D. Carroll, and Katherine M. Flegal, "Obesity and Socioeconomic Status in Adults: United States, 2005–2008," Center for Disease Control data brief (December 2010): 3.

17. Samantha Kwan, "Framing the Fat Body: Contested Meanings between Government, Activists, and Industry," *Sociological Inquiry* 79, no. 1 (2009): 39.

18. Sheila Parker, Mimi Nichter, Mark Nichter, Nancy Vuckovic, Colette Sims, and Cheryl Ritenbaugh, "Body Image and Weight Concerns among African American and White Adolescent Females: Differences that Make a Difference," *Human Organization* 54 (1995): 107.

19. Tamara Beauboeuf-Lafontant, "Strong and Large Black Women? Exploring Relationships between Deviant Womanhood and Weight," *Gender and Society* 17, no. 1 (2003): 119.

20. Andrea Elizabeth Shaw, *The Embodiment of Disobedience: Fat Black Women's Unruly Political Bodies* (Lanham: Lexington Books, 2006), 8; Cathy J. Cohen, "Deviance as Resistance: A New Research Agenda for the Study of Black Politics," *Du Bois Review* 1, no. 1 (2004): 38–40.

21. In attempting to interview fat black female teenagers (especially as a graduate student), I faced large opposition from a high school review board that considered the group a "vulnerable" population that needed their protection. For IRBs, children are considered vulnerable populations to work with because of their ages, especially in terms of their levels of discomfort when they are asked questions about sex and sexuality. One woman I encountered was very protective of her group of fat female teenagers and was wary about any researchers gaining access to the group. I believe that having access to those young

women would have enriched my studies deeply, if only to hear from them directly what they thought about the intersections of their race, gender, age and body size.

22. Deborah I. Tolman, *Dilemmas of Desire: Teenage Girls Talk about Sexuality* (Cambridge: Harvard University Press, 2002), 8.

23. Foucault, *History of Sexuality*, 38–39.

24. Tolman, *Dilemmas of Desire*, 17.

25. Ibid., 88.

26. Ibid., 89.

27. This assertion comes from a 2010 informal interview with a f(ph)at black teenager who revealed to me that she was "thicker than a snicker" and did not care about anyone else's opinion of her.

28. Sapphire, *Push: A Novel* (1996; repr., New York: Vintage Books, 1997), 111.

29. Tolman, *Dilemmas of Desire*, 21.

30. Hunter, Guerrero, and Cohen, "Black Youth Sexuality," 387.

31. Ibid., 391. While the authors do not explicitly address fat female teenagers, I consider the fatness of these young women to be a contributing factor in their sexual decision making.

32. This is not to suggest that all female teenagers have older partners, but that relationships with older partners create power dynamics that are significant in decision making, as is evidenced in Kim S. Miller, Leslie F. Clark, and Janet S. Moore, "Sexual Initiation with Older Male Partners and Subsequent HIV Risk Behavior among Female Adolescents," *Family Planning Perspectives* 29, no. 5 (1997): 212.

CHAPTER 3

Corporeal Presence

ENGAGING THE BLACK LESBIAN PEDAGOGICAL BODY IN FEMINIST CLASSROOMS AND COLLEGE COMMUNITIES

Mel Michelle Lewis

Should I speak to the history of my blackness as a black feminist or as a queer, or do I identify with both because I am a lesbian of African American descent? Often, black lesbian, and the way that description of myself troubles identity, are terms that inform each other best about my differences.[1]

—*Laura Harris*

The intersections of identity inform and construct the classroom; all pedagogues find themselves differently situated within their fields of study and within "normative" conceptions of the archetypal "professor." However, that situatedness remains invisible until highlighted by the experiences of those who stand farthest from those established normative conceptions. The experiences of Black lesbian feminist pedagogues teaching social constructions of identity foreground the nexus of race, gender, and sexuality as they perform their own "embodied texts" in the classroom.[2] In this instance, identity itself disrupts normative expectations about the authoritative professorial subject, carving into high relief what Laura Harris describes above as the act of "troubling identity." These interlocking identities also influence the expectations of students, colleagues, and administrators regarding emotional and intellectual labor. In effect, the body functions as a text for college professors who self-identify as Black lesbian feminists as they draw attention to or deflect attention away from their corporeal presence as racialized, gendered, and sexualized subjects in their feminist classrooms and campus communities.

This essay explores the myriad ways that function plays out in the classroom as three Black lesbian feminists teach about race, gender, and sexuality in specific collegiate contexts. I draw upon a prior qualitative research project in which I applied an intersectional feminist approach to three cases (two case studies and a self-study).[3] The two other case participants were identified through a small, informal network of Black lesbian academics. Both were known to me and were well suited to the parameters of the larger study, which focuses on feminist college-level instructors who teach interdisciplinary materials related to race, class, gender, and sexuality. For this study, I conducted extended interviews and classroom observations, examined personal narratives and syllabi, reviewed course materials, and shadowed my subjects on campus. The self-study component employed reflexive autobiography, journaling, memory work, and personal narratives to examine my own corporeal presence in the classroom. Drawing on qualitative data from that research, this chapter explores how three Black lesbian feminist pedagogues work to harness their "otherness" and grapple with the act of "teaching the 'other' as the self" while engaging their creative pedagogical power through embodiment and performance.[4]

The feminist methodologies that ground this project highlight experience as evidence, the evidence of felt intuition, *testimonio*, theory in the flesh, and reflexivity.[5] The project grapples with the ways pedagogues and researchers who study the nexus of racialization and sexuality "pursue critical consideration of Black queer sexuality" in which "the objects of our analysis are so ethereal that they appear to offer us no hard evidence at all."[6] Given the importance of this process to minority life experience, I maintain that experiential and speculative knowledge and the evidence of felt intuition as presented by participants are valid forms of testimony.[7] Indeed, these ways of knowing are what shape our pedagogical projects.

QUEERING THE QUESTION: RESEARCH METHODS AND DESIGN

The research questions guiding this project centered on the premise that the body, identity, and performance can function as "equipment" for teaching and learning. I explored how three Black lesbian feminist pedagogues use physicality, classroom resources, materials, assignments, and personal narratives to acknowledge the body, employing embodied performance as a "text" to inspire teachable moments.[8] The two case studies each included six classroom visits over a sixteen-week semester, three extended interviews, and the shadowing of each participant during my visits on campus. The third case is a self-study.

This study attends to how intersecting identities play out in the classroom and in the broader campus community with particular attention to the negotiations of identity.[9] The case participants—Dr. Mariposa, Professor Deborah, and myself (Dr. Mel)—are introduced in the sections below.[10] Although each case is markedly different, two things are common to each: first, how negotiating the body's explicit and implicit identities remained a part of the pedagogical project, and, second, the ways the more legible performances and expressions of identity created disruptions, served as pedagogical tools, or inspired teachable moments.

Language and self-identification regarding sexual orientation and gender expression emerged as an important theme among the cases.[11] I considered the individual characteristics of each pedagogue and focused on the deployment of pedagogies through Black lesbian feminist women's embodiment and performance. I carefully use the names and terms "Black," "African," "queer," "lesbian," and "feminist," which people have chosen for themselves, because these are the specific terms articulated by the participants or used within the literature. I also use the term "queer" to assert the potential of gender identity and expression, in addition to an articulated lesbian sexual orientation. In the context of these cases, the two are read together upon the body in significant ways. The following sections explore topics related to experiences in the classroom and campus communities, drawing on our own words.

CASE STUDY: DR. MARIPOSA

Dr. Mariposa is a tall, handsome African American butch-identified lesbian woman whose presence quietly fills the room. Always dressed in a freshly pressed oxford button-down shirt, dark slacks, and leather loafers or lace-up leather dress shoes, she saunters into the classroom with confidence. A junior faculty member at a state university on the East Coast with few Black students or faculty, she commutes from a nearby city and rarely socializes or comes to campus on days she is not teaching. She describes herself as Black, lesbian, feminist, middle class, and butch. She asserts that her gender expression is read through the lens of Black masculinity, and she believes that students correctly read her queer butch gender identity as lesbian.

In terms of the politics of gender expression, Dr. Mariposa often thinks about how other people "read" her body on campus. In our interviews, she cited her physical appearance and gender expression, pointing out how her Afro-centric hairstyle—locks—could indicate her politics and, perhaps, her age. She posits that the hairstyle could affect how her sexual orientation and gender identity are received: "Um, well I certainly read as Black; but a particular kind of Black because I do have locks, which marks me as a certain type of Black person, I'm sure, to students. I mean I think it reads as young; I think it reads as hip. Um, but it also could read as militant, I'm not sure."

Dr. Mariposa describes herself as "naturally more retiring," the opposite of militant. She says she is "naturally reserved," both personally and politically. Her unobtrusive demeanor frames how she "comes across in spaces," and she tries her best "not to [attract] a lot of attention." Nonetheless, she notes, "People pay a lot of attention to me." As scholar Evelynn Hammonds warns, "The hypervisibility of Black women academics and the contemporary fascination with what bell hooks calls the 'commodification of Otherness' means that Black women today find themselves precariously perched in the academy."[12] Moreover, according to bell hooks, the Black woman student or professor is almost always at odds with the existing academic structure, which has not become accustomed to the Black female presence or physicality.[13]

Discussing her butch gender identity, Dr. Mariposa and I delved into how she sees herself expressing her gender and how this is interpreted or erased by her campus community. Asked to describe how she performs masculinity, she says: "I think I read as masculine to people. I mean, I wear men's clothes and things, [deliberately trying] to look masculine, and I think that comes across to students. . . . I wear earrings and a watch but no other jewelry. . . . I think they are put off by it—at first. . . . So, a lot of women in the school that I have seen are more traditionally feminine." Dr. Mariposa recognizes that in the classroom her stature and aesthetic draw attention, particularly for students who are "put off" by her butch expression.

Notably, Dr. Mariposa says that in other contexts, her butch identity appears to be invisible or may be purposely ignored by her male colleagues: "I think the men that I interact with see me just as, just as another woman, and I think they erase my masculinity, even though I think it's obvious for folks. I think I'm just a little lady for them." She reports that male colleagues refer to her as "young lady," saying such things as: "Oh, young lady, how are you doing young lady?" Being perceived this way feels uncomfortable and upsets her. She wrestles with whether to correct her male colleagues, saying, "It grates on me because my masculinity is a key part of my identity, but I don't know how to assert that. I'm not invested in kind of [saying] 'No! I'm not a young lady!'" Indeed, the consequences of such a retort would likely be dire.

We explored the implications of her intersectional identities in the classroom. One of her first responses noted the initial shock her body and identity pose to students entering her classroom for the first time:

> So, [students] were not expecting a Black person. They weren't expecting some-
> one so young, and they weren't expecting this masculinity. It's like, "Whoa!
> What's happening! Like Oooooh! I'm not sure I'm OK with this!" [Laughs.]
> Yeah, I feel them kind of do a double take like, "Oh! She's the professor? *She's*
> the professor?"

Overcoming students' expectations presents a barrier for her, particularly at the beginning of the semester. For her, the need to establish the legitimacy of her body and identity as "the professor" in the critical first class meetings takes precedence over introducing foundational material.

I contend that the experiences Dr. Mariposa articulated are a consequence of the many assumptions made about the intellectual shortcomings of women and people of color and of stereotypes applied to the Black female body. These coalesce on the bodies of Black queer women, particularly in the context of the academy, and are ever present in the classroom, as Dr. Mariposa's case illustrates. Thus, the Black queer female body of the professor signals the collective presence of "controlling images," to use Patricia Hill Collins's terminology, that have been fundamental to Black women's oppression.[14] At the same time, Dr. Mariposa's corporeal presence as the professor offers an oppositional challenge to the accuracy of these tropes. It is this disruption that arouses the curiosity of students and, often, the surveillance of colleagues and administrators.

Dr. Mariposa is uncomfortably conspicuous. That is, the attention that her body and identities attract and the dissonance engendered by her embodied text as "the professor" emphasize the significance of the relationship between pedagogy and identity in the classroom. Bryant Keith Alexander observes that the bodies of Black gay teachers are "racially historicized, sexualized, physicalized, and demonized," and these norms are further disrupted when Black gay teachers "present ourselves in the classroom as gay," which further upsets the academic tradition of disembodied intellectual exercise.[15] I argue that this disruption can be compounded by the presence of Black queer women's bodies when presented as simultaneously Black, female, and queer. This body represents multiple racial, historical, sexual, and physical narratives that contest the possibility of the mind/body split as it "mediates the educational endeavor."[16] Dr. Mariposa's case demonstrates the time and effort involved in negotiating these factors, which shape her larger pedagogical project and take an emotional toll.

Teaching Inclusivity in the Women's Studies Classroom

Dr. Mariposa's lessons center on intersectional analysis and inclusivity. However, students sometimes "buck back at" her when they encounter identity groups that make them uncomfortable. We discussed an incident I observed in her classroom that followed a screening of the film *Paris Is Burning*. A student referred to transwoman Octavia St. Laurent, a central figure in the film, by name, then with a snicker said "she, or he, or whatever."[17] Dr. Mariposa interrupted the student with measured frustration, indicating to the class that St. Laurent's gender identity is female and that "she" and "her" were the appropriate pronouns to use.

As a gender-nonconforming lesbian woman, Dr. Mariposa's response was spirited and emotional: "She! She! She identifies as she," Dr. Mariposa said, referring to St. Laurent. "Yeah . . . I have to try to . . . hold that in myself in order to have the class progress." She notes that these microaggressions "are ubiquitous" and that she rarely has an outlet for her frustration.[18] "There are a lot of little things like that," she says. "I think I just stockpile those kinds of experiences. . . . I can't respond to it all the time, so I just have to store it up, for some other time." Stockpiled experiences of racist, sexist, and homophobic microaggressions can leave faculty whose bodies signal the nexus of race, gender, and sexuality "'drained' by the intense scrutiny their everyday actions receive in the context of negative preconceived notions."[19] This scrutiny weighs on Dr. Mariposa. She employs various coping methods, including talking with loved ones and seeking musical entertainment, as a strong therapeutic force.

Within the context of this surveillance, Dr. Mariposa struggles with how to discuss race, gender, and sexual orientation in the classroom, particularly as they are inscribed and read upon her body. However, she also sees her gender expression as a bridge for her male students in particular: "I'm trying to make use of my identity in that way," she says. "Imagine another situation where they really take against me, like [speaking as student], 'Who's this Black butch? Talking all this bullshit about gender, shut up Dr. Mariposa,' but they don't." Moreover, she notes the bond she has with many of her male students, whom she believes unconsciously think, "Well, she's thought about masculinity, she's an ally towards masculinity, she's doing her own kind of masculinity, so it's okay for me to think critically about this stuff." Having a gift for teaching about masculinity through a butch gender expression is important to Dr. Mariposa. The ways she describes her own gender identity, coupled with my observation of her gender expression, lead me to read her body and its masculine gender expression as a "critical masculinities embodied text." Her corporeal presence thus operates as a textual bridge between masculinity and feminist consciousness for students.

Although Dr. Mariposa teaches through her masculine body as text in the classroom, she does not specifically discuss butch identity or female masculinity. She is out as a lesbian, and she says her body raises issues of lesbianism and female masculinity in the class, noting "how much we patrol that." Nonetheless, she does not delve deeply into female masculinity as a gender identity and expression. She avoids this, in part, because she says it feels "too close," and she feels uncomfortable discussing this openly with students. If she were to directly engage material on her own identities, she, by her own account, wouldn't "have the language to deal with it."

Dr. Mariposa believes that students receive her presentations of multiple dimensions of gender differently from presentations that might be offered by masculine-identified men or feminine-identified women because of how her particular embodiment plays out in the classroom, disrupting status-quo expectations about gender, race, and authority. Teaching about gender through her particular embodiment, she concludes, "might have the side benefit of making more space for people like me."

CASE STUDY: PROFESSOR DEBORAH

Professor Deborah is a petite, stunning African woman whose subtle intensity ignites everyone in the room. She is calm, still, and centered, speaking slowly and deliberately with measured gestures. "I don't like to make a lot of noise," she says. She is at once intimidating and warm, and her passionate approach to teaching is deeply engaging. Professor Deborah teaches at a private predominantly white institution on the East Coast. Categorizing herself as an African feminist lesbian and embracing a Black identity, she often refers to herself as "this little Black woman."[20] Her stature, openness, casual style, and easy smile exude youthful energy, although she tells students that she is not as young as they might assume. She wears jeans and khakis in class and is politically committed to wearing only natural fibers. Her expensive but comfortable shoes mute her steps around the classroom. She seems to appear out of nowhere; colleagues carelessly bump into her and students sometimes look up from their notes in surprise to find her peering down at them. Her students are at once intimidated by her intensity and brilliance and drawn to her warmth and compassion.

As a senior faculty member, Professor Deborah has taught at her institution for many years. In the classroom, she is demanding. She walks slowly around the room, placing the tip of her eyeglass arm into her mouth contemplatively. She leans in, peering at the students seated at tables, insisting they rise to the occasion with an answer, which they do.

Lived Identities

Professor Deborah describes herself as "an African feminist lesbian . . . that's how I've lived." She also believes her institution to be "the safest environment" for her, noting that her identities are respected. "I have a lot of space to be who I am, I meet a lot of quotas: a lot, so many, and it's really good to knock off some of those quotas with one body, so I'm going to get you all those quotas, then I am going to get some space," she affirms. Professor Deborah's multiple "quotas" also translate into many service responsibilities. As Darrell Cleveland asserts, "What makes African American [faculty] issues more pronounced are the very low numbers of Black PhD holders, and the 'stimulus value' placed upon us."[21] Moreover, Danielle Conway asserts that the "strong Black woman" stereotype leads to expectations and negative consequences within the academy.[22] Black female doctorate holders in particular are asked to be "all things to all people," including a role model, a resource to faculty and administrators, a bridge to the community, and an ethnic representative, in addition to fulfilling the teaching, research, and service responsibilities that are necessary for tenure and promotion.[23]

Although her schedule and responsibilities are shaped by her status as a body that meets multiple quotas, the "space" Professor Deborah claims as a powerfully positioned faculty member is supported by what I perceive as "heroic masculinity." As Jack Halberstam elucidates, "Female masculinities are framed as the rejected scraps of dominant masculinity in order that male masculinity may appear to be the real thing. But what we understand as heroic masculinity has been produced by and across both male and female bodies."[24] I describe Professor Deborah's pedagogical performance, then, as heroic masculinity, produced by a Black queer female body because it simultaneously troubles representations of normative genders and sexualities and makes room for alternatives infused with power and status.

Professor Deborah posits that some male colleagues engage her in "masculine bantering," in part, because she believes they see her as a "buddy," a masculine insider, rather than as a "female/feminine" colleague. As such, they relate to her with hand shaking and backslapping. I assert that this relationship to masculinity results in unique access to and acceptance into the campus power structure. Professor Deborah maintains that her "ideal [gender expression] is sort of a balance of the two": mixing and expressing both the masculine and the feminine. Her professional manicure is emblematic of this conscious mixing and divergence from her colleagues' perceptions of her as "masculine" or "neuter," as she reported.

Except for her remarkable relationship to heroic masculinity, Professor Deborah notes that she doesn't "have the usual markers of credibility," referring to perceptions held by students who do not know her: "I'm not married, I don't have children, my hair is not straightened, I'm not wearing high heels," she says. "So whatever the things, the markers you need to make you understand that I can command [respect from] you [and ask you] to behave in a certain way, they're not being read, so they are not there as far as I'm concerned." Professor Deborah interprets the complex readings of gender, race, and sexuality as she embodies them as challenging to members of the campus community who grapple with the multiple dimensions of her identity. Her subjectivity at the nexus of race, gender, and sexuality illustrates the ways Black queer women in the academy must grapple with the assumptions and costs of an "outsider within" status, one consistent with the analysis Professor Deborah articulated.[25]

Rapport and Power: What Would Professor Deborah Do?

Professor Deborah's students appear to hold her in the highest regard. She cultivates strong relationships with them, particularly the majors in her department, and acts as their mentor and confidant. She says her students frequently express admiration for her principles and integrity. Describing herself as intimidating despite her slight stature, she wants her colleagues and students to recognize the impact "this little Black woman" has had on the department and the college. Indeed, I read her intensity and stillness as intriguing. She is not at all unapproachable; rather, her intimidating persona serves to attract, inspire, and intrigue: "I have a reputation for being a hard teacher," she says. "And I appreciate that, and I want that. You know, because the package is a little small and can be thrown around, and so I want them—a little bit—to be concerned. For all students . . . even though I also have a reputation for being a very good teacher." I contend that Professor Deborah's description of her corporeal presence as something that could potentially be "thrown around" connotes both her physical stature and the identities that are read upon her body. She employs a strong mysterious persona in order to intentionally counter this possibility.

Professor Deborah's reputation for being a very hard, very good teacher, mentor, and role model has yielded some interesting tributes. She shared a story about some of her majors and advisees who responded to a racist or homophobic campus incident of student misconduct (she could not recall which at the time of this particular interview). The campus climate became "very tense," she said:

> A bunch of my students got together and made really big signs, and they walked around campus, [the signs] said "What would Deborah Do?"[26] I asked them, "What do you mean by that?" They said, "But you are like a little Buddha! You have anger and you have passions and we understand that, but you don't take them out on other people and we think people should be like you! We are trying to be like you." [Laughs] Ok, I thought, I can get behind that, but can you not put it on a sign! Yeah, so I thought, that's great, I don't mind my body being used for this purpose, but not a sign! That was nice; it's not just that I'm scary and mean and intimidating, and a lot of students say that, but that there might be a model here, if they're making signs!

In this example, she asserts that her body was used as a "model" for how to deal with conflict. She does not mind her body being used in this way. Being comfortable with power is a feminist stance for her. She connects her "comfort" with power and her feminist pedagogical authority. She is "very aware" of her authority and is, as she notes, "comfortable with it. It's not a thing, it's a non-issue. . . . it's a non-thing." Professor Deborah's corporeal presence simultaneously signals conflict and a model of engagement and resolution.

"Whose Side Are You On?" Positions and Identities on Campus and in the Classroom

One of Professor Deborah's advisees, a leader within the student LGBTQ organization on campus at the time, invited her to speak to the group. Professor Deborah responded to the student, saying: "As long as it's an intellectual conversation about these issues, I'd be happy to; and I'd be happy to talk about any other issues you want to talk about, but I don't want to come in there and talk about myself. I'm not into that. . . . [The student] wanted me to talk about gay marriage."

The student mentioned that another lesbian faculty member of color had given a very impassioned talk about marriage. Professor Deborah replied that she was on the opposite side. The student was appalled. Professor Deborah described their exchange: "She said '[Gasp!] You don't believe in marriage!' and I said, 'Do I have to?' We had this conversation, I said, 'Do all gay people have to be behind it? Have you thought about the race/class issues and this particular agenda?' She was my advisee, and she never came back to me. She *never* came back!"

Professor Deborah concluded that instead of a conversation about the broad political issues gay marriage brings up, the student wanted a fairly simplistic discussion about sexual orientation. She reports: "That's the place I won't go, not on this issue, because it seems performative to me. . . . I feel like I don't . . . need to do a gig about this [sexual orientation]. I live it! I've taken a lot of shit for it. I am marginalized in some amazing ways because of it. I've earned it. You know, so, no!" Professor Deborah notes emphatically, "I am not interested in using my body for student learning" in the case of student groups or events around sexuality.

Although Professor Deborah is "out" to her colleagues and students, she does not articulate her sexual orientation in the classroom. Instead, she "sends up little signals" in class: "I'll tell them that I know people, that I know this [gay] person and I knew this other person. That's going to be odd. That should, hopefully, send up little signals, right?" Regardless of whether the students make the connections, Professor Deborah feels that the students who need her to "be one of those identities with, to, or for them" are "paying attention" and will "get it." She confirms that they do seek her out, recognizing her corporeal presence as potentially supportive and affirming around multiple identities and intersections.

Case Study: Dr. Mel

I am a Black woman in my early thirties. Over the past seven years, I have taught at three predominantly white institutions: a large state Research One university, a state honors university, and a small private liberal arts college, where I am currently a tenure-track assistant professor. I identify as a queer feminist femme lesbian southern belle from Alabama. I am petite and quite frenetic, moving about the classroom as if it were a stage. Students often comment that I "dance" around the room; indeed, I rarely sit down in the classroom. Students and faculty observing me comment frequently on how "energetic" or "passionate" I am about the course material and how I transmit that excitement through my body to the students. I sometimes note my own tap dance–like rhythms as I prance across the front of the room. Dressing up is a part of my professional performance: tailored suits, fancy shoes with ribbons, flowing scarves, trendy hats, and a stylish (and sometimes unruly) short, curly haircut signal both the seriousness and the playfulness with which I wish to be received. I invest in this performance and believe that it has the potential to trouble some of the assumptions presented by my precarious positioning as an out Black queer young woman in the academy. I acknowledge here the challenge of self-study. Making plain one's own practices, performances, and identities is quite difficult. However, it has been beneficial in the development of my own pedagogical project.

An Uncanny Resemblance

This research project was precipitated, in part, by experiences in the classroom through which I recognized my body and identity as a canvas for teaching and learning. I intentionally highlight my identities and connect them to the texts and materials. I consider the concept of embodied text in the classroom as central to how I understand my own pedagogical project. I inferred that students were influenced by the ways my body and identities were aligned with the texts.[27] This sense of alignment was heightened when those texts articulated a Black feminist and/or Black lesbian perspective and when I explicitly expressed a connection by sharing a personal experience or affinity for the text based on my identities.

During my self-study, I noted that I deliberately say, "Black women/we/I," "As a woman/I," or "as a queer identified person/lesbian/femme/I" during classroom discussions. This intensifies the ways my students align the class materials to my own identities and embodied performances. This alignment indicates the ways my body functions as a text in the classroom and performs in such a way that I am sometimes indistinguishable from the topical or textual material. In these instances, my identity and embodiment influence meaning-making in the classroom, and this process is heightened when the material is about the intersections of race, class, gender, and sexuality. I negotiate this alignment, consciously walking a difficult line between mobilizing my Black queer body as a text, pointing to my own identities at times, and drawing students back to the theoretical readings produced by Black queer women's intellectual labor in ways that delve more deeply into the personal, historical, or cultural context in which they were produced.

Dilemmas to Consider When Teaching Desire

During a course on sexuality, I was surprised by my students' reactions to Deborah L. Tolman's *Dilemmas of Desire: Teenage Girls Talk about Sexuality*.[28] Most of the students in the class—twenty-one women and one man—had recently graduated from high school and still labored, by their own accounts, under the double standards presented in Tolman's study about the adolescent sexuality of girls. The study became a target of the students' deep personal frustrations.

As a lesbian who has been "out" to myself and others since age fourteen, my main concern in high school was to try to find another lesbian somewhere on the planet or, at the very least, to secretly record *Ellen* episodes on the guest room VCR and sneak off to concerts by Lilith Fair artists with anyone who had a driver's license. As such, it took me quite a while to interpret my students' anxieties. I had ideas, but I was unprepared and under-informed about the level of frustration my students were experiencing. "[Tolman's] asking all the wrong questions," they would retort. Apparently, so was I. "Everyone knows if you have sex, you get pregnant and die," a student proclaimed. Her classmates agreed; this is what they had been taught.

I realized that my own experience and research on queer identity development, sexuality, and gender expression had left me with a blind spot. Most students openly described their experiences with (and, in some cases, acceptance of) various versions of "abstinence only education" and abstinence-centered familial expectations. Some students objected to Tolman's inattention to asexuality, with which some identified. I was deeply challenged by these classroom conversations and gained new insights far beyond my own experience.

CREATING EXCITEMENT WITH UNSTABLE IDENTITIES: CROSS-CASE ILLUSTRATIONS

Placing these three cases in conversation with one another, making comparative connections, and noting distinctions allowed me to explore the depths and nuances of each case. Several themes emerged related to pedagogy and relationships with students and faculty. All of us commented on how creating "curiosity" around our identities, defying "stereotypes," and keeping students doing "guess work" about the identity of the professor can be useful pedagogical tools. Dr. Mariposa asserts, for instance, that keeping students "off balance" about "who she is" invites curiosity, cultivating space pedagogically to push the envelope and take students in new directions. In this way she both transgresses students' expectations about identity and enables them to see her as both more impartial and an authoritative voice.

Similarly, Professor Deborah notes that having students guess her identities can prove exciting and pedagogically advantageous: "I don't want to divulge everything; I want a little bit of the guess work. . . . I want a little bit of the 'What's going on? Who is she, what is she? What does she think about this? How far will she go, how far will she not go?'" However, she points out that keeping students interested in her is not always beneficial:

> Sometimes keeping them interested in me becomes problematic because they become more interested in the material because I'm interesting—and I'm not always . . . that's not always pedagogically valuable to me. But then, there's also the piece that says you can do [feminist activism]. That's really important, I've done this; I know you can do this. That piece is really crucial and it's pedagogically very important to me to do that empowering work.

Deborah feels that student interest in her can impede the learning process: "At times they are more interested in pleasing me than learning about the material," she says. "They want to look studious in my eyes and are only learning on the surface." However, she also feels that sharing details about herself and her work is a central element of her pedagogy, empowering her students by affirming, "I have done this/you can do this."

Similarly, I find sharing my experiences to be very important, particularly for students of color. I also enjoy dancing around identities in ways that give me maximum space to discuss race, class, gender, and sexuality in the classroom. For me, positioning myself as a Black lesbian femme feminist "publicly" in the classroom is advantageous: first, it allows students to assess and understand the depth of my relationship to the material; second, it models the practice of reflexivity. For all three of us, our pedagogical practice and corporeality allow for and, in some cases, insist that students explore reflexively their own identities.

Continuums of Recognition, Disclosure, and Performance

Dr. Mariposa is nominally involved with LGBTQ organizations on campus as a member of the faculty group, but she does not participate in the student group. Although she is "out" on campus and speaks openly about gay men, masculinity, and effeminacy, she feels that openness about her own lesbian identity and female masculinity is "talking too close to home." She describes her department as "a heteronormative department for sure. I mean everybody knows [I am a lesbian and] that I have a partner . . . [but] we're not exactly a department that asks about spouses." But it occurs to her that perhaps her colleagues don't ask about her spouse because she is a lesbian. She notes that African American studies colleagues do ask about her partner. "Maybe they really *do* ask each other about 'How's your partner?' and I'm not getting asked because my partner's a woman! [Laughs] . . . Um, in [African American studies] I think they do a little bit more about 'How's your partner?' . . . You know how Black folks askin' 'bout how your family is. That's what Black people do."

Dr. Mariposa also considers how her lesbian identity and other identity intersections position her within the department: "Well, there are other Black women in the department, and also other lesbians in the department; we're just full of everybody! Diversity!" she jokes. However, she notes that a white lesbian faculty member is "the branded lesbian of the department. So I don't play that role." Self-described as "naturally more reserved," she would not want to take on the role as "the lesbian." Significantly, Deborah expresses the same sentiment. Deborah discusses the campus celebration of National Coming Out Day (NCOD) referencing another faculty member who also fits the description of "the lesbian."[29] Deborah notes that she and "the lesbian," who is white, used to "get into it" over Deborah's lack of participation in NCOD events. She resists the expectation, saying, "I don't! I don't go to 'coming out day' or any of those things, you know . . . unless I'm specifically invited." She describes her confrontation with "the lesbian":

> So here is an instance where I wasn't interested in using my body for student learning or anything like that. . . . I think about a lot because around sexuality there's a novelty that makes us a little bit [like] circus performers, that I don't like. I, you know, at the risk of sounding like an assimilationist . . . view my sexuality as integral to my person. There wasn't a moment when I realized, "I am gay"; it came along with me as I grew, and so I want—I don't want to come out and say, "Oh, this is what happened and I was treated in this way." I am not into coming out stories.

Professor Deborah feels that participating in these campus events makes her and her queer-identified colleagues look like "circus performers." S. J. Ingebretsen supports this perception, writing:

> The lesbian or gay teacher easily becomes entangled in a grammar of the pornographic. That is, the teacher performs a skin dance, a public baring of his or her emotional body that is generally not permitted under other conditions. The only problem, of course, is that the dance is forced, indeed, framed as potentially scandalous, the public deviant presents a spectacle that is much in demand in eroticized popular culture.[30]

I see the concepts of "public baring" and "skin dance" as aligned with Professor Deborah's perception of participation in LGBTQ-centered activities or coming out in the classroom as a "circus performance." She is deeply committed to the idea that her body's enunciations perform a model for integrated identities; thus, because she "liv[es] her identities," she feels no need to overperform them in ways that separate, highlight, or make a spectacle of one identity over another.

While Professor Deborah wants to create safe spaces for students around her in regard to sexuality, she says, nonetheless, "I don't want to be asked to perform my sexuality as a model for students because I think I [already] do it." Professor Deborah sees her body as always already representing a model for integrated identities and, as such, resists requests to perform a particular element of that identity on demand. Dr. Mariposa and I tend to consciously perform identities or allow our bodies to speak, whereas Professor Deborah returns to her assertion that she lives her identities and hopes that students get it: "I think I do it, I mean look at me!" She notes that, indeed, some people are clueless, while "the kids in need [of support] are not."

In contrast, I realize that I am "the lesbian" in my department. I find that NCOD can be cathartic or used as a teachable moment. Recently, students celebrating in the student union asked me to "come out" after class. They asked me to dance through a giant cardboard door they had constructed. For them, this act symbolized "coming out of the closet" as a lesbian on campus; my performance made the newspaper. To this end, I see myself as a role model, particularly for LGBTQ students of color, both in and outside the classroom. I want my support to be highly visible. Nonetheless, there are many valuable ways to demonstrate support. The common thread in these cases involves the process of negotiating these choices.

Conclusions

Dr. Mariposa, Professor Deborah, and I all struggle with the ways our identities influence our pedagogical projects and shape our relationships with students and other faculty on campus. This struggle is a central overarching theme in our respective pedagogies. Creating excitement by sharing our identities or by leaving them unarticulated in creative ways is central to our work. We all use a variety of approaches to enunciate or deflect attention away from elements of our identities in ways that fulfill our pedagogical projects.

My hope is that this project will shed new light on the negotiations of marginalized bodies in the academy. For many of us, the practice of "teaching the other as the self" shapes the academic endeavor. Documenting these experiences and challenges as well as our reflections on them and using detailed portraits, reveals new insights into the body as text in the classroom. I hope that pedagogues like the three of us who find themselves precariously placed within the academy will be able to find kinship on the page and recognition for their own Black queer feminist pedagogical selves.

NOTES

1. Laura Alexandra Harris, "Queer Black Feminism: The Pleasure Principle," *Feminist Review* 54 (1996): 4.

2. Bryant Keith Alexander, "Embracing the Teachable Moment: The Black Gay Body in the Classroom as Embodied Text," in *Black Queer Studies: A Critical Anthology*, ed. E. Patrick Johnson and Mae G. Henderson (Durham, N.C.: Duke University Press, 2005).

3. This use of the term "intersectionality" refers to how race, class, gender, and sexuality operate together in relation to black women. See Kimberlé Crenshaw, "Mapping the Margins: Intersectionality, Identity Politics, and Violence against Women of Color," *Stanford Law Review* 43, no. 6 (1991): 1241–1299.

4. See Mae G. Henderson, "What It Means to Teach the Other When the Other Is the Self," *Callaloo* 17, no. 2 (1994): 432–438.

5. For a discussion of "felt intuition," see Phillip Brian Harper, "The Evidence of Felt Intuition: Minority Experience, Everyday Life, and Critical Speculative Knowledge," *GLQ: A Journal of Lesbian and Gay Studies* 6, no. 4 (2000): 641–657. For a discussion of *testimonios*, see Judith Flores and Silvia Garcia, "Latina Testimonios: A Reflexive, Critical Analysis of a 'Latina Space' at a Predominantly White Campus," *Race, Ethnicity & Education* 12, no. 2 (2009): 155–172.

6. Harper, "The Evidence of Felt Intuition," 651.

7. Methodological concerns derived from positivist or comparative social science research do not apply here. Because this study centers on participants' perceptions, neither measurable "reality" separate from perceptions nor generalizability is relevant.

8. For further discussion, see Mel Michelle Lewis, "Pedagogy and the Sista' Professor: Teaching Black Queer Feminist Studies," in *Sexualities in Education: A Reader*, ed. Erica Meiners and Therese Quinn (New York: Peter Lang, 2012), 33–40.

9. In the discussions below, it can be assumed that assertions not attributed to the subjects or to other sources are derived from my own observations.

10. To preserve anonymity, the participants selected their own pseudonyms.

11. For further discussion, see J. Halberstam, *Female Masculinity* (Durham, N.C.: Duke University Press, 1998); Laura Harris and Elizabeth Crocker, eds., *Femme: Feminists, Lesbians, and Bad Girls* (New York: Routledge, 1997); and Joan Nestle, Clare Howell, and Riki

Wilchins, *GenderQueer: Voices from Beyond the Sexual Binary* (Los Angeles: Alyson Books, 2002).

12. Evelynn Hammonds, "Toward a Genealogy of Black Female Sexuality: The Problematic of Silence," in *Feminist Theory and the Body: A Reader*, ed. J. Price and M. Shildrick (New York: Routledge, 1999), 99.

13. bell hooks, *Teaching to Transgress: Education as the Practice of Freedom* (New York: Routledge, 1994), 193.

14. See Collins, *Black Feminist Thought*, 5.

15. Alexander, "Embracing the Teachable Moment," 250.

16. Ibid., 255.

17. Octavia St. Laurent, a transwoman featured in *Paris Is Burning*, was a central figure and performer in New York's "ball culture" of the 1970s and 80s.

18. See Daniel Solorzano, Miguel Ceja, and Tara Yosso, "Critical Race Theory, Racial Microaggressions, and Campus Racial Climate: The Experiences of African American College Students," *Journal of Negro Education* 69, nos. 1–2 (2000): 60–73.

19. Ibid., 67.

20. For Deborah, "Black" and "African" are distinct and contextual identities that overlap.

21. See Darrell Cleveland, *A Long Way to Go: Conversations about Race by African American Faculty and Graduate Students* (New York: Peter Lang Publishing, 2004), x. Cleveland applies Na'im Akbar's conception of "stimulus value" to the experiences and labor of Black faculty.

22. See Melissa V. Harris-Perry, *Sister Citizen: Shame, Stereotypes, and Black Women in America* (New Haven, Conn.: Yale University Press, 2011).

23. Danielle Conway, "Being All Things to All People: Expectations of and Demands on Women of Color in the Legal Academy," in *From Oppression to Grace: Women of Color and Their Dilemmas within the Academy*, ed. T. R. Berry and Nathalie Mizelle (Sterling, Va.: Stylus Publishing, 2006), 21–30.

24. Halberstam, *Female Masculinity*, 2.

25. See Patricia Hill Collins, "Learning from the Outsider Within: Sociological Significance of Black Feminist Thought," in *The Feminist Standpoint Theory Reader*, ed. Sandra Harding (New York: Routledge, 2004), 103–126.

26. The signs the students made parodied the phrase "What would Jesus do?"

27. For further discussion, see Mel Michelle Lewis, "Body of Knowledge: Black Queer Feminist Pedagogy, Praxis, and Embodied Text," *Journal of Lesbian Studies* 15, no. 1 (2011): 49–57.

28. Deborah L. Tolman, *Dilemmas of Desire: Teenage Girls Talk about Sexuality* (Cambridge, Mass.: Harvard University Press, 2005).

29. On October 11 of each year, LGBTQ students on all of our campuses put together a program for NCOD.

30. S. J. Ingebretsen, "When the Cave Is a Closet: Pedagogies of the (Re)pressed," in *Lesbian and Gay Studies and the Teaching of English: Positions, Pedagogies, and Cultural Politics*, ed. W. Spurlin (Urbana, Ill.: National Council of Teachers of English, 2000), 17.

CHAPTER 4

Untangling Pathology

SEX, SOCIAL RESPONSIBILITY, AND THE BLACK FEMALE YOUTH IN OCTAVIA BUTLER'S *FLEDGLING*

Esther L. Jones

Stereotypes about the black family and black women's roles within it as pathological have formed the basis of public policy creation since the civil rights era, when Senator D. Patrick Moynihan outlined the black family's so-called tangle of pathology in his *Report on the Negro Family: The Case for National Action* (1965).[1] There is an often-unacknowledged linkage between the increased access to social programs that occurred with the gains of civil rights for blacks and the increased angst over the costs to society to provide economic aid to young poor unwed mothers. From the claims about the black family's pathological matriarchy that originated in what is now known as simply the Moynihan Report to the decades of subsequent legislative attention to remedy the so-called problem of single motherhood and the attendant social ills it creates, black women and girls in particular have been vilified and targeted for sexual management.[2] They have come to embody the emerging concept of the purportedly undeserving poor who take state resources that could better be used elsewhere.

Octavia Butler's *Fledgling* (2005) is a vampire novel that richly engages with the relationship between adolescent sexuality, individual responsibility, agency, and the state as a paternalistic regulator of these issues in service to the public good. The protagonist, Shori Matthews, allegorizes every anxiety about adolescent sexuality and its undesirable consequences: the reproduction of more undesirable bodies that drain the vitality of the body politic. The novel explores the extremes to which the state will go to contain this sexuality.

The novel opens with the protagonist, young Shori Matthews, in an amnesiac state after having survived a genocidal assault against her family. As she uncovers the mystery of her attack, we learn that she is a 53-year-old vampire-human hybrid who looks like a ten-year-old black girl. She is the product of controversial genetic experimentation by her vampire families, or Ina, as they call themselves, to impart the African human genetic defense of melanin to the Nordic-appearing Ina. The Ina consider themselves to be a cousin species to humans: they have survived the centuries by coexisting alongside mostly European populations but are unable to mate with them. Their exceedingly pale skin renders them defenseless in sunlight, and this necessitates long periods of death-like sleep during daylight. These vulnerabilities render their superior powers of speed, longevity, and exceptional healing capacities ineffectual during these periods. The Matthews family's success in cross-breeding the Ina and human species is considered to be a great benefit for their descendants, who will be able to stay awake in daylight and have greater defense against the sun.[3] The Matthews and Gordon families planned to mate Shori and her siblings with other Ina families to impart the "gift of the day" more broadly to the Ina species. The Silks, an Ina family living in northern California, found such experimentation to be an abomination. They consider themselves to be a species superior to humanity and set out to kill Shori and her two families in order to preserve Ina identity by preventing the reproduction of black vampires. The narrative climaxes when the Silks are brought to trial before the elders' Council of Judgment for orchestrating the murder of Shori and her families.

Octavia Butler's *Fledgling* offers a means of rethinking questions of social and cultural normativity, family structure and responsibility, and the relationship between black girls and the state. It reveals the extent to which the stereotyping of black girls' sexuality pathologizes Shori, rendering her Other and therefore unsympathetic to the ethical standards of her culture that would allow her simply to exist. This essay explores why black girls' sexual behaviors are targeted for social control and how *Fledgling* challenges the ethical logic that justifies oppressive state practices. A long-standing perspective metaphorically posits the state as an organic body, as the "body politic."[4] The family is presumed to function as an organic extension of that body. When parts of the political body are perceived as sick or pathological, steps are taken to fix that portion through social regulation. Shori represents the so-called pathology of young black sexually active females who are viewed as an imminent threat to the state precisely because of the stereotypes circulating about blacks generally and black women particularly. Traditional images of vampires represent them sucking the life force from unsuspecting victims, but, in this novel, Butler shifts our understanding of vampire-human relations from a parasitic to a symbiotic relationship. In so doing, she shifts the focus from the false question of whether the undeserving poor should receive support to the deeper ethical question of why we see some bodies as deserving of support while others are viewed as unsympathetic, expendable problems to be solved through increased social control or outright annihilation.

I begin by giving a brief historical background of how black women and girls in the United States have come to represent a social and sexual pathology through their allegedly non-normative roles within their families. Arguing that the state understands young black female sexuality as a dire problem to be resolved at all costs, I outline the relationship that has developed between sexual stereotypes and social policies since the Civil Rights era. I then move into analysis of Butler's *Fledgling,* which challenges notions of familial normativity, what constitutes pathology, and the logic that the state uses to justify its punitive behaviors in the name of a questionable greater good.

STEREOTYPES AND SOCIAL POLICY: A TANGLE OF PATHOLOGY

In March 1965, Daniel Patrick Moynihan, in his role as assistant secretary of labor and director of the Office of Policy Planning and Research, submitted a report to the Department of Labor outlining the now-notorious "tangle of pathology" in black communities. His report sought to demonstrate that the purported "cycles of poverty," delinquency, and social degeneracy attributed to black family life, if left unaddressed, would become the nation's most "dangerous social problem." Moynihan asserted that strengthening fathers to play a more normative role that fit the mainstream patriarchal structure was key to the successful assimilation of African Americans into the national political body and that the domineering black mother was the barrier to that process.[5] This alarmist rhetoric positioned the systemic socioeconomic problems of blacks as an urgent national policy issue that would guide the intellectual debate and policy formulations affecting black life for decades to come.[6]

The Moynihan Report helped codify stereotypes about black women, especially by purporting that at the heart of black America's problems was a matriarchal structure that usurped the black male's proper role as head of household and provider.[7] Historically, black single women had most often been viewed as jezebels, sexually aggressive women whose moral laxity functioned as a vector of both social and physical disease. According to this stereotype, this so-called jezebel would become particularly problematic as her sexual promiscuity resulted in offspring who would ostensibly be rewarded by entitlements from the state. The shiftless welfare queen would take advantage of the largess of the state by adding more babies to her delinquent brood. As the sexually irresponsible jezebel and excessively fertile welfare queen aged, they would mature into the emasculating black matriarch who, as head of the household, would make decisions and run the lives of children, grandchildren, and others under her rule.[8]

Not long after the Moynihan Report highlighted this pathology thesis, angst about teen pregnancy increased. A series of laws from the 1970s through the 1990s took on both the perceived epidemic of adolescent pregnancy and the problem of welfare entitlements.[9] These concerns over black matriarchal pathology and an increase in the number of single young mothers converged to make black girls the face of single motherhood: as undeserving claimants in an overly generous welfare state. Deborah Rhode and Annette Lawson argue that the angst over teen pregnancy is less about girls giving birth than it is about the burden of economic responsibility it imposes and the "cultural ideology they challenge" surrounding traditional values of young female sexual propriety.[10] I would argue, however, that policymakers are troubled by all of these issues: the cultural ideologies about the sexual activity of young females and the perceived economic burden early motherhood poses for the state; the reproduction of undesirable offspring, such as criminal black boys and morally lax black girls; and the perpetuation of cycles of criminality and poverty that are stereotypically linked to the black and poor. These are the so-called undeserving poor who drain the vitality of the state in vampiric fashion and who must be neutralized.

These stereotypes live a vibrant life in the public imagination and have functioned as the faulty data source upon which policy agendas are set, thereby legitimizing the political assault against black women and girls.[11] Political scientist Melissa Harris-Perry has described how black women are not seen as citizens who need support because of the inaccurate filter that stereotypes create.[12] I argue that not only are black women seen as undeserving of support, they are actually also viewed as a threat to the stability of the body politic that must be neutralized through control of their sexual and reproductive activities. And it is the family, as an extension of the state, that is responsible for policing sexual and reproductive behavior by enforcing proper norms, values, and behaviors.

A number of assumptions undergird the state's attitude toward families and their role in the management of the sexuality of adolescent girls.[13] Because the state assumes that youths cannot manage sexual activity responsibly, they are subject to the supervision vested in parental figures or other state-sanctioned responsible authorities *in loco parentis*, or in place of the parents.[14] However, because it is the state that endows the family with the power to manage and control youths,[15] we might just as readily observe that the family is, in fact, a civic apparatus that serves *in loco ordinatio*—that is, suborned to and acting in place of the government to enact the will of the state. In other words, the sexuality of young people is managed by families but is defined, structured, and controlled by the state in the name of protection from harm.[16] Thus, familial structure and the management of adolescent sexuality are inextricably linked in service to nationalist imperatives that purportedly strengthen the body politic.

Uncoupling the examination of early adolescent sex from the dreaded outcome of unwed teen pregnancy allows us to examine the ethical contours of our cultural expectations. From the perspective of the state, it would seem that sex among black adolescents is not really a problem until it results in the production of offspring, which the state then becomes responsible to support. Yet failure to engage the social, cultural, and psychological context of premature sexual

activity creates an ethical logic that invokes stereotypes of precocity and promiscuity, thereby rendering sexually active girls unsympathetic subjects who are
unworthy of social support. Our attention must turn to the development of an
ethical logic of relationality that attends to a psychological and emotional support for girls that more effectively informs their experiences of sexuality. Within
this new ethic, Michelle Fine and Sarah McClelland's argument for an evolved
politics of "thick desire"—that includes "unhindered access to those social and
interpersonal structures" necessary to "make safe, agentic, responsible sexuality
possible"—opens a crucial space where we can begin to untangle myths of black
female pathology.[17]

Black Vampires: Speculations on Adolescent Girls' Sexuality

The vampire novel might seem like an unlikely choice of genre for exploring
important political issues such as adolescent sexuality, teen motherhood, and
state welfare policy. Some might even argue that this approach is counterpro-
ductive, as such issues are too important to risk reducing them to the elements
of the extreme, the absurd, and the obscene. However, science fiction, fantasy,
horror, and other speculative genres offer an alternative approach to social issues
by utilizing the distancing literary mechanisms of mythic figures and nonhu-
man others, epistemological dislocation, and alternate realities to create what
Darko Suvin has coined "cognitive estrangement," signaling the genre's capacity
to make strange what we assume we already know.[18] The interaction of cognition
and estrangement in *Fledgling* highlights assumptions and stereotypes about the
unusual sexual precocity, dangerous reproductive patterns, and sexual unassail-
ability of black girls.

In U.S. society today, as was the case historically, sexually active black female
youths are perceived and treated as a social pathology. *Fledgling* enables us to
examine not only the ways in which black female adolescent precocity is already
naturalized but also the degree to which black girls are assumed to be sexually available, unassailable because of their purported precocity, and therefore
expected to unjustly shoulder the responsibilities of mature womanhood. This
highlights black girls' particular vulnerability in relation to the body politic.
Black women are, in ordinary reality, considered always already alien, an ultimate Other, as indicated through the stereotypes of the jezebel, welfare queen,
and matriarch described earlier. Unsurprisingly, the sexual stereotypes for black
girls are the same as those for black women. In fiction, the process of rendering
this already known yet always alien figure recognizable depends largely upon
rehearsing stereotypical sexual narratives. Thus, in *Fledgling*, Shori is sexualized
and pathologized in both human and Ina cultures.

Shori appears to us as the text begins as a ten-year-old, amnesiac, feral black
girl who is trying to survive after a violent assault. With no memory of who she

is or what has happened to her, she follows her instincts, manages to salvage clothing from the ruins of the fire that has wiped out her community, and wanders onto the road. She is picked up by a 23-year-old white man named Wright who perceives from her burns, her bald head, and her ill-fitting clothing that she is a little girl in trouble. This does not stop him from engaging in what would constitute pedophilic assault in human culture before he even knows what she is and what would explain his erotic response to a child: she is a vampire. According to the empirical reality of his world, vampires do not exist; what he sees is that she is a human black girl and that she is accessible to him and willing to engage in sexual activity. After a disturbingly brief internal struggle that exhibits an astonishing lack of restraint, he places her on his lap, engages in overt sexual banter, and allows her to lick and bite him as he writhes with pleasure under her body.[19] Although we later learn that Wright is responding to an addictive chemical produced by Shori's venom and her Ina scent, he does not realize this in their initial encounter. It seems odd that the cultural taboos surrounding pedophilia and statutory rape do not curb his eagerness to act on his urges. But Wright can behave in this manner, I argue, in large part because Shori fits the stereotypical human referential framework of a sexually precocious, unassailable black girl-woman. It is not until much later that we learn that she is 53 years old in human years but still a child by Ina measures.

Even as Shori becomes legible as human through the invocation of well-known sexual stereotypes, the speculative vampire genre constructs behaviors that are considered problematic in human terms as normative and explicable in the parallel Ina world. For example, the parasitic practice of living off human blood is transformed into a "mutualistic symbiosis" in which humans receive the benefits of extraordinary longevity, health, and intense sexual pleasure (123). Yet although Shori's precocious human behavior is explained by her Ina genetic disposition, she remains alien to the Ina who have tried to destroy her precisely because of her human traits, the most notable of which are her dark skin and her atypical diminutive stature by Ina standards. The mythic archetype of the vampire as Butler renders it addresses racialized and gendered questions of Otherness, narratives of identity and belonging, and social empathy (the cognition side of Suvin's theory). Shori's melanin makes her a more powerful and valuable member of the Ina species because of her capacity to reproduce more of her kind imbued with the gift of daytime alertness and decreased vulnerability to sunlight. But a faction of the Ina reject this power because she is part human and, even worse, black. Thus, they attempt to kill her before she reaches full sexual maturity, when she would be able to bear more black Ina.

This interplay of cognition and estrangement clearly articulates racialized and sexualized parallels to historical U.S. human ideologies of white supremacy, black inferiority, and social ills attributed to race mixing, placing these discourses at a distance to allow a fresh examination of old issues. Shori has been targeted for extermination because an Ina family group, the Silks, feels that cross-breeding with black humans—deemed the most inferior race in an inferior species—is an abomination that must be stopped by destroying Shori and her families. The notion of "species contamination" is well known to us through the slavery-era ideologies that argued that African Americans were not really human but constituted another species entirely. These racist patterns also parallel the eugenic discourse of blood contamination during Jim Crow, reflecting anxieties about white racial purity and the continued angst race mixing generated.[20] The Silk family regards humans as tools for Ina use and justifies their actions with the argument that they are preserving the purity of the species. Finally, just as during the post–Civil Rights era, when black families were pathologized as a parasitic force that fed upon the body politic of the welfare state, the figure of Shori appears as a vampire, echoing the image of black female dependency even as it undermines it. In *Fledgling*, we see these sociohistorical strategies of denying personhood, which resulted in unethical treatment of the Other, repeated as a speculative parallel.

While the social and political dynamics of species and racial chauvinism are recognizable as empirical, historical and contemporary realities in human cultures, the vampire figures who enact these recognizable crimes in Butler's text are less so, constituting the estrangement side of Suvin's theoretical coin. Both the embodied attributes of the Ina and the structures that constitute Ina culture and politics provide a necessary distancing from empirical human norms. This distancing strategy functions to release readers from an immediate sense of culpability that provokes a knee-jerk resistance to many realist depictions of sexual taboos and related social problems and allows for a discussion of social ills in a less personalized manner. That it is the Ina and not we (humans) who are behaving badly allows us to respond with a fuller, less guarded range of emotions and to see familiar social conditions with new eyes.

INA OLIGARCHY AND THE BURDEN OF RESPONSIBILITY

At the core of the angst surrounding adolescent sexuality is the question of who, ultimately, will be responsible for the undesirable offspring that will be produced. In U.S. norms, the state, which bases its policies on the model of the nuclear patriarchal family, mandates that the family manage adolescent sexuality and subsidize premature motherhood.[21] The family is deployed *in loco ordinatio*, in place of the state, to manage the economic and social burdens of undesirable breeding. Social stability is linked with the containment of sanctioned normative sexual behaviors within these traditional family structures.

In Ina culture, families function as the locus of state or political functioning to an even greater degree. But the so-called familial norm is radically revised in *Fledgling*. Butler generates an ironic reversal of cultural norms wherein Shori's sexual promiscuity, which in human terms is a moral shortcoming, becomes a strength in Ina culture that enables her to survive. Even though Shori exhibits sexual stereotypes that are problematic in human terms, from an Ina perspective, her sexual choices are safe, agentic, and socially responsible as she reconstructs her family after the genocidal massacre of her community.

Ina families consist of a male Ina family that is mated with a female Ina family. The two families live in separate, homosocial communities, thereby generating multigenerational communities of fathers and elderfathers in one community and mothers and eldermothers in a separate neighboring community. The male and female elders are all equally available to the Ina young people for socialization and education. Humans are part of these Ina families as "symbionts" who are physiologically and emotionally tied to the particular Ina who have bound them. Gender is of no consequence in the Ina-symbiont relationship. Male and female Ina will have both male and female symbionts upon whom they depend not only for physical sustenance but also for emotional support and sexual pleasure (270). Even Ina children have their own symbiont dependents. What appears as homosexuality, pedophilia, and general queerness in human experience is acceptable—and even necessary—sexual play in Ina culture (80). Moreover, each Ina, including children, is responsible for providing for and protecting their human symbionts within their own households.

These alternate familial structures and social roles highlight the vulnerability and interdependency of humans and Ina, challenging patriarchal notions of family and social responsibility. But it also highlights the primacy of the state in mediating reproduction, if not sexuality. Without her human symbionts, from which the Ina receives a regular supply of sustenance, and without an Ina family or community to which she can be mated to continue the family bloodline, a single Ina is vulnerable to death and extinction. The two parts of her family—human and Ina—separate the functions of sexual, psychological, and emotional pleasure and support from reproductive functions. Ina who lack this web of relations will die.

Shori is targeted for extermination because of the threat she poses to the Ina family-state. The danger she poses is directly related to her hybrid status as both human and vampire and her potential to bring more of her kind into the Ina world once she reaches childbearing age. However, the Silk family's chauvinism is also racialized. In the judiciary proceedings that are assembled to determine who is responsible for killing Shori's families and symbionts, Katharine Dahlman, counsel for the Silk family, expresses the ethical logic that justifies the murders by citing Shori's illegible otherness: "No one can be certain of the truth of anything you say because you are neither Ina nor human. Your scent, your reactions, your facial expressions, your body language—none of it is right. . . . We are Ina. You are nothing!" (272). That Shori is not even human, that she is, in fact, "nothing" speaks to the unknowability of her mixed Otherness. This is enough to justify killing the "black mongrel bitch," preventing her from reproducing more "mongrel cubs" of her kind (300).

The compulsion to exterminate Shori and her families is the primary strategy for exerting state political control over her presumably dangerous reproductive potential. But interestingly, she poses a threat to both her supporters and persecutors. Her melanin—which renders her vulnerable to the Silk's racist attack—also makes her a desirable choice of mate for the Gordon family. Now that her families have been destroyed, however, she is a dangerous choice of mate because her sisters, who had been promised as mates for the Gordon brothers along with her, have been killed. The responsibility for bearing all of the Gordons' children now falls solely on Shori once she reaches sexual maturity. This is reminiscent, in one respect, of black women's status as breeders during the antebellum slave era. Yet her position yields considerable power because she is now the only remaining Ina who has the power to birth children who can survive in daylight. The Gordons understand this as a strengthening of their family and are willing to risk Shori's singularity to gain access to it, but no one seems to raise the question of the risk—indeed, the excessive burden—mothering the children of multiple Ina men will pose for Shori. The Silks reject her completely, but the Gordons demand too much of this girl. Posited as a risk to the Gordons because of her singularity and considered too great a cost to Ina species purity for the likes of the Silks, Shori's young black female body becomes the political battleground on which state policy and the notion of social welfare is contested. This reflects the dual relational pattern between black females and the state: either Shori is wholly unassimilable into the body politic or is overly burdened by the excessive expectations of her reproductive contribution.

Shori and the Family-State: Sexual Propriety and Social Welfare

The Ina Council of Judgment—the three-night trial during which Russell Silk and his family are tried for the murder of Shori's families—reveals the ways in which the family-as-state defines not only who belongs within the body politic but also what constitutes acceptable state enactments and coercive powers to discipline, punish, and even kill with near-impunity to preserve the greater social good. Silk family counselor, Katharine Dahlman, uses three strategies to deny the family's responsibility for the murders, each of which hinges on discrediting not only the charges of murder that Shori has brought but also her right to call a Council of Judgment in the first place: she argues that she is not Ina, that she is sick because of her amnesia, and that she is a child. They use these collective arguments in an attempt to establish Shori's status as illegitimate and expendable.

The Ina species purists regard Shori's existence as a threat to the stability of the state that must be destroyed. Thus, it is unsurprising that in the trial, the Silks, who are on trial for mass murder, turn the tables and put Shori in the defensive position of proving her Ina citizenship. According to Katharine Dahlman, the Silk family's initial counsel, purportedly normal Ina would be completely devastated to the point of madness if they lost their entire web of Ina and human relations (272). But the council members, who rely on their hypersensitivity to literally smell the truth, are split in their interpretation of Shori's behavior after the loss of her families. Her composure during the trial is interpreted two ways: some read her lack of emotion in the aftermath of such great loss as evidence of her non-Ina status, while others perceive it as evidence of her amnesiac state. Either way, Shori's credibility is challenged because her behavior and her looks are supposedly too abnormal to disregard. Shori's amnesiac state further complicates their ability to see her as Ina. Ina have excellent memories and brain injuries are an extreme rarity in their communities. The Silks use Shori's amnesia as an opportunity to further highlight her difference from Ina by calling to the stand a human doctor to examine her and to raise questions about the nature of her amnesia—a maneuver designed to imply her non-Ina status. In this way, they use her amnesia, which explains her seemingly abnormal behavior, to negate her identity and belonging as Ina.

As the defense seeks to discredit her biological belonging as Ina, they also seek to challenge her cultural belonging when they accuse her of violating the Ina sexual taboo of premature bonding with her future Ina mate, Daniel Gordon. While sexual activity is regarded as a safe and customary part of Ina relations with their symbionts, Ina male and female mating practices are far more carefully monitored. The venom of the female's bite binds the male to her in the same manner that symbionts become addicted and bound to their Ina, but when an Ina girl binds a male before she has reached sexual maturity, it is dangerous for the male, as doing so renders him infertile with other Ina (109). Such an accusation of premature bonding, if true, would prove her utter disregard for the welfare of other Ina, deeming her irresponsible and dangerous for the welfare of the state writ large (244). Shori had, in fact, resisted biting Daniel and prematurely bonding with him. Her exercise of restraint exhibits her capacity to act in accordance with Ina sociocultural morals and norms and affirms her status as Ina.

When these discrediting strategies fail, Katharine orchestrates the murder of one of Shori's newly acquired symbionts, Theodora, during the trial. This is a double-edged test to see if Shori would respond in proper emotional Ina fashion: she would either be driven mad with grief, unable to continue the trial, or she would behave in such a non-normative manner as to exhibit to all that she is not Ina (272). In spite of these machinations, Shori is indomitable in her self-defense. Exhibiting a brilliant stroke of reason, she forces the Silks to admit that if their concern for greater Ina welfare is truly about the dangers of genetic experimentation, then the legal action of summoning a Council of the Goddess is an available recourse that they have neglected to take (292).

In the concluding remarks of the trial, Russell Silk calls upon the council to consider the welfare of the Ina people, implying that his family's genocidal acts should be overlooked for the greater good of preserving Ina identity. With trembling intensity, he implores the Ina council to remember: "Children of the great Goddess, we are not them! . . . We are not them, nor should we try to be them. Ever. Not for any reason. Not even to gain the day; the cost is too great" (292). Thus, the murder of twelve Ina and nearly 100 human symbionts is justified in the name of protecting the state against the potential reproductive dangers of an adolescent black girl. It is not sexual activity that presents a problem to the state; it is the reproduction of more "mongrel cubs" like her. She is considered nothing more than a "clever dog" (238) and therefore is dispensable, in spite of her ability to impart the indispensable gift of "the day" to the Ina.

The lack of unanimity about the Silks' clear guilt at the trial's conclusion reveals the ideological rift in the Ina narrative of belonging. Still, a majority vote for guilt, and the Silk family and Katherine Dahlman are brought to justice for their crimes. The Silk family is, as such, dissolved and their unmated sons are adopted into other families on different continents, effectively ending their sovereignty as a political unit. Moreover, Katharine Dahlman is executed for refusing the council's guilty verdict for the crime of killing Shori's symbiont.

As the reader is groomed into an understanding of Ina cultural logic and social/behavioral norms, the recognition of Shori's sexual Otherness as explicable in Ina terms actually renders her a more sympathetic subject. Shori is both human and not human, both a girl and not a girl, both vulnerable and powerful. The vampire genre naturalizes Shori's sexual precocity, making it a biological imperative that is part of her nature as a vampire. Yet reducing black sexuality and identity to biological essence are precisely the ideas that many scholars have resisted. Shori's utter Otherness raises a question: Even though she embodies all of the troubling stereotypes that have been used to justify black women's (mis)treatment, is she still beyond the pale of empathetic ethical treatment? The Silks had other legal means of stopping the genetic experimentation that produced Shori, yet they chose genocide because they assumed they could do it with impunity. That many of Shori's fellow Ina fail to recognize her as worthy of ethical treatment as Ina or human highlights a tendency toward the ethical disjunctures that occur in the practice of all varieties of chauvinism, particularly when the welfare of the state is thought to be at stake.

Fledgling challenges the particular distortions vested in black adolescent sexuality by shifting the conversation surrounding what constitutes pathology. Disturbing as it may seem, because Butler disentangles sexual activity from the consequences of reproduction, she reveals the attempts to manage and repress Shori's reproductive capacities for what they are: racist, ethnocentric endeavors. That the Silks and Dahlmans are willing to risk their stake in the body politic by refusing to acknowledge their crimes reveals the true pathology to be an obsession with racial purity. Shori asserts her belonging in the Ina familial-political body by exercising ethical sexual relations with both Ina and humans that go beyond the instinctual, revealing a resourceful intelligence that subverts notions of social responsibility and untangles the mythology of black female pathology.

NOTES

1. D. Patrick Moynihan, *Report on the Negro Family: The Case for National Action* (Washington, D.C.: Office of Policy Planning and Research, United States Department of Labor, 1965). Moynihan argues that the so-called tangle of pathology threatens the fabric of society of the Negro urban poor and, by extrapolation, all of African American society and the stability of the nation as a whole.

2. The Adolescent Health Services and Pregnancy Prevention Act was passed in 1978, during Jimmy Carter's administration; the Family Support Act was passed in 1988, during Ronald Reagan's administration; and the Personal Responsibility and Work Opportunity Reconciliation Act was passed in 1996, during Bill Clinton's administration.

3. Octavia Butler, *Fledgling* (New York: Warner, 2005), 67. All subsequent references to this novel will be cited parenthetically within the text.

4. Daylanne English, *Unnatural Selections: Eugenics in American Modernism and the Harlem Renaissance* (Chapel Hill: University of North Carolina Press, 2004), 4. See also Nancy Ordover, *American Eugenics: Race, Queer Anatomy, and the Science of Nationalism* (Minneapolis: University of Minnesota Press, 2003).

5. Moynihan, *The Negro Family*, 48.

6. Elaine Bell Kaplan. *Not Our Kind of Girl: Unraveling the Myths of Black Teenage Motherhood* (Berkeley: University of California Press, 1997), 5.

7. Ibid., 29.

8. Patricia Hill Collins masterfully outlines the history and politics of these black female stereotypes in her groundbreaking book *Black Feminist Thought: Knowledge, Consciousness, and the Politics of Empowerment* (New York: Routledge, 1991).

9. Numerous critics have challenged the rhetoric of crisis surrounding teen pregnancy rates. See Maris Vinovskis, *An "Epidemic" of Adolescent Pregnancy? Some Historical and Policy Considerations* (New York: Oxford University Press, 1988), 22.

10. Deborah Rhode and Annette Lawson, "Introduction," in *The Politics of Pregnancy: Adolescent Sexuality and Public Policy,* ed. Annette Lawson and Deborah L. Rhode (New Haven, Conn.: Yale University Press, 1993), 3.

11. Collins, *Black Feminist Thought*, 69.

12. Melissa V. Harris-Perry, *Sister Citizen: Shame, Stereotypes, and Black Women in America* (New Haven, Conn.: Yale University Press, 2011), 21.

13. The management of adolescent girls' sexuality through public policy has increased for all girls in all racial and socioeconomic groups, yet girls of color and poor girls are disproportionately affected by legal policy.

14. Michelle Fine and Sara I. McClelland, "The Politics of Teen Women's Sexuality: Public Policy and the Adolescent Female Body," *Emory Law Journal* (2007): 997.

15. The issues of reproductive rights and sexuality education and related issues constitute a political battleground. The state has imposed variously restrictive laws that are at odds with scientific research findings. Parental consent and parental notification abortion

laws for minors reflect the state's strategy of giving parents mechanisms for sexual control over children.

16. Fine and McClelland, "The Politics of Teen Women's Sexuality," 996.

17. Ibid., 1035.

18. Darko Suvin, "Estrangement and Cognition," in *Speculations on Speculation: Theories of Science Fiction*, ed. James Gunn and Matthew Candelaria (Lanham, Md.: Scarecrow Press, 2005), 24.

19. Butler, *Fledgling*, 12. All subsequent references to this novel will be cited by page number within the text.

20. English, *Unnatural Selections*, 15.

21. Diana Pearce, "'Children Having Children': Teenage Pregnancy and Public Policy from the Woman's Perspective," in *The Politics of Pregnancy: Adolescent Sexuality and Public Policy*, ed. Deborah L. Rhode and Annette Lawson (New Haven, Conn.: Yale University Press, 1993), 49–50.

PART II

DISENGAGING
THE GAZE

CHAPTER 5

(Mis)Playing Blackness

Rendering Black Female Sexuality in *The Misadventures of Awkward Black Girl*

Ariane Cruz

The Misadventures of Awkward Black Girl *(ABG)*, which premiered on YouTube on February 3, 2011, is a comedy web series that chronicles the life and times of J, a young Black woman living in Los Angeles played by actor/producer/director/writer Issa Rae. Two seasons and twenty-five episodes later, *ABG* has transformed from a self-funded "guerrilla style" project into an award-winning web series with a sizable and devoted fan following, a professional staff, significant media coverage, and financial investors (both public and private).[1] *ABG* has come a long way from its humble grassroots origins and has projected Rae beyond the realm of web celebrity status. The show began in January 2011 with only "a camera, a temporary office job and no budget." She has been the focus of media attention on blogs and web sites, as well as CNN, NBC, NPR, the *New York Times*, the Associated Press, *BET*, *Vibe* magazine, *Essence* magazine, *Jet*, the *Huffington Post*, *Rolling Stone*, and *Forbes*.[2] In addition to establishing Rae as a web series guru and a veritable force in American popular entertainment, *ABG* has transformed the web series into "legitimate entertainment" and has profoundly challenged prevailing representations (and lack thereof) of Black women in American popular culture.[3]

ABG is a dynamic example of Black women's use of new media to challenge dominant codes of Black female sexuality anchored in a foundation of pathology and policed by the politics of respectability, silence, and patriarchal heteronormativity. The show paints a complex and contradictory portrait of Black female sexuality that is simultaneously unwieldy and easily consumed, hyperracialized and deracialized, unique and universal, aggressive and diffident. This essay illuminates *ABG* as a fecund site for analyzing a profound ambivalence toward Black female racial sexual alterity and its (cyber) performance and spectatorship. First, I illuminate how the epithet of awkward mediates performances of Black female racial and sexual authenticity on the show, unveiling the ways that Black female sexuality becomes authenticated in and through its ontological failure and nonbelonging, however comic. Next, I consider how J contests dominant representations of Black women in contemporary popular culture, specifically the Black single lady phenomenon. Finally, I read *ABG's* rendition of Black female sexuality within the contemporary landscape of Black female cybersexualitites in pornography by interrogating not only the Internet's facilitation of alternative performances of racialized sexualities but also cyberspace's catalyzing of technologically inspired rearticulations of popular Black female sexuality. In both the web series and in pornography, Black women's do-it-yourself (DIY) mode of media production facilitates new cartographies of Black female desire and renderings of nonhegemonic, transgressive paradigms of Black female sexualities.

When the character J first started spinning around in Rae's head two years before she created the show, she consciously set out to challenge hegemonic and trite paradigms of Black womanhood. Twenty-seven year old Senegalese-American Rae—who graduated from Stanford with a BA in African American Studies and political science and studied filmmaking at NYU—aimed to challenge the "pop cultural idea [*or better yet ideal*] of Blackness" and fill a void in the televisual rendering of Black womanhood.[4] This gap is primarily addressed through the main character, J, a young Black woman living in Los Angeles, who channels her frustration over her dead-end job, irksome co-workers, profound social awkwardness, and difficult love life by writing and rhyming ferocious, profane raps.[5] J's failed sexual relationships are the core of this romantic comedy. The "awkward" in the show's title is performed via moments of sexual liaison: getting dumped, sleeping with a co-worker, choosing between two suitors (one white and the other Black), and experiencing difficulty consummating a new relationship. It is the fractured, bipolar composition of timorous, gawky proletarian and aggressive, outspoken "ratchet" MC that makes J such a magnetic character and enables Rae to both recite and rebuff prevailing stereotypes of Black female sexuality, while simultaneously adhering to politics of respectability and bucking these conventions.[6] Indeed, what is most fascinating about the character J is her ambivalence: her simultaneous perpetuation and contestation of stereotypes and representations of blackness within the dominant socio-cultural imagination all within the span of an episode. Moreover, J effects an urgent self-representation, an "exaggerated" version of Rae and her experiences: "it was more for me, for representation of me," Rae notes, "because it . . . filled a void that I just didn't see in media."[7] Rae imagines J as "the Black Liz Lemon," a similarly socially maladroit female character in the highly acclaimed NBC sitcom *30 Rock*.[8] Rae "relate[s] to Jerry Seinfeld's pet peeves or Liz Lemon's insecurities, but it bothers [her] that there aren't people of color in those roles."[9] In the tradition of Black female racial sexual alterity and its performance on screen by an enduring though evolving set of stereotypes—mammies, sapphires, jezebels, matriarchs, tragic mulattas—this awkwardness is a different kind of difference. J's awkwardness, that is, represents a different enactment of exclusion, deviance, nonbelonging, otherness, outsiderness, and marginalization than previously seen in the tradition of Black women's representation.

THE POWER OF AWKWARDNESS

Rae relies on universality, as she consistently deracializes the character J and, through her, the show itself. In various interviews she posits this universality through the trope of awkwardness. The rubric of universality belies the salience of Blackness in her constitution and performance. She states, "I definitely feel like everybody has these awkward moments so that in itself is universal. And I think that just because the show is titled *Awkward Black Girl* and it is a predominately Black cast doesn't mean that you shouldn't be able to relate to these people."[10] In other interviews Rae confirms the racial dilution of awkwardness, stating that "even though J is Black, the things she goes through are universal" and that "awkwardness doesn't have a race."[11] This deracialization is significant for many reasons. First, it is contradictory. In many interviews, Rae is outspoken about having created J in response to a dearth of Black female characters in mainstream television and *ABG* as a political project of Black (self)representation and reinvention. It conflicts with the title and much of the plot, which chronicles the quotidian happenings of an awkward Black girl, not just an awkward girl. This quasi-colorblind notion of universality defies the unique events J experiences as a Black woman. For example, she must field racist questions about her hair from her (White) boss, Boss Lady, and has to throw up her "nigga shield." Part of this colorblindness comes, I contend, from Rae's desire to market the show in a way that appeals to wide and diverse audiences. We could read this universalizing tendency as a sort of sales technique. A similar impetus of deracialization resounds in Black female screenwriter/director/producer Shonda Rhimes's description of her Black female protagonist Olivia Pope, played by actress Kerry Washington on the hit ABC drama *Scandal*. Rhimes describes this first African American female lead on a major network television show in thirty-eight years as "any human being . . . who happened to be born female and Black."[12] Like Rae, Rhimes wrote her Black female lead into being with the hope of changing both prevailing images and the collective imaginings of Black women.[13] Rhimes calls to attention an ambivalent economy of racialized desire regarding Black female sexuality, while advancing her own political objectives to foreground and elevate Black women despite the hierarchies that have long privileged white women's bodies. The politics of confronting these ontological and other limits of womanhood expose the fact that notions of colorblindness that Rhimes and Rae articulate are not necessarily evidence of either a modernist racial ideology or postracial politics in contemporary American television; rather, it represents an urgent, if even veiled, campaigning for recognition of Black women's humanity.[14]

This universalizing tendency signals both the limits of our collective imagination in envisioning Black women and the enduring legacy of oppressive images of Black women in popular entertainment. Where are the boundaries of our vision when it comes to conceiving Black womanhood? What does it mean for Blackness, Black femininity, and Black female sexuality to be universal? What kind of Black womanhood is not universal? I am especially interested in these questions, the identity politics that animate such inquiries, and how awkwardness mediates performances of Black female racial and sexual authenticity on *ABG*. If awkward is something that Black people are not or should not be—as another web series, *Black Folk Don't*, (which also comically explores Blackness, authenticity, and the notion that "Black folk don't do awkward") suggests—J's awkwardness seems to dis-authenticate her Blackness. Yet, Black womanhood remains ultimately legible through its nonbelonging however comic.[15] I read J's awkwardness, what Rae calls "the idea of being a social misfit," as being both prompted by her Blackness and instantiating it.[16] If we understand Blackness to be a state of nonbelonging, abjection, and marginalization, then we might read J's awkwardness as a characteristic of her Blackness and not as a quality that somehow nullifies it.

The first episode of season 1, "The Stop Sign," depicts an important sequence of events, the first of which is J's reading of the stop sign itself. She states, "The stop sign: to any ordinary person, it's a simple sign of direction, but for me it's the epitome of social misdirection, because I am awkward." More than cueing J's signature style of self-depreciating self-analysis via the voice-over as a primary narrative mode, which evidences Spike Lee's influence on her work (Rae produced and staged two theatrical adaptations of Lee's films while at Stanford), this confession asserts her awkwardness as a misplay while establishing *ABG* as a deliberate project on the nature of belonging that, in turn, makes evident its investment in the ontology of Black women. It is a critical moment of legibility: not just how we read J but also of how she reads broadly. The second event is J's introduction of herself, a performative declarative utterance of Blackness and awkwardness executed through her statement "My name is J and I'm awkward . . . and Black. Someone once told me those were the two worst things anyone could be." This articulation of subject position through speaking or vocalization is also a point of interpolation and interpellation: J is interpolated, situated between the two (seemingly irreconcilable) points of Blackness and awkwardness, as well as is simultaneously interpellated or hailed as subject through discourse.[17] *ABG* thus becomes a deliberate project about the nature of belonging. This proclamation is a critical moment of Black female subject constitution and self-narration. As such, J's performative declaration resonates with what Henry Louis Gates Jr.

identifies as the Black American's urgent need to write himself (herself) into "the human condition" in and through the genre of the slave narrative as a testament of Black female humanity.[18] Echoing the slave narrative's characteristic opening statement, "I was born," J's narrative is one of both self-definition and self-constitution.[19] But what do we not hear in this critical J's assertion? While the title *Awkward Black Girl* explicitly announces a specific gender, J's affirmation, her introduction of self, lacks any assertion of or reference to gender. If being Black and awkward are "the two worst things anyone [can] be," we are left with the oft-cited words of Janie's grandmother in Hurston's *Their Eyes Were Watching God* ringing in our ears: "De Nigger woman is de mule uh de world so fur as Ah can see."[20] What happens when female is added to the mix?[21] Hearing how Rae echoes the voices of her African American literary ancestors allows us to not only place *ABG* in a vibrant lineage of African American cultural production and critical artistic self-authorship, it also inspires us to take pop culture and new media seriously in this continuing project of black reinvention. More than a self-portrait and an attestation of humanity, J's statement reveals a critical reckoning with the politics of identification as a process that is continually staged yet "never fully and finally made" in the imaginary, or what Judith Butler describes as "the phantasmatic efforts of alignment, loyalty, ambiguous and cross-corporeal cohabitation."[22] The tension between the identifications J makes here, which are enacted throughout the show, mirrors the myriad contradictions operating in *ABG* with respect to Black female sexuality.

AGAINST RATCHETS: NEW KIND OF SINGLE LADY?

Pharrell Williams is one of Rae's most enthusiastic fans and one with the deepest pockets. The three-time Grammy award–winning rapper, singer, composer, producer, and fashion designer is now a media empire potentate and the executive producer of *ABG*. Williams says, "When I saw the show I didn't see . . . this Black woman catering to that annoying characterization that you see on every television show, you just saw, you saw someone that was incredibly honest."[23] Funding the entire second season without asking for any creative control of the show Williams recently welcomed *ABG* to his new creative online platform "i am Other," a "channel and cultural movement dedicated to Thinkers, Innovators and Outcasts—in short, OTHERS."[24] As a project that radically reinterprets Black female difference, *ABG* meshes well with i am Other's mission of showcasing otherness.[25] Williams' comment highlights two themes that recur in critical reviews of the show: stereotypes and authenticity. The common view is that *ABG* projects less stereotypical (less galling) images of Black women and that these new representations are somehow less trite and more real because of their nonrecital of such stereotypes. Although J is a critical intervention in the popular stereotype of the single lady that permeates the televisual topography of Black female representation, she challenges, through her ratchet alter ego, prevailing paradigms of Black female sexuality as pathological.

As the phrase "single ladies," the title of both Beyoncé's 2008 quadruple platinum hit song and a VH1 sitcom suggests, Black women's solitary romantic status is a hot issue in American popular culture. The low marriage rates of Black women, especially those who are financially successful and highly educated, has recently received attention in the media and academia.[26] In a recent study from Yale on the longitudinal trends in marriage among highly educated Black women, those born after 1950 were twice as likely as white women to be unmarried by age forty-five and twice as likely to be divorced, widowed, or separated.[27] Though the study and its surrounding dialogue are anchored in a heteronormative logic that disavows same-sex marriage and Black (homosexual and heterosexual) women's choice to abstain from marriage, both offer useful insight into the representation of Black women's relationships. Despite studies that suggest that Black women prioritize their educational development and standard of living, other sources posit that Black women are at fault for their single status. Televisual performances of single Black womanhood, in "reality" TV in particular, represent Black women as complicit in their own loneliness, thereby condemning them as unsuitable, idealistic, and impossible (unloving and unlovable) partners.

The character J is distinct in a reality television landscape that is dominated by shows such as *Basketball Wives, Single Ladies, Love & Hip Hop* (all on VH1), and *The Real Housewives of Atlanta* (Bravo), wherein romantic relationship drama reigns, animosity prevails between Black women and their (Black) men, and Black women's sexual labor eclipses their actual labor. J challenges these prevalent characterizations of single ladies on multiple fronts. Her awkwardness mediates her Blackness as a kind of performance of racial authenticity. Moreover, J also challenges stereotypes about class, physicality, and sexuality. She is definitively working class, and her work is an important element of the show's narrative, much of which revolves around J's nine-to-five job as a telephone salesperson at Gut Buster, a company that sells weight-loss products.

She looks nothing like most single ladies we see in the visual media (she wears very little makeup and has no weave, no cocktail dresses, no Louboutins, no implants, and no bling). With her darker skin and short natural hair, she may be seen as resisting Western ideals of beauty, body, and skin color. Mistaken for a butch lesbian in season 2, episode 1 ("The Sleepover"), she asks, "Is there a non-homophobic way to tell someone you're not gay?" This reveals that J often reads as if not queer, then queer-allied, and while she resists popular stereotypes of Black female sexuality, she succumbs to sexual hierarchies. Indeed, her fervent denial of lesbianism through statements such as "no lesbo" and "pussy tastes like fish, fish, fish ... no homo" represents more than just a reassertion of her heterosexuality; it is a reinstatement of institutional heteronormativity.

Unlike her wanton single-lady sisters, J presents a reserved, inexperienced, and, yes, incredibly awkward approach to sex and sexuality. *ABG* works against the prevailing image of Black women perpetrated by reality television as not just unlucky in love but unlovable because of their bellicosity and aggression.[28] In a domain where Black womanhood is characterized as physically and verbally hostile and is presented as verisimilitude, J embodies a kind of self-antagonism. The wars she wages are staged in the psychic battleground of her exceedingly active imagination, not in physical fisticuffs with others. While she is not the pugnacious drama queen we are accustomed to seeing, J enacts the prevailing single-lady construct through her "bad bitch" pantomime. In what J identifies as her "ratchet alter ego," the brazen, lascivious, mc ying to her meek, sexually awkward, nine-to-fiver yang, she conjures a flashy single-lady sisters-on-television persona.[29]

The Black female ratchet is rampant in contemporary American pop culture, particularly in the arenas of hip-hop and reality television. An amalgamated offspring of the jezebel, matriarch, mammy, and welfare mother figures, she is a modern "controlling image," to evoke Patricia Hill Collins's terminology, of black female sexuality.[30] Like the mechanical device it is named after, the term "ratchet"—also defined as "a situation or process that is perceived to be deteriorating or changing steadily in a series of irreversible steps"—is an equivocal tool used to debase black women.[31] The foundation of this evolving stereotype, which evokes shame, pride, fear, laughter, and desire, is rooted in a history that denigrates and pathologizes black women's eroticism. If the ratchet is both revered and reviled in contemporary American pop culture and represents, the ambivalent figuration of black female sexuality, J's enactment of ratchetness is also deeply ambiguous. Unlike the purportedly authentic televisual ratchet performances she mimics from reality shows, J's ratchet soliloquies, as mostly privatized, highly dramatized alter-egos, illuminate the performed nature of such a stereotype. Private in the show yet open for public consumption, J's ratchet outbursts perpetuate, nonetheless, a recital of the stereotype that remains problematic, even beyond its reliance on black female sexual pathology as comedic fodder. In many episodes, she enacts this alternate ratchet persona, often using hip-hop as her medium to communicate her malapropos thoughts and sexual desires.[32] Through this ratchet personality, Rae plays with stereotypes while simultaneously resisting the politics of respectability that can script performances of Black female sexuality. In the season 2 trailer, J raps "I am not a basketball wife," but has she escaped "the Black girl curse"?

Continuing to gain currency in popular culture and scholarly arenas, "the Black girl curse" was dubbed the term for this highly problematic Black single lady phenomenon in 2009 when ABC News Nightline journalist Linsey Davis interviewed four single professional Black women in Atlanta about being single in their thirties. One of the participants said "We have a saying called the 'black girl curse.' A lot of our white friends are married by 25, happily married with kids by 27, and we're like, 'What's the deal with the BGs?'—and that's black girls."[33] By problematic I am referring to the ways this trend has been discursively deliberated and theorized. Davis's interviewees offered an etiology of this so-called curse that, on the one hand, blames Black women for having standards that are "too high" and unreasonable or for having unrealistic expectations for a life partner; on the other hand, it suggests that the pool of eligible Black male bachelors is small ("slim pickings") in ways that exonerate Black women. In either case, Black women are considered accountable for their own single status. Books such as Jimi Izrael's *The Denzel Principle: Why Black Women Can't Find Good Men* (2009) and Eric Culpeper's *The Black Girl Curse* (2009) have blazed the trail of Black women's culpability, suggesting that Black women are on a futile search for a mythical Black man and need to lower their utopian standards to secure a "good" brother.[34] Such rhetoric refashions the prevailing oppressive notions of Black women as accountable for the failure of the heteronormative Black family unit that was cemented into our national consciousness in March 1965 with the publication of Senator Patrick Moynihan's contentious report *The Negro Family: The Case for National Action.* The "Black girl curse," much like the Moynihan Report, perpetuates the idea that the "tangle of pathology" that Black women find themselves ensnared in is inevitably of their own making.[35]

So what are the J-like single Black ladies of the world to do? Black male "comedian-turned-relationship guru Steve Harvey," whom *Nightline* solicited to evaluate this "serious dilemma," suggests that Black women need to "compromise": they need to stop trying to find Black men who match their own education level, corporate status, and income.[36] Ralph Richard Banks, the author of *Is Marriage for White People?* (2011), asserts that, according to recent statistics, Black women are reluctant to date outside their race and should do so; and, indeed, the character J does just that. Black women are the least likely racial group to do this. Only 5.5 percent of married Black women in the United States have husbands of different races.[37] While J's relationship with her beau White J reinforces the heteronormative mandate of mainstream television's representation of Black romance, we may read her interracial romance as contesting the order of Black-on-Black love often endorsed by the single ladies we see on television. Still J's relationship illustrates the always already political, "always extraordinary" nature of Black-and-white interracial intimacy in American culture. As historian Kevin Mumford reminds us, "Because of History—slavery, racism, gender relations, sexual repression, power politics—sex across the color line always represents more than just sex."[38] It also compounds the problem of J's racial sexual authenticity. Her comments such as, "What do white people listen to when they have sex? Taylor Swift? Michael Bolton? Eminem?" communicate the vexed nature of enactments of cross-racial intimacy on the show. Couched in a signature *ABG* brand of racially charged humor, these statements reveal profound anxieties about race, racial difference, and racial anxiety while mining (for comedic currency) the tensions not between Black and white but rather surrounding race that is at once performed and essential. Such statements speak to the show's investment in contesting, albeit sardonically, assumptions of essentialized racial authenticity, both black and white. But what is this leitmotif of single lady/Black girl curse masking? What does it reveal about the politics of Black female sexuality? It signals profound anxieties about shifts in the contemporary landscape of Black female sexualities, specifically resisting a heteronormativization of Black women's sexuality and their financial, intellectual, and sexual autonomy or, more specifically, their increasing nonreliance on Black men. This might best be read as a crisis not in Black female sexuality but rather in the institution of heteronormativity itself.

Sisters in Cyberspace?

ABG is a dynamic example of Black women's use of new media to rewrite dominant codes of Black female sexuality. It is also part of the contemporary landscape of Black female cybersexualitites. In this section, I explore how the Internet facilitates alternative performances of racialized sexualities and how cyberspace catalyzes technologically inspired rearticulations of popular Black female sexuality in Black web series and pornography.[39] Since the invention of the printing press in the fifteenth century, pornography has maintained a critical relationship with technology. It has pioneered and used ever-evolving visual technologies to reinvent itself. Pornographers have consistently been among the first to exploit new publishing and visual reproduction technologies. I engage and consider pornography here not only because of such technological manipulation but also because of the ways it has enabled and empowered Black women, long before the web series, to command their own sexualities. In mapping the landscape of black female cybersexualities through web pornography, we can better understand the critical field of black female cybersexualities as an arena for showcasing novel, nonhegemonic paradigms of Black female sexualities.

In her conception of the Internet as a critical medium in rewriting codes of Black womanhood, Rae resembles many of today's Black female pornographers who use it as a mode of self-representation to create images that counter prevailing representations of marginalized Black female sexuality and maintain control over the projection of these images. The web series, Rae asserts, "is going to be the opportunity for people of color, not just African-Americans but others. . . . I think that this is the space for niche communities to find content and for niche creators to find their audiences."[40] According to Rae, unlike Hollywood, the fact that the Internet lacks gatekeepers means that it offers "way more opportunities" to people of color.[41] This "frontier" "allows you to express yourself more creatively and more freely" and provides an audience for this expression. Rae states,

"You can literally put anything out there and you're going to find an audience."[42]
Recognizing the autonomy and audience potential of the web, Rae is among a
new generation of contemporary Black female media producers who use new
media to create alternative schemas of Black female sexuality and desire.

For example, Black lesbian filmmaker Shine Louise Houston uses digital
technology, particularly cyberspace, as her primary architectonic instrument
to transform queer pornography. Resisting mainstream representations of so-
called normative Black female sexuality in porn, she asserts that "there is power
in creating images, and for a woman of color and a queer to take that power.... I
don't find it exploitative; I think it's necessary."[43] Houston's "hardcore indie feminist dyke porn" exhibits stunning cinematography, incredibly diverse performers, and fresh diegeses, critically queering renditions of Black female sexuality,
while presenting paradigms of pleasure outside the dominant, heteronormative
portrayals of Black womanhood in porn.[44] Like Rae, Houston's production was
motivated by the need for alternative images of black womanhood: "There needs
to be more voices. I believe in my politics. If you don't like it, do what I did.
I didn't like what was going on in the porn industry in terms of representation of gay, lesbian, queer, and trans folk, so I made my own stuff."[45] Houston
identifies technology as power that allows her to create and re-create images.[46]
Cyberspace enables her to "build something that was going to be able to create
content on a regular basis."[47] In the case of both the web series and pornography,
medium makes possible not just a single intervention but a continuing process
of transformation, one in which reverberates the, dynamism and polyvalence of
Black female sexuality. By providing what Rae calls "constant content," the web
makes it possible for female artists to present an evolving, rather than a static,
performance of Black womanhood.[48] Rae's use of the Internet as a platform for
reinventing Black female sexuality occurs in a similar context wherein cyberspace serves as a laboratory for the projection of new paradigms of Black female
sexuality.

If the Internet has facilitated changes in the types of representations of Black
female sexuality, it has also transfigured the ways we consume such images and
the spectatorship of Black womanhood. Internet porn has profoundly changed
what I call the geographies of pornography by muddying the boundary between
private and public, further commodifying our experiences of sexual pleasure,
transforming the environment of and for the experience of pornography, and
engendering a more intimate physical relationship between us and the pornography we consume. The web series represents, then, a spatial and temporal transformation of our experience of entertainment. It both reflects and reveals a new
way of looking and a new zeitgeist with respect to our recreational practices.
Moreover, its typically shorter format caters to a kind of millennial attention def-
icit disorder. In her online *Huffington Post* article and five-point tutorial, "How
to Write a Wildly Successful Web Series," Rae advises would-be cyber scribes to

"keep it short and to the point" in order to attract and maintain an audience.[49] Similarly, most porn sites feature videos that are roughly four to five minutes long. Reading ABG in tandem with coeval developments in the arena of contemporary Black female-authored porn is profoundly insightful when considering the digital production and consumption of Black female sexuality.

Authenticating race in cyberspace no longer requires the same charge it did in the days of multi-user domains and other text-based exchanges in cyberspace, when anonymity and masquerade dominated interpersonal interchange. The Internet is increasingly becoming an extension of our physical selves, a sphere where we project, present, and represent our material bodies; and as fantasies of cyber-disembodiment, transcendent identities, and postraciality dwindle, questions of authenticity reanimate in new ways.[50] ABG reveals a profound investment in the question of authenticity: J's Blackness mediates her awkwardness, she misplays the "real" single ladies who dominate the televisual landscape, and she pursues interracial romance. Amid the hype surrounding the anticipation of the show's move from the web to the HBO cable television network, another thorn of authenticity surfaces. I find myself asking (though knowing better), "Will the show somehow become less authentic in this transition?" Because scholars such as Bhabha have long revealed authenticity to be a fundamental discursive "strateg[y] of discriminatory power," I know better.[51] Because I am familiar with the ways myths of authenticity police race as process, as performance, I know better. Like most fans, I harbor mixed feelings about the show's rumored transition from the Internet to cable television. Part of me feels that it is a type of selling out and another part of me fears the kind of watering down that Rae herself initially expressed about the show's content—its autonomy, radicalism, and innovation—as a result of being on the web.[52] Nevertheless, I look forward to more diverse representations of Black womanhood in the televisual landscape—something that will provide some stiff competition to the current trope of single ladies in the media.

NOTES

A portion of this essay draws from a section of Ariane Cruz, "Gettin' *Down Home with the Neelys*: Gastro-Porn & Televisual Performances of Gender, Race & Sexuality," *Women and Performance* 23, no. 3 (2013): 1–27.

1. *ABG* has 150,000 views per episode, almost 20,000 fans on Facebook, and nearly 8,000 Twitter followers. See Antia McCollough, "The Awkward Black Girl Lands ABC Show," *Amsterdam News*, October 22, 2012, http://www.amsterdamnews.com/testing/the-awkward-Black-girl-lands-abc-show/article_efd08824–1c65–11e2–8bde-0019bb2963f4.html, accessed October 31, 2012. The show raised over $50,000 through kickstarter.com, an online fund-raising platform for creative projects. See Issa Rae, "How Awkward Black Girl Raised over $44,000 through Kickstarter," *Huffington Post*, August 10, 2011, http://www.huffingtonpost.com/issa-rae/kickstarter-awkward-Black-girl_b_922966.html,

accessed August 12, 2012. See also "'Awkward Black Girl' Garners Laughs," *NPR*, September 1, 2011, http://www.npr.org/2011/09/01/140113809/awkward-Black-girl-garners -laughs, accessed September 7, 2012.

2. In early October, Shondaland, Shonda Rhimes's production company, sold a half-hour comedy written by Rae entitled *I Hate LA Dudes* to ABC. Rae will write and co-executive produce the show.

3. Rae has created four other web series, *FLY GUYS Present "The 'F' Word," Dorm Diaries, Ratchetpiece Theatre,* and *Roomieloverfriends* (a collaboration with Blackandsexytv.com). Rae's prolific web series production testifies to her view of it as a "legitimate form of entertainment;" see Rae, "How Awkward Black Girl Raised over $44,000 through Kickstarter."

4. Issa Rae, "Black Folk Don't Like to Be Told They're Not Black," *Huffington Post,* August 4, 2011, http://www.huffingtonpost.com/issa-rae/Black-folk-dont-movie_b_912660 .html, accessed August 13, 2012.

5. One such example of J's emceeing is, "I'm a bad bitch. You're a pussy nigga. What the fuck rhymes with 'pussy nigga'? . . . Burn in hell, nigga! Burn in Hell, nigga!" See *ABG,* season 1, episode 1.

6. I discuss what I call J's *ratchet alter ego* in more depth later in the essay; however, I use the term ratchet, a contradictory and problematic often-used contemporary colloquialism in African American vernacular and pop culture, specifically hip-hop, to generally refer to a stereotype of wild, degenerate, "ghettoized" black womanhood. Simultaneously adored and abhorred, desired and disparaged, the term ratchet reifies historical myths of black womanhood signifying black women's supposed physical and sexual aggressiveness, madness, irrationality, excess, and utter lasciviousness. Yet it is simultaneously a trope of black female agency.

7. Lily Rothman, "Issa Rae of *Awkward Black Girl* on the Future of the Web Series," *Time,* July 10, 2012, http://entertainment.time.com/2012/07/10/issa-rae-of-awkward -Black-girl-on-the-future-of-the-web-series/, accessed August 13, 2012.

8. Rae states, "It's exaggerated versions of stuff that's happened to me and stuff I'd never want to have happen to me." See Jamie Peck, "Interview with Issa Rae, Creator and Star of *The Misadventures of Awkward Black Girl,*" August 15, 2012, http://crushable .com/entertainment/interview-issa-rae-the-misadventures-of-awkward-Black-girl -414/, accessed September 7, 2012. Such characters have proved to be comedic gold. Highly lauded and in its seventh season, *30 Rock* has garnered seventy-seven Emmy nominations and fourteen wins and numerous other awards. For more, see "About the Show," 30 Rock web site, http://www.nbc.com/30-rock/about/.

9. Clover Hope, "That Awkward Moment When . . . 'Awkward Black Girl' Blows Up," *Vibe,* April 17, 2012, http://www.vibe.com/article/awkward-moment-when-awkward -Black-girl-blows, accessed July 22, 2012.

10. "V Exclusive: Vibe Gets to Know the Creator of YouTube's Hit Awkward Black Girl," *Vibe,* August 4, 2011, http://www.vibe.com/article/v-exclusive-vibe-gets-know-creator -youtubes-hit-awkward-Black-girl, accessed July 22, 2012.

11. See Hope, "That Awkward Moment When"; see also "'Awkward Black Girl' Web Hit," *CNN,* October 8, 2011, http://www.cnn.com/video/#/video/living/2011/10/08/whitfield -issa-rae-interview.cnn, accessed July 22, 2012.

12. According to Nielsen, an average of 7.3 million people watched *Scandal's* finale, of which 1.8 million were African American. See Sarah Springer, "'Scandal' Updates Image of Black women on Network Television," *CNN,* March 25, 2012, http://inamerica.blogs .cnn.com/2012/05/25/scandal-updates-image-of-Black-women-on-network-television/,

accessed June 8, 2012. Recently *Scandal* boasted its biggest audience ever 7.4 million viewers in the 18–49 age group and a 2.5 rating from that same group. See Joyce Eng, "Ratings: *Scandal* Shoots to New Highs," *TV Guide,* December 7, 2012, http://www.tvguide
.com/News/Ratings-Scandal-Highs-1057354.aspx, accessed December 9, 2012.

13. Rhimes states, "I hope that Olivia Pope being a lead of a television series and being
smart and vulnerable and the most desirable woman in any room that she walks into
changes something for someone in the way they perceive women of color." See Springer,
"'Scandal' Updates Image of Black Women on Network Television."

14. Analyzing race through the lens of U.S. miscegenation laws, Peggy Pascoe argues
that the Supreme Court adopted a modernist racial ideology (oft labeled "antiracist" or
"egalitarian"), the "powerfully pervasive belief that the eradication of racism depends
on the deliberate nonrecognition of race." See Pascoe, "Miscegenation Law, Court Cases,
and Ideologies of 'Race' in Twentieth-Century America," *Journal of American History* 88,
no. 1 (1996): 48. Similarly, scholars have critiqued this modernist racial ideology at work
in television, resulting in a modulation of race and racial difference. See Emily M. Drew,
"Pretending to Be 'Post-Racial': The Spectacularization of Race in Reality TV's Survivor,"
Television & New Media 12, no. 4 (2011): 326–346; Jennifer Esposito, "What Does Race
Have to Do with Ugly Betty? An Analysis of Privilege and Postracial(?) Representations
on a Television Sitcom," *Television & New Media* 10, no. 6 (2009): 521–535; and Hollis Grif-
fin, "Never, Sometimes, Always: The Multiple Temporalities of 'Post-Race' Discourse in
Convergence Television Narrative," *Popular Communication* 9, no. 4 (2011): 235–250. Such
a strategy resonates in Rae's full statement: "And I think that just because the show is titled
Awkward Black Girl and it is a predominately Black cast doesn't mean that you shouldn't
be able to relate to these people. We are all human beings." See "V Exclusive: Vibe Gets to
Know the Creator of YouTube's Hit Awkward Black Girl."

15. *Black Folk Don't,* a web series in "the spirit of irreverent inquiry," is a satire about
Black authenticity. For more, see http://Blackfolkdont.com/pages/about/. Another contemporary Black web series, *Dear White People,* similarly satirically explores racial authenticity; see http://dear-white-people.tumblr.com/.

16. When asked to "elaborate on what exactly awkward means to [her]," Rae replies,
"To me, it's social discomfort. Everyone is awkward in a way. Everyone has these moments
where you don't feel comfortable in your own skin, you don't feel comfortable in your
own surroundings, certain people make you feel uncomfortable. But I think it's just this
idea of being a social misfit." See Rothman, "Issa Rae of *Awkward Black Girl* on the Future
of the Web Series."

17. Louis Althusser, *Lenin and Philosophy and Other Essays* (New York: Monthly Review
Press, 1971).

18. Henry Louis Gates Jr., *The Signifying Monkey: A Theory of African-American Literary
Criticism* (Oxford: Oxford University Press, 1989), 163.

19. James Olney notes that the phrase "I was born" occurs in the first few sentences
of many slave narratives, corroborating the humanity of the slave author. See Olney, "'I
Was Born': Slave Narratives, Their Status as Autobiography and as Literature," *Callaloo* 20
(Winter 1984): 50.

20. Zora Neale Hurston, *Their Eyes Were Watching God* (New York: Harper Collins,
1937), 14.

21. Legal scholar Toni Lester's question resounds here, "What does it mean to have a multiple, marginalized, identity in a world that tends to frame all identities through the lens
of the white, heterosexual majority culture?" See Lester, "Race, Sexuality and the Question

of Multiple, Marginalized Identities in U.S. and European Discrimination Law," in *Gender Nonconformity, Race, and Sexuality: Charting the Connections,* ed. Toni Lester (Madison: University of Wisconsin Press, 2003), 84.

22. Judith Butler, *Bodies That Matter: On the Discursive Limits of Sex* (New York: Routledge, 1993), 105.

23. "Issa Rae and Pharrell at the Awkward Black Girl Screening," YouTube video, posted by iamOTHER, August 16, 2012, http://www.youtube.com/watch?v=TXh3XNJ5Utg& feature=g-all-u, accessed August 22, 2012.

24. http://www.youtube.com/user/iamOTHER.

25. Pharell Williams, "2014," http://iamother.com/manifesto, accessed 19 May 2014.

26. See Brian Alexander, "Marriage Eludes High-Achieving Black Women," *MSNBC,* August 13, 2009, http://www.msnbc.msn.com/id/32379727/ns/health-sexual _health/t/marriage-eludes-high-achieving-Black-women/, accessed November 4, 2009; Joy Jones, "Marriage Is for White People," *Washington Post,* March 26, 2006, http:// www.washingtonpost.com/wp-dyn/content/article/2006/03/25/AR2006032500029 .html, accessed November 4, 2009; and Eric Johnson, "Nightline Face-Off: Why Can't a Successful Black Woman Find a Man?," *ABC News,* April 21, 2010, http://abcnews.go .com/Nightline/FaceOff/nightline-Black-women-single-marriage/story?id=10424979, accessed May 7, 2010.

27. Hannah Brueckner and Natalie Nitsche, "Opting Out of the Family? Social Change in Racial Equality in Family Formation Patterns and Marriage Outcomes among Highly Educated Women," paper presented at the annual meeting of the American Sociological Association, San Francisco, California, August 8, 2009.

28. "Reality" shows such as *Basketball Wives, The Real Housewives of Atlanta,* and *Love and Hip Hop* illustrate the combative, verbal, and physical "nature" of Black womanhood.

29. In another of Rae's web series, *Ratchetpiece Theatre,* Rae concedes that while she can't provide a "dictionary definition," ratchet "is like if ghetto and hot shitty mess had a baby, and that baby had no father and became a stripper, then made a sex tape with an athlete and became a reality star." See "[Ep. 1] RATCHETPIECE Theatre | Rasheeda (Love & Hip-Hop: Atlanta)," uploaded by Issa Rae, July 20, 2012, http://www.youtube .com/watch?v=JtJOaBer5kk, accessed May 19, 2014.

30. Though the ratchet is a cross-racial stereotype, the specific ways it is commonly racialized, sexualized, classed, and gendered within the dominant sociocultural imagination relies heavily on the bodies of black women. Black feminist scholar Patricia Hill Collins identifies four controlling images, Jezebel, mammy, matriarch, and welfare mother, arguing that these images function to provide the ideological basis for oppression of Black women on the basis of race, gender, class, and sex. For more, see Patricia Hill Collins, *Black Feminist Thought: Knowledge, Consciousness, and the Politics of Empowerment* (London: Routledge, 1990).

31. *Oxford Dictionaries,* s.v. "ratchet," http://oxforddictionaries.com/us/definition/american _english/ratchet, accessed March 5, 2013.

32. Regarding her use of hip-hop in such fashion, J asks in the pilot episode "Am I the only one who pretends I am in a music video when I am by myself?" Other examples are her rhyming "take my virginity nigga" to a high school love interest in one of the show's many flashbacks and her repping of "Booty Shawts" as her mobile phone ringer/ anthem. To hear two sexually explicit original *ABG* soundtracks featuring Rae, see "ABG SOUNDTRACK: 'Booty Shawts'—Doublemint Twins," YouTube video, uploaded by iss-arae12, February 8, 2011, accessed May 19, 2014; and "ABG SOUNDTRACK | 'Take My

Panties Off" Doublemint Twins (feat. Bruce Illest)," YouTube video, uploaded by issarae12, June 14, 2012, accessed May 19, 2014.

33. Chato Waters quoted in "Single, Black, Female—And Plenty of Company," *ABC News,* December 22, 2009, http://abcnews.go.com/Nightline/single-black-females/story?id=9395275, accessed June 2, 2014.

34. See Jimi Izrael, *The Denzel Principle: Why Black Women Can't Find Good Men* (New York: St. Martin's Press, 2010).

35. Chapter 4, entitled "The Tangle Of Pathology," analyzes Black matriarchy, "the reversed roles of husband and wife," as the root cause of the failure of the Black family, which, according to Moynihan, includes high rates of poverty, delinquency, and crime and the educational deficiency of Black youth. See Daniel Patrick Moynihan, *The Negro Family: The Case for National Action* (Washington, D.C.: Office of Policy Planning and Research, United States Department of Labor, 1965), http://www.dol.gov/oasam/programs/history/webid-meynihan.htm.

36. In addition to being an entertainer, Harvey's qualifications to evaluate this "crisis" in Black female sexuality includes his authoring of the book *Act Like a Lady, Think Like a Man: What Men Really Think about Love, Relationships, Intimacy, and Commitment* (New York: Harper Collins, 2009).

37. This figure refers to Black women's rate of interracial marriage in 2008. For more, see Jeffrey S. Passel, Wendy Wang, and Paul Taylor, "Marrying Out: One-in-Seven New U.S. Marriages Is Interracial or Interethnic," *Pew Research & Social Demographic Trends,* June 4, 2010, http://pewresearch.org/pubs/1616/american-marriage-interracial-interethnic, accessed July 3, 2012. The report finds that "some 22% of all Black male newlyweds in 2008 married outside their race, compared with just 9% of Black female newlyweds."

38. See Kevin J. Mumford, *Interzones: Black/White Sex Districts in Chicago and New York in the Early Twentieth Century* (New York: Columbia University Press, 1997), xi.

39. The Internet, which some have imagined as a democratized space, has proven itself a site for narratives by and about others. Examples of web series focusing on Black women include: *Chick, In(HER)view: A Conversation with Black Women, Blind Date, Afrocity, Celeste Bright, Buppies, Got2Be Real, Diary of a Single Mom,* and *Kindred.* For more about Black web series, see Joshua R. Weaver, "7 Must-Watch Black Web Series," *The Root,* August 9, 2012, http://www.theroot.com/articles/culture/2012/08/best_black_web_series_the_roots_favorites.html, accessed September 1, 2012; and Aymar Jean Christian, "Black Web Series," Televisual, February 2012, http://tvisual.org/Black-web-series/, accessed May 19, 2014. For more about the history of episodic web series that sees them as deviated from yet ultimately not diverging from legacy media (specifically TV) despite the neoteric promise of the Internet, see Aymar J. Christian, "The Web as Television Reimagined? Online Networks and the Pursuit of Legacy Media," *Journal of Communication Inquiry* 36, no. 4 (2012): 340–356.

40. Rothman, "Issa Rae of *Awkward Black Girl* on the Future of the Web Series."

41. Ibid.

42. Ibid.

43. "Shine Louise Houston," CrashPadSeries.com, http://crashpadseries.com/queer-porn/shine-louise-houston/, accessed May 19, 2014.

44. "Preview: The Crash Pad: Director's Cut," http://crashpadseries.com/queer-porn/?feature=the-crash-pad-directors-cut, accessed May 7, 2012.

45. Jillian Eugenios, "Chatting up Shine Louise Houston," *Curve,* September 20, 2011, http://www.curvemag.com/Curve-Magazine/Web-Articles-2011/Chatting-up-Shine-Louise-Houston/, accessed March 5, 2012.

46. Shine Louise Houston, telephone interview with author, May 24, 2012.

47. Ibid.

48. Rothman, "Issa Rae of *Awkward Black Girl* on the Future of the Web Series."

49. Issa Rae, "How to Write a Wildly Successful Web Series," *Huffington Post*, September 15, 2011, http://www.huffingtonpost.com/issa-rae/how-to-write-a-wildly-suc_b_964048.html, accessed July 19, 2012.

50. Cameron Bailey's remark about the ambivalence of cybersubjectivity is resonant here: "Cybersubjectivity promises the fantasy of disembodied communication but it remains firmly connected to bodies through the imaginative act required to project into cyberspace." See Bailey. "Virtual Skin: Articulating Race in Cyberspace," in *Immersed in Technology Art and Virtual Environments*, edited by Mary Anne Moser and Douglas MacLeod (Cambridge, Mass.: MIT Press, 1996), 42.

51. See Homi Bhabha, *The Location of Culture* (New York: Routledge, 1994), 95.

52. Sarah Springer and Sarah Edwards, "'Awkward Black Girl' Creator Issa Rae Responds to Racism," *CNN*, April 24, 2012, http://inamerica.blogs.cnn.com/2012/04/24/awkward-Black-girl-creator-issa-rae-responds-to-racism, accessed July 22, 2012.

CHAPTER 6

Why Don't We Love These Hoes?

Black Women, Popular Culture, and the Contemporary Hoe Archetype

Mahaliah Ayana Little

Being black and a woman results in a very specific coming-of-age experience in the southeastern United States. Further nuance this with post–civil rights, post–black power angst, urban decay, the cocaine epidemic of the eighties, and the consummate saturation of American culture with rap and hip-hop music, and you have my adolescence. As a teenager, I often naively excused the overt hostility toward femininity rampant in popular culture. I accepted misogyny and chauvinism as the status quo in most of my favorite rap songs, even believing that disrespectful phrases were somehow necessary to make a song seem cool or become popular. I believed that I was not the target of the verbal attacks my favorite artists waged on women—because the rappers I listened to had never met me. I eagerly memorized and recited the lyrics to songs, gradually internalizing their messages and coming to misguidedly prefer male rappers over their equally and sometimes more talented female counterparts. I was convinced that women rappers were generally less skilled.

I was certain that if I absorbed the male-directed misogynistic lyrics and showed prowess in knowledge of the various rappers, rap battles, and mixtape releases in a male-dominated industry, I would somehow avoid the kind of inferiority that befell the women my favorite male and female emcees berated. I mistakenly assumed that the women who were disrespected in the music were somehow culpable and stubbornly refused to include myself in their number. Even as I rationalized the overt insults against women in the lyrics, I found their frequent use problematic.[1] But as a then blissfully naïve conformist, I was largely desensitized to the invective directed at women in my favorite songs, movies, and reality television shows. Charisse Jones and Kumea Shorter-Gooden would label my behavior as "shifting": "hiding my true feelings" to negotiate the "relentless oppression" of my cultural environment.[2] My personal "shifting" took the form of denial, and I trained myself "not to notice subtle sexism."[3]

In college, as I embarked on an intellectual and ideological journey, I questioned the masculinist spaces that constituted pop culture, particularly hip-hop, and scrutinized my actions and others for destructive misogynist discourse and indoctrination into hegemonic practices and patriarchal supremacy. I became far more aware and critical of the problematic elements in pop culture media outlets, including 30-second advertisements on television, movies, and, most jarringly, the Dirty South rap music with which I had previously been enamored. In November 2011, as a result of my hypersensitivity and burgeoning consciousness, I began a research project at the Robert Woodruff Library of the Atlanta University Center (AUC). As part of an informal study, I began tallying the number of times I overheard my black female cohorts using the slang insult hoe. In just over an hour, I heard it forty-five times. From that point forward, I believed with conviction that this cavalier use of the undesirable epithet hoe warranted further investigation.

In this essay, I explore how a growing number of black women of the millennial generation participate, if even inadvertently, in their own oppression through their use of the term hoe. I argue that careless, indiscriminate use of this word contributes not only to the monolithic labeling of black women—in ways that challenge their subjectivity and undermine their agency in defining their own complex identities—but also poses a threat to black women that is equal to the threat they experience from their black male counterparts. In the face of interracial, intraracial, and gender prejudice, this particular form of intragender oppression is especially destructive, and it threatens black women collectively.

The hoe archetype, a flimsy construct, is an amalgamation of various destructive tropes used to describe black women.[4] The term hoe, a "Black or Southern U.S. pronunciation of whore," is defined as "a Black slang (U.S.) derogatory term for a woman."[5] This contemporary denotation illustrates a shift of a slang insult from a colloquial term that is synonymous with "prostitute" to a word used to refer to all black women. Many phrases use it, from cautionary statements such as "don't trust a hoe" and "you can't turn a hoe into a housewife" to the mantra made notoriously popular by hip-hop artist Snoop Dogg, "we don't love these hoes." Although many authors, pundits, and social commentators have weighed in on how men perpetuate the degradation of women in commercial rap and hip-hop music, I seek to explore how the traditions of chauvinism and misogyny have affected black women and how they are perceived in the diasporic black community.

The use of the term hoe by black females, celebrities and non-celebrities alike, serves to further normalize patriarchal views of women as subhuman and inferior.[6] As Audre Lorde theorized in *Sister Outsider*, "It is easier to deal with the external manifestations of racism and sexism," such as the racist offenses of nonblacks or the sexist offenses of black male rappers, "than it is to deal with the results of those distortions internalized within our consciousness of ourselves and one another."[7] The internalized distortions of commercial rap and hip-hop consumers, especially black women, have resulted in a warped perception of reality.

Many subjugated groups attempt to reclaim slurs that have been traditionally used to dehumanize. Debate continually swirls around the current usage of many different epithets within the black and female communities, but it is important to differentiate between these phenomena and that of the increased use of the term hoe. In stark contrast to women who may choose to or find it empowering to identify themselves or their friends as "bitches," for example, no one wants to be a hoe. While there is a marginal population of black women that affectionately refer to their friends as such, my empirical research and lived observations indicate that there are few, if any, efforts to refashion the connotation of the word hoe. Regardless of how cavalier the attitude of the labeler of hoes may be, being labeled as such has some very specific and undesirable implications. According to Mireille Miller-Young, hoe is interchangeable with the following terms: "video model, street prostitute, exotic dancer, freak, chicken head, and gold digger." Moreover, it encapsulates "any other individual existing outside of black moral respectability." As such, a hoe is "embarrassing and retrograde to the black progress narrative" because she legitimizes the pernicious stereotypes (including the pathologized sexuality) of black women in ways that "make the real black community look bad."[8] Miller-Young's characterization supports the observation that the insult is used in many other ways than simply referring to a sex worker. The public shame and distaste hoes inspire in some members of the black community is further evidence that contemporary usage trends perpetuate not simply a derogatory term but an entire thought system surrounding what a hoe is and what a hoe does.

Black men and women alike seem to harbor fear toward the hoe and to be repulsed by her. The omnipresent hoe is out to gain every material comfort that young black men work for, all the while ensnaring them deceitfully in insincere emotional investments. She tries to come between black men and their friends, weakening their homosocial bond. She entices them with her sexual prowess and tempts them, all the while scheming to trap them in a cycle of financial commitment that may or may not involve the obligation of unplanned offspring. For black women, the hoe elicits intense uncertainty. She could lie in wait, in disguise as a close friend, absorbing precious information about your turbulent relationship while plotting to steal your man. The fear of paling in comparison to a more skillful, less inhibited, and kinkier lover is ever present because hoes set a deviant sexual standard that so-called decent and respectable black women are reticent about or generally unwilling to achieve.

The contemporary archetype is a social construct: a figment of our collective contemporary hip-hop imagination based on a modicum of truth and reality. The hoe has evolved into a monstrous figure: a rogue, modern-day embodiment of Eve who is conniving and self-indulgent. It is precisely because of these implications of the term that—regardless of the action or reason that leads someone to label a black woman a hoe—it is assumed that she is a type of sexual deviant, even if that assumption is not explicitly acknowledged. These beliefs spawned the line of reasoning that hoes cannot be trusted and that their behavior cannot be reformed. Given the contradictory nature of the beliefs and assumptions about what a hoe is and what sort of debauchery hoes are considered capable of, they occupy a precarious position of being both admired and scorned in contemporary black society. While this modern archetype is an amalgam of older degrading historical tropes, such as Sapphire and the jezebel, that have been used to unfairly categorize and dehumanize black women, it is unique in that it reflects the imprint of centuries of white oppression and black internalized inferiority but is explicitly informed by post–civil rights black life. The rise in popularity of the colloquialism in the last two decades firmly roots the emergence of this archetype in the late twentieth century. The socially constructed hoe serves multiple, layered, and nuanced purposes for women and men.

I turn now to the lyrics of the Atlanta-based rapper Future to illuminate the contempt, ambiguity, and complexity of the hoe archetype. In his club hit "My Hoe 2," Future verbalizes the conflicting attitudes and feelings the song's male persona has toward a woman with whom he is sexually involved. As the song begins, his reactions to this woman are evident. He contrasts his interactions with her with those of another man to exemplify his emotional desensitization toward and dehumanization of her: "I pissed on her / You kissed her. . . . You feel in love with / I think I miss her. . . . You took her on a trip / I tried to pimp her."[9] He illustrates his callousness and devaluation of the woman deemed the embodiment of a hoe figure by urinating on her, while his competition (the other male persona in the song) supposedly demonstrates emotional vulnerability by falling in love with her. Though Future degrades this woman, he ruefully admits that he misses her, which further complicates his otherwise egregious treatment of her. What also becomes evident is that the hoe archetype becomes a conduit through which particular types of masculinity, machismo, and male (sexual) domination are reified. In contrast, affection and loving behavior toward women is characterized as somehow a threat to authentic masculinity within the hip-hop genre and in the culture at large.

Moreover, further highlighting that this perspective is rife with contradiction and complexity, Future scoffs at the other man for treating the woman to a romantic vacation. He, being a savvy businessman who seeks to exploit her, "tried to pimp her."[10] In the second portion of the chorus, Future expresses his appreciation for the way this woman looks, calling her "sexy" and "fine." However, he immediately counters these associations of her with positive attributes with remarks about her deceitful personality: "she say she loves me / I know she lyin."[11] He denies, if not undermines, the credibility of everything this woman says by emphasizing the conniving traits associated with black women labeled as hoes.

The final insult Future lobs at his competition is the most devastating. He gloats that his inferior opponent could "marry" this woman "today" but that she would still be drawn to him sexually.[12] The remainder of the chorus repeats "If that's your hoe / That's my hoe too," exemplifying the detached sense of owner-ship that the male persona Future described in the song maintains with hoes. While he is uninterested in maintaining a monogamous relationship with this woman because she is, in his skewed conceptualization, an adulterous liar, he is undeniably attracted to her and longs for sexual interaction with her. The chorus also emphasizes the assumption that women are at everyone's disposal. Success-fully disarming the woman he has described throughout the song of any human-ity, he objectifies the hoe while characterizing her as a potentially dangerous sexual plaything. Popular rap and the everyday speech rap music inspires "have successfully depersonalized relationships," placing little value on women because they are deemed expendable.[13]

The influence of radio rap and hip-hop music crosses ethnic, economic, and social boundaries. As Pulitzer Prize winner Eugene Robinson acknowledges in *Disintegration,* his account of the fissuring of black America, "There are times and places where we still come together—on increasingly rare occasions when we feel lumped together, defined, and threatened solely on the basis of skin color," iden-tifying "venues like 'urban' or black-oriented radio" as one of the unifying ele-ments, classifying it as a "kind of speed-of-light grapevine."[14] Although rap and hip-hop were once defined as a witnessing of the life of the underrepresented, as testimonies of the institutional demons that plague predominantly black urban areas, this widely distributed and commercially profitable music has made a monumental shift in the past decade. Extravagance, the acquisition of designer goods, virility and conquest, and bragging self-description define modern-day commercial rap. The narrative is no longer a carefully constructed exposé of everyday life in the proverbial ghetto. Now it describes what life is like after one has amassed the wherewithal to escape the ghetto. Radio rap and hip-hop are dominated by artists who cleverly mask artifice as "realness," greatly embellish accounts of the amount of money they earn, fictionalize descriptions of how they earn it, and imply that they have harem at their beck and call. I do not suggest that commercially successful artists such as Nicki Minaj, Lil Wayne, and Jay-Z are somehow deficient in artistic talent. In fact, their "lyrical and performative talents and the compelling music that frames their rhymes" are precisely what makes "this seduction so powerful and disturbing."[15] Because they are heavily influenced by corporate propaganda, the most profitable hip-hop and rap songs on the radio today are not artistically designed to do the political work that other forms of black music, such as the blues, have historically done. Unfortunately, contemporary hip-hop and rap often do the opposite of community-building work in their lyrical devaluation of black women and black life generally.

The genre of the blues, for example, is defined by its history of protest and its function of providing an emotional outlet for its artists and their listeners. Angela Davis writes that this "musical genre is called the 'blues' not only because it employs a musical scale containing 'blues' notes, but also because it names, in myriad ways, the social and psychic afflictions and aspirations of African Americans."[16] The blues genre left a legacy of "intermingling the private and the public" and the "personal and the political," and one of its essential elements was a mindset of resistance. In contrast with the myopia or narrow-mindedness oftentimes promoted by much of contemporary commercial rap and hip-hop, the blues provided a medium through which "individual tragedies affecting black working class communities" were "recast as social, collective adversities."[17] Individualist attitudes among blues artists "would have significantly diminished black people's ability to constitute themselves as a community in the struggle." The blues illustrates the power of music to unify.[18]

During the 1920s and 1930s, the heyday of blues artists such as Gertrude "Ma" Rainey, clearly identifiable experiences were common to the majority of black people in America. Extreme poverty and illiteracy were common denominators for most persons of African descent. Our collective condition has evolved over time and the musical genres of commercial rap and hip-hop have come to influence lifestyles and worldviews that are not class specific. Cora Daniels posits that the word "ghetto" is "not about class" but is much more fluid, "uncontrollably transcending class, race and culture."[19] Her conceptualization applies equally well to contemporary commercial rap and hip-hop. The extravagant lifestyles and chauvinist perspectives promoted in best-selling rap and hip-hop music today are seductive regardless of the listener's socioeconomic status. Instead of a message that inspires a sense of collective responsibility or assigns transcendent qualities to particular black social conditions, as jazz, spirituals, and the blues do, the most popular rap music promotes exclusionary practices and unabashed sexism, misogyny, and heteropatriarchy that ignores collective struggle and meaningful angst. This change cannot be divorced from the fact that much of it is driven by the music industry and the market; often when artists attempt to infuse a deeper sense of meaning or social commentary into their work, they experience a lag in sales, if their lyrics ever make it to the recording studio or the public domain. In the cacophony of mainstream music industry propaganda, "conscious" rap has been silenced.

"Who's Pimping Who?"

The music that I love is and always has been an uneasy fit with the feminist tenets with which I was raised. I have a deep affinity for the loud bass, thumping percussion, and clever quips that so many rappers offer in their music, yet the cognitive dissonance I experienced as I listened to this music began to make me uncomfortable. By the time I was in high school, I had begun analyzing the lyrics of some pop-rap songs more closely and engaging in my own passive form of protest by refusing to dance to tracks I deemed particularly disrespectful. I still maintained that the chauvinism I heard in the majority of the music I listened to was troubling only in the most extreme instances ("Lay on the bed / And give me head / Don't have to ask / Don't have to beg" for example) but not in your run-of-the-mill tracks sprinkled with "bitch" or "hoe."[20] To those who would indict the genre wholesale, my defensive rebuttal remained that whatever evils were apparent in the music simply reflected the flaws of our already perverse world: a rebuttal that is juvenile in its apathy because it suggests that since societal ills such as sexism and hyperbolic violence are present everywhere, they should not be confronted anywhere.

As hip-hop scholar Imani Perry asserts, rap is an "inherently masculine art form" characterized by "masculine aesthetics," such as rampant boasting, extreme competitiveness, and the objectification of black women.[21] The promotion of these ideals has caused black female emcees and consumers of rap and hip-hop music to "often occupy roles gendered male" in order to advance in social status and cultural capital.[22] Perry observes that "in the later years of the twentieth century, hip-hop took a turn not only towards sexist assertions" but "also towards having a threatening impact, particularly on black girls and young women."[23] Stanley Crouch claims that this threatening impact manifests itself as a "sadomasochistic relationship" between black female fans and hip-hop.[24] Black female consumers of commercial rap and hip-hop must be aware that they support a popular idiom that typically assaults women with contempt. It is from the latter unresolved psychological wreckage that the contemporary use of hoe emerges as a figurative nod of agreement with misogynist notions and patriarchal discourse within rap and hip-hop, black society, and dominant American culture. Having been "born into a society of entrenched loathing for whatever is black and female," black women interact with one another amid the obstacles of "silence, isolation, fury, mistrust, self-rejection, and sadness," as Audre Lorde observes.[25] Black women simultaneously face the smothering effects of normative white male patriarchy and further marginalization by sexism within the black community: a nebulous and precarious domain we black women inhabit. Black women's libel and slander of other black women is largely normalized because, as Tricia Rose asserts, "sexism works best when women are isolated from and pitted against one another," as "isolation and conflict ensure that women will sustain and internalize the terms of insult and control used to keep things as they are."[26] When black women use the invective hoe to define or characterize other black women, the labeler is seemingly spared from exile to the margins of respectable black society and relegates the labeled black woman to oblivion in her stead. The black male quest for agency has become entangled with a "myth of sexual prowess that conflates assertions of freedom and power with the subordination of black women as solely objects of pleasure," and black women who seek power by using the insult hoe perpetuate the same sexism.[27]

"STUPID HOES IS MY ENEMY"

The flamboyant Nicki Minaj is an internationally known example of a female black pop culture icon who wantonly projects the contemporary hoe archetype and uses the insult hoe to label other black women. Minaj, a Trinidadian-American, female emcee born in 1982, has achieved unparalleled commercial success in the hip-hop, gangster rap, and pop culture genres by assuming stylistically misogynist spaces. Her use of the word hoe reflects the rage, distrust, and self-rejection that is a result of historical matrices of oppression in American society.

When one examines Minaj's usage of the word hoe through the lens of the detrimental implications of the term, it becomes clear that the practice poses an insidious threat to black women's humanity and worth. In her book about the active participation of American women in the development of contemporary raunch culture, *Female Chauvinist Pigs,* Ariel Levy describes such a woman as one who "doesn't mind cartoonish stereotypes of female sexuality" or "cartoonishly macho responses to them." Moreover, a female chauvinist pig is a woman who responds to the presence of chauvinist men by asking "Why try to beat them when you can join them?" This is a particularly relevant question for women in the male-centered genres of rap and hip-hop.[28] As a self-proclaimed black Barbie, Minaj conjures the language, aesthetics, and iconography of the cartoonish: she is widely known for her outlandish costumes, over-the-top performances, and deliberately unrealistic exaggeration of her body parts and figure.

Born in Trinidad and raised in Queens, New York, Minaj struggled for years as an underground rap act before finally catching the attention of Cash Money Records mogul Dwayne Carter (aka Lil Wayne) in 2009. Nicki Minaj is a product of the era of the titillating female emcee that was pioneered by artists such as Foxy Brown and Lil Kim in which "many women visually look femme, but simultaneously occupy male spaces linguistically."[29] In *Shifting,* Jones and Shorter-Gooden describe the persona that female emcees such as Foxy Brown and Lil Kim created as "insatiable divas who live for sex, diamonds and champagne." They assert that artists such as Nicki Minaj who thrive off that image "propagate the idea of black women as sexually charged and [ever] available, as obsessed with money and men."[30]

In her March 2011 release "Did It On 'Em," for example, Minaj describes scenarios of power and dominance that involve a penis she does not physically possess: "If I had a dick / I would pull it out and piss on 'em." In her desire to be perceived as powerful and aggressive—and to be taken as seriously as an emcee as her male rap cohorts—Nicki Minaj "finds it more efficient to identify with men than to try and elevate the entire female sex to [her] level."[31] Along similar lines, she targets black women when she states, "These little nappy headed hoes need a perminator."[32] By directly quoting the infamous and egregious comments made by polemical radio personality Don Imus, Minaj aligns herself, not with black women, but rather with a white, male, patriarchal, oppressive power structure. By labeling other black women as "nappy headed hoes," she differentiates herself from her demographic and perpetuates their denigration.

Even more inflammatory than "Did It On 'Em," Minaj's December 2011 release "Stupid Hoe" undeniably uses the term to distinguish herself from other black women. In the bridge of the song, Minaj repeats in a singsong refrain, "Stupid hoes is my enemy / Stupid hoes is so wack / Stupid hoe shoulda befriended me / Then she coulda probably came back." Minaj not only detests and distances herself from these women, she also situates them as her direct enemies, proclaiming that other black women should seek association with her to avoid harsh treatment. During the last twenty seconds of the song, she uses the term hoe so rapidly that it is nearly unintelligible. She chants, "I said fuck a stupid hoe / Yeah fuck you, stupid hoe" repeatedly to the extent it operates in two ways. First, in lyrical and discursive terms, she deploys a language ("*fuck* you, stupid hoe") that mimics the actual sexual acts (copulation rather than sexual intimacy) male rappers engage in with women they deem hoes. Second, drawing upon an idiom of aggression and derogation, her lyrics denigrate women in a similar fashion as the misogynist, sexist, and male-dominating verses of male rappers.

Her appropriation of such male hegemonic rhymes is evidenced in the lyrics that immediately follow this diatribe, where she refers to herself as "the female Weezy" (the female Lil Wayne). In so doing, she explicitly positions herself as the female equivalent (in her musical career and her public persona) of her mentor Dwayne Carter, whose lyrics exhibit a degree of black male chauvinism and misogyny, even if they are complex and provocative. Her framing of herself as the female parallel of Lil Wayne illustrates how she consciously operates as a female chauvinist pig within the already restrictive roles ascribed to women (and men) in the mainstream hip-hop industry.

Though Nicki Minaj's lyrics may be shocking, she is not especially pathological in her use of hoe. It marks a strategic alignment with what the music industry and record labels problematically require of mainstream artists, female and male emcees alike, if they are to reach the airwaves and achieve commercial success. In addition, she is merely reflecting what she hears in popular culture.

My peers usually meet my study of the word hoe with laughter, remarking that they believe it is useless to attempt to bring attention to a term that is already so widely used. For me, this blindness to their participation in the oppression of themselves and other black people illustrates a thoughtless commitment to reckless behavior and a compromised consciousness that is far too commonplace in

American society at large. However unpopular or unusual it may be, an investigation of how rappers and everyday people use the slang insult hoe is worthy of critical attention. It would be unrealistic for me to expect Nicki Minaj, Future, or any other black women or men to suddenly become attuned to the sociohistorical stereotypes that are projected onto black women. Nor would it be reasonable for me to expect them to suddenly exchange their profitable ignorance for cultural critique or an attitude of social responsibility. My goal is not to indict mainstream rap and hip-hop as a genre. As Tricia Rose notes, "Gangsta rap isn't just a corporate fantasy, nor did it create sexism in the black community." The music "does not break from the fundamental logic of mainstream masculinity" but rather "conveys it with excess, bravado, and extra insult."[33] Yet the numbing impact of the high-frequency use of hoe in radio rap and hip-hop that then trickles down into contemporary black vernacular not only necessitates acknowledgement but also begs for intervention. The use of the slang insult hoe to describe black women cannot continue as if it is a trivial development.

NOTES

1. I refer to terms such as "bitch," "slut," and "hoe."

2. Charisse Jones and Kumea Shorter-Gooden, *Shifting: The Double Lives of Black Women in America* (New York: HarperCollins, 2003), 6–8.

3. Ibid., 50–53.

4. For an exploration of the sociohistorical context from which many of the implications of the modern stereotypes against black women, see Dionne P. Stephens and Layli D. Phillips, "Freaks, Gold Diggers, Divas, and Dykes: The Sociohistorical Development of Adolescent African American Women's Sexual Scripts," *Sexuality and Culture: An Interdisciplinary Quarterly* 7, no. 1 (2003): 287–299. These stereotypes, I believe, have coalesced in the insult "hoe."

5. *The Collins English Dictionary,* s.v. "ho," http://www.collinsdictionary.com/dictionary/english/ho, accessed November 21, 2011.

6. Innumerable rap lyrics have echoed and affirmed these sentiments. An example is Dr. Dre's "Bitches Ain't Shit but Hoes and Tricks," *The Chronic,* audio CD, Death Row Koch, 1992. Many examples of rap lyrics proclaiming female inferiority are also directed toward men. For example, in "Stay Schemin (feat. Drake and French Montana)," Drake asserts, "I'm just hitting my pinnacle / you and pussy identical / you like the fucking finish line / we can't wait to run into you"; Rick Ross, *Stay Schemin,* audio CD, Slip 'N Slide/Def Jam Records, 2012.

7. Audre Lorde, "Eye to Eye: Black Women, Hatred, and Anger," in *Sister Outsider* (Freedom: The Crossing Press, 1984), 147.

8. Mireille Miller-Young, "Hip-Hop Honeys and Da Hustlaz: Black Sexualities in the New Hip-Hop Pornography," *Meridians: Feminism, Race, Transnationalism* 8, no. 1 (2008): 276.

9. Future, *Astronaut Status,* audio CD, Freebandz, 2012.

10. Ibid.

11. Ibid.

12. Ibid.

13. Cora Daniels, *Ghetto Nation* (New York: Doubleday Broadway Publishing Group, 2007), 106.

14. Eugene Robinson, *Disintegration: The Splintering of Black America* (New York: Double Day, 2010), 5.

15. Tricia Rose, *Hip Hop Wars: What We Talk about When We Talk about Hip Hop and Why It Matters* (New York: Basic Civitas, 2008), 4.

16. Angela Y. Davis, *Blues Legacies and Black Feminism: Gertrude "Ma" Rainey, Bessie Smith, and Billie Holiday* (New York: Vintage Books, 1984), 33.

17. Ibid., 111.

18. Ibid.

19. Daniels, *Ghetto Nation,* 37.

20. Three 6 Mafia, *Most Known Hits,* audio CD, Sony, 1999.

21. Imani Perry, *Prophets of the Hood: Politics and Poetics in Hip Hop* (Durham, N.C.: Duke University Press, 2004), 156.

22. Ibid.

23. Ibid., 175.

24. T. Denean Sharpley-Whiting, *Pimp's Up, Ho's Down: Hip Hop's Hold on Young Women* (New York: New York University Press, 2008), 8.

25. Lorde, "Eye to Eye," 151.

26. Rose, *Hip Hop Wars,* 175.

27. Cornel West, *Race Matters* (New York: Vintage Books, 1994), 127–128.

28. Ariel Levy, *Female Chauvinist Pigs: Women and the Rise of Raunch Culture,* edited by Ariel Levy (New York: Free Press, 2005), 93.

29. Perry, *Prophets of the Hood,* 157.

30. Jones and Shorter-Gooden, *Shifting,* 30.

31. Levy, *Female Chauvinist Pigs,* 95.

32. Nicki Maraj, *Pink Friday,* audio CD, Cash Money, 2010.

33. Rose, *Hip Hop Wars,* 119.

What Kind of Woman?

ALBERTA HUNTER AND EXPRESSIONS OF BLACK FEMALE SEXUALITY IN THE TWENTIETH CENTURY

K. T. Ewing

The scent of steaming hot plates and a feeling of anticipation permeated the atmosphere at Barney Josephson's Cookery in Greenwich Village, New York. Everyone looked around to catch a first sighting of the elderly woman quickly making her way through the tables with a smile. Her mischievous eyes said it all. Alberta Hunter had come to play. For the next hour she entertained the crowd with songs made popular before most of them were born. With hands on her hips, she tossed her head from side to side, emphasizing the swinging of her oversized gold hoop earrings. Her throaty voice was strong and articulate as she pleased the audience with stories about tough men and hard times.[1] It is not hard to imagine this lively octogenarian performing without undergarments in frigid weather for the sole purpose of delighting soldiers stationed overseas, as she once did.[2] However, the evening celebrated much more than playful sexuality. Intertwined with the fun-loving songs was a message about how Hunter had become an important figure in African American social and political history as well as a popular music icon. These two parts of her story are inextricable.

Historians of black womanhood in the early twentieth century emphasize two models of black women's sexual expression as a means of resisting racist stereotypes in the early twentieth century. The dominant voice belonged to middle-class clubwomen who espoused values almost identical to those of mainstream white society.[3] The assimilationist agenda of these consciously fashioned race women set the tone for African American civil rights and community progress strategies for many decades. The popular voice, however, came from decidedly working-class blues singers whose sudden rise to national acclaim captured the attention of listeners around the country. Instead of defining themselves as race ambassadors, these women claimed to speak only for themselves and women like them. These dominant and popular voices defined competing views of African American womanhood for much of the early twentieth century.[4]

Through an examination of Alberta Hunter's life, this research complicates the bifurcated approach to analyzing the discourse between blues women and clubwomen to provide a more nuanced understanding of how highly visible black women embodied or manipulated expressions of gender. As a singer whose career spanned much of the twentieth century, Hunter's long life provides an illuminating glimpse into the options available for black women and how they exercised subjectivity in their choices during this era. This essay examines not only how Hunter fashioned an alternative idea of race womanhood by consciously manipulating two kinds of gendered performances to enact a multifaceted strategy of resistance, but also how she moved back and forth between the two most visible models of black womanhood. Hunter used, that is, both a blues aesthetic and middle-class respectability to assert herself as a race woman. Her multifaceted response to the pressures black women faced reveals that the dominant models of black womanhood are insufficient explanations for the range of possibilities some women had during the last century; that other possible definitions of black womanhood may have been neglected historically; and, that a reassessment of Hunter, her life, and prevailing assumptions about the politics of black womanhood in the twentieth century is necessary.

Scholars have depicted the ideological tensions between middle-class clubwomen and female blues singers as a difference of opinion regarding sexuality and morality. Clubwomen sought to affirm the inherent worth of all black women by engaging in racial uplift programs so that the dominant society could not deny their human dignity. Blues singers, on the other hand, sought to affirm the value of black life by celebrating it as it was, with all of its diversity intact. Implicit in both characterizations were protests against racism and also competing ideas about gender expression.

Hunter consciously challenged the assumption that the best representatives for the race were women who adhered to Victorian moral ideals at all times.[5] She adeptly manipulated two strategies for confronting racism by concomitantly using middle- and working-class models to challenge gender norms. This decision set her apart from other figures who generally chose to publicly embody only one type of womanhood to confront racist stereotypes. In addition, Hunter kept her most personal relationships private. Later labeled a lesbian by scholars and LGBT activists, Hunter herself never publicly embraced any kind of affiliation with same-gender-loving communities. It does seem possible, however, that Hunter performed one kind of black womanhood while quietly embodying another.

Best known for her musical career during a time "when women who performed in genres other than sacred or classical music challenged the boundaries of 'respectable' womanhood," Alberta Hunter boldly embraced a blues aesthetic.[6] Her decision to enter the world of popular music was a result of financial and racial concerns that for most southern black women were inextricable. Her intimate, animated, double-entendre-laced performances used sex appeal in ways that were expressly at odds with Victorian standards of respectability. Although women who embraced middle-class values were supposed to be the best representatives of the race, it is important to examine working-class women's use of the blues as a means of combating racist stereotypes. Though middle-class women assumed the mantle of speaking for the race, the reality was that middle-class leaders and blues singers spoke to and for different audiences.[7]

The significance of blues music extends beyond the realm of leisure and amusement. Blues culture formed a site of resistance to assaults on the humanity of African Americans. As Michelle R. Scott notes, "Blues music became more than entertainment but a music of self-definition and personal liberation."[8] According to Patricia Hill Collins, blues music provided a means of solidifying aspects of the black community while providing a commentary on the lives of its working-class members. Implicit in this commentary was a challenge to "externally defined controlling images used to justify Black women's objectification as the Other."[9] The blues constituted a site of antiracist discourse, and its singers were participants in a movement to reclaim images of black people and remake them in their own image.

The middle-class discourse of respectability competes with what I call a "discourse of desire" that blues women employed. Blues women were accessible models of womanhood for their working-class sisters. These hard-working, hard-drinking, long-traveling women did not embrace a vision of soft femininity. Instead, they boldly promoted behaviors that were antithetical to middle-class ideals of sexual purity. While middle-class women assumed the mantle of speaking for the race, the reality was that middle-class leaders and blues singers spoke to and for different audiences. Calls for sexual purity, marriage, motherhood, thrift, and sobriety may not have been particularly appealing to women with few outlets for their desires and frustrations. Working-class women more easily identified with the hard-working message embedded in blues music. Blues singers represented who working-class women were at that moment. The women described and embodied by black clubwomen seemed almost irrelevant to women who could not relate to them or their ideals, even if they desired the security those ideals implied.

During the early half of the twentieth century, the public realm was primarily considered male territory. Both the visibility and popularity of blues women were problematic for clubwomen who were concerned with presenting a morally and sexually pure image of African American womanhood. As Evelyn Brooks Higginbotham argues, "It was particularly public behavior that they perceived to wield the power either to refute or confirm stereotypical and discriminatory practices. . . . There could be no laxity as far as sexual conduct, cleanliness, temperance, hard work, and politeness were concerned. There could be no transgression of society's norms."[10] Instead of appreciating blues music as a site for building self-esteem and resisting racist cultural norms, many clubwomen denigrated it as a hindrance to respectability. Because blues spoke openly about a world clubwomen rejected, they offer a glimpse into behaviors and values that might otherwise be lost to us. As Angela Davis notes, "Considering the stringent taboos on representations of sexuality that characterized most dominant discourses of the time, the blues constitute a privileged discourse site."[11]

The designation of blues as "low" culture by Harlem Renaissance intellectuals contributed to its marginalized place among middle-class African Americans.[12] Cheryl Wall highlights the significance of the female voices in blues in her work *Women of the Harlem Renaissance*. By placing women writers of the Harlem Renaissance in the context of other African American female artists, Wall establishes a larger community of peers that had earlier been juxtaposed with each other in order to accentuate their differences. Although Alberta Hunter was aware of the distinctions made between blues culture and middle-class values, she willfully disregarded the notion that she could not be considered refined in spite of her chosen art form. Her refusal to restrict her repertoire to one musical genre allowed her to transcend some of the stereotypes assigned to blues singers, even as she used her notoriety as a blues woman to enhance her career.

Alberta Hunter was born on April 1, 1895. Her childhood under the care of her mother and grandmother in Memphis, Tennessee, influenced her ideas about respectability and options for black women.[13] However, her proximity to Beale Street, the blues core of the city, also affected her perception of her range of possibilities. Though her mother, Laura Hunter, endeavored to keep both her daughters away from what she considered the negative influences of Beale Street, young Alberta proved more resourceful than Laura anticipated. Watching her mother work menial jobs without hope for advancement shaped Hunter's ideas about expectations for black women's lives.[14] Determined to avoid a life of drudgery, she ran away to Chicago and took the spirit of Memphis with her.

Although the content of Hunter's music was undeniably grounded in her southern upbringing, her performance style was more influenced by what she learned after running away to Chicago. She skillfully used sex appeal to engage audiences. Her suggestive songs and performances earned her the nickname "warbler of naughty songs."[15] Yet she valued the distinction between using sex appeal during a performance and using sex as a tool for career advancement. Hunter refused to use sex as a means of getting ahead in an industry in which such practices were considered "part of the game."[16] This refusal indicates the distinction between what she considered acceptable for entertainment value and what crossed the lines of respectable behavior.

Hunter did not allow her career in secular music to preclude the possibility that she was a fit race representative. She used regular correspondence with the black press to craft a public image, particularly during overseas stays. Many of her letters reported on what other performers were doing abroad. In doing this, she implicitly took the position of a race woman through her writings and interviews. Among her personal papers is a response from the *Dallas Morning News* to Hunter's criticism of the racism she experienced while traveling through Dallas. Her decision to address racial matters through both music and the news media suggests that she consciously moved between two models of representation in a way that challenged the assumption that black women were either righteous or licentious.

On the surface, Hunter was a woman who was so dedicated to her career that she chose a life in music over a respectable marriage. However, because marriage and domesticity were visible signs of the assumption of adult status and respectability during much of her life, Hunter, ever conscious of her public image, sought a marriage that would be advantageous. While working a short engagement in Cincinnati, Ohio, she met Willard Saxby Townsend, a military veteran.[17] She was not a woman to waste any time, and they were quickly married on January 27, 1919. Hunter once said of him, "I could see he was a fine young man and a perfect gentleman. I've always been crazy about class."[18] However, her perceptions of classy behavior and what constituted impropriety would have implications for the degree of intimacy they would share once living together as husband and wife. Hunter refused to share a bed with Townsend while they lived in her mother's apartment.[19] She later asserted that the marriage was never consummated.

The union was short-lived, and Townsend filed for divorce two months later, citing Hunter's refusal to give up her career for domestic life. He testified that "she insisted on going on entertaining at cabarets. She told me that she could make more money than I could give her and that she did not like domestic life. I kept after her and told her I would rather she stay at home and not do that kind of work. After I told her that the last time she left."[20] Although the union was short-lived, it provided Hunter with a lifelong connection to someone who went on to become a well-known figure among African Americans. Townsend spent much of his life fighting for labor equality and became the highest-ranking black officer in the Congress of Industrial Organizations in 1942.[21]

Hunter's unwillingness to fulfill traditional domestic expectations was listed as the primary reason Townsend filed for divorce, but Frank C. Taylor, Hunter's first biographer, proposes that another cause may have been her romantic inclination toward women.[22] Her brief marriage might be interpreted in several ways. The marriage may have been a genuine moment of love. It may have been a failed attempt at pursuing heteronormative sexuality. Or it may have been a skillful manipulation to silence rumors about her romantic associations with other women. Based on evidence indicating that she continued to maintain long-term romantic attachments to women, her marriage to Townsend may have, in fact, been designed to cover up another side of her persona.

If her dedication to domesticity was lacking, her enthusiasm for lively performance was not. Even when she had reached her fifties (an age at which most of the women she had begun her career with had long since retired from the stage), she insisted upon giving United States troops stationed overseas a show worthy of their attention. Never one to shy away from making an impression, she once performed in a slinky dress without undergarments despite frigid temperatures. She explained her decision as one of empathy for the soldiers. "You know that those soldiers got so tired of looking at nothing but men in soldier clothes. I knew they didn't want to see no woman come out there with no jeans and pants and things on. . . . So I had those slinky dresses, and I had on nothing but the dress, see? Not even my little shorts."[23]

Embodying a blues aesthetic that did not balk at open expressions of sexuality was only one way that Alberta Hunter crafted her public image. Although she enjoyed her life as a singer, there was another side of her that she valued as much. Offstage, she displayed middle-class characteristics more in keeping with the way her mother and grandmother raised her. Having grown up in her grandmother's deeply religious home, she had regularly attended Collins Chapel Colored Methodist Church which heavily influenced her childhood. As an adult, she used her intimate ties with the black press to blur the boundaries between blues culture and middle-class race leadership. In fact, it was her notoriety as a blues and cabaret performer that garnered her attention from the black press, which in turn allowed her to use print media as an outlet to become well known as a race woman. By rejecting the notion that only those who always conformed to Victorian values were the best spokespersons for the race, Hunter advocated for a more open idea of who was fit to represent the interests of African Americans.

Black communities highly prized education as a means of overcoming obstacles. Although Hunter's formal schooling was truncated when she ran away to Chicago, she took steps to educate herself. She stressed the importance of appearing educated and refined at all times and took care to associate herself with those she considered to be of higher class standing than herself and from whom she could learn. She also acquired fluency in French as an adult. She even saved her lesson notes until the end of her life as proof that she had accomplished this feat.[24] Her dedication to learning a language that would both enhance her overseas career and impress her social peers is indicative of the value she placed on education. That dedication came in handy on a trip under the auspices of the United Service Organizations when she confronted a French citizen about sharing a racist joke with a white American serviceman. She reported the serviceman to his commanding officer, repeating the offensive joke verbatim in French.[25] Hunter taught as much French as possible to other African American performers in her troupe and groomed them for a life of public scrutiny. She saw herself and the other musicians as ambassadors representing African Americans as well as the nation. The French joke incident reminded the younger members of her unit that education was a means of protecting and standing up for oneself.

Though scholars classify Hunter as a blues singer in the early portion of her career, an examination of her life and career reveals that she does not fit neatly in that category. Her stage performances embodied a blues persona, but her personal values much more closely reflected ideals espoused by middle-class women. She rejected the label of blues singer. In an interview with *DownBeat* magazine, Hunter said, "They call me a blues singer, but I'm not a blues singer, that's a mistake. I'm a singer of songs. I sing pretty songs and old songs; blues is just a part of what I do. I'm just Alberta, singer of songs."[26] Embedded in this refusal to be pigeonholed was a rejection of the values commonly associated with blues music. Taylor wrote that Hunter "turned up her nose at anyone unrefined or too close to her own humble origins with whom others might associate her."[27] Placing herself at a distance from those she considered unrefined set Hunter apart from other blues singers of her time; and her rejection of the label of blues singer is indicative of her desire to avoid strict professional and personal categorization.

Although she distanced herself from many people, she never hesitated to give credit to Chicago's prostitutes and club singers for teaching her how to style herself as a fashionable blues woman. In interviews with Taylor, she always spoke highly of those underworld characters, including pimps and gangsters, whom she said behaved like ladies and gentlemen. She conferred upon them a status that many middle-class African Americans would have been reluctant to bestow on people of that social class. The knowledge she gained in Chicago wildly contradicted the values she was raised with, but she blended them into a lifestyle that she used to form her own method of confronting racial challenges. Her respect for prostitutes and gangsters notwithstanding, Hunter's tendency to exercise social distance from people with mannerisms she considered crude intensified over time.

Hunter's intense desire for privacy is one of the more prominent themes woven throughout Taylor's work. He asserts that she was what is now commonly referred to as a closeted lesbian.[28] Based on subtle cues during interviews with Hunter as well as hints from her friends during interviews, Taylor places a label on Hunter that she may not have personally chosen for herself for a variety of reasons. What is most important is not whether she identified as lesbian but rather how she presented herself in order to manipulate gender conventions throughout much of her life. Hunter's life unfolded over a period of time in which the understanding of same-sex relationships was in flux. Categorizing her as lesbian, particularly in the early period of her life is problematic because "lesbian" was not a clearly defined identity until around the middle of the twentieth century.[29] If accounts of her same-gender-loving relationships are accurate, then she publicly performed and privately embodied various complex kinds of black womanhood. It is the more obscure part of her life that raises perhaps more questions than answers about black womanhood and sexuality. If she did establish long-term romantic relationships with women, why did she choose to conceal that aspect of her life, particularly given that several prominent female blues singers celebrated same-sex desire for women? What was at stake in her portrayal of herself as hetero-sexual? And, is it possible that because same-sex relationships remained outside the established boundaries of Victorian morality that Hunter was unwilling to publicly abandon her presentation of certain middle-class behaviors necessary to enhance her carefully crafted image as a race woman?

There is much about Hunter's life that remains in the shadows. Although she enjoyed her status as a public figure, she worked hard to maintain a distance between her public and private selves. Although her personal values were decid-edly middle class, her private life may have included romantic practices that were outside the accepted range of options for middle-class women. As a woman who had few intimates, journal entries of her innermost thoughts could have been an outlet, but was not the case for Hunter. In fact, the Alberta Hunter Papers at the Schomburg Center for Research in Black Culture makes evident what she saw fit to save and what she chose to conceal or omit. Included in her personal col-lection are numerous newspaper clippings, handwritten letters from family and friends, contracts, receipts, and many scraps of paper with handwritten remind-ers. She also saved three diaries, but they are noticeably blank except for sparse entries about travel dates and performances.

The paucity of information recorded in Hunter's journals may be interpreted as a determined preservation of privacy. As historian Deborah Gray White notes,

> In order to be one's own best argument . . . clubwomen had to make "the cause" and their lives indistinguishable to themselves, their peers, and to future gen-erations. Few left records that revealed their private selves; most of the collec-tions left are filled with public memorabilia rather than personal materials. Even though it makes the historian's job of piecing together their private lives almost impossible, for women who wanted their public lives to stand in for the private, this was a good strategy.[30]

Middle-class women were particularly sensitive to ad hominem attacks and, therefore, endeavored to reduce the possibility that they would be considered unfit race representatives. These women went to great lengths to appear respect-able at all times. Alberta Hunter's practice of keeping her personal life off the record compelled people to contend with her public ideas.[31]

Historian Darlene Clark Hine argues that black women adhered to a "culture of dissemblance" that "involved creating the appearance of disclosure, or open-ness about themselves and their feelings, while actually remaining enigmatic."[32] This practice was used as protection against charges of immorality and, more seriously, rape.[33] She asserts that an emphasis on manners and morals served as protection against the very real threat and acts of rape against black women that mostly went unpunished. Seen in this light, it is not unfathomable that many women were disturbed by a seemingly lax attitude toward sex in an environment that was hostile to women's expressions of sexual freedom. As Hunter knew first-hand the psychological impact of sexual abuse, she behaved, understandably so, in a manner designed to shield herself from further injury.[34] Examining how she embodies a kind of sexuality in keeping with the culture of dissemblance may provide some explanations for why she consciously crafted a particular public image that was at odds with her private life.

Although Hine's term "culture of dissemblance" refers to black women's efforts to shield themselves from white society particularly, in Hunter's case, the term may be applicable to how she handled her intimate relationships generally. Her playful treatment of sex and sexuality through music is one way that she portrayed a sense of openness. She belted out sensual lines with the winks and nods of a woman who seemed familiar with "rough and ready" men.[35] However, Hunter was caught in the clash between acceptance of and opportunities for expressions of both same-sex love and the respectability politics among African Americans.[36] The way she navigated this dynamic provides insight into how black women balanced their personal desires with the struggle to combat negative stereotypes about their sexuality.

Studies of community building among white lesbians tend to focus on the emergence of bars as sites of socialization and culture building. However, scholars interested in black lesbian history have highlighted the limitations of looking primarily at bars for information about similar processes among lesbians of color.[37] Rochella Thorpe examines the significance of house parties and the friend-of-a-friend nature of black lesbian community building for fostering a sense of intimacy among women. She writes that "unlike white lesbians, who could hear about a bar and show up without knowing anyone else there, black women had to form connections with other lesbians in order to know where to socialize. Once that initial connection was made, however, their choices of where to socialize could increase dramatically."[38]

Hunter's personal papers indicate that she knew A'Lelia Walker, a woman known for hosting parties that catered to Harlem's lesbian and gay community.[39] Associating with A'Lelia Walker may have been one way she kept ties to Harlem's same-gender-loving community while endeavoring to maintain the privacy she needed to protect her career. Given her preference for privacy, it is highly unlikely that Hunter would have frequented lesbian bars in any city, as her notoriety would have drawn unwanted attention. As an illustration of the risks same-gender-loving carried in this time period, Hunter's seemingly neutral professional relationship with singer Marian Anderson turned sour once Anderson became aware of rumors regarding Hunter's sexuality.[40]

The black press that Hunter courted throughout her career in music exhibited a strong anti-homosexual bias.[41] Members of the black bourgeoisie influenced the agenda in these publications and thus had a ready outlet for their world-views. Their influence did not escape Hunter's notice and may have played a role in her decision to keep her romantic attachments to women out of public view. For example, she skillfully used speculation in the black press about a mysterious overseas suitor to her advantage. As was her style, she played coy when asked about the unknown beau while allowing the story to linger.[42] It is possible that the mysterious suitor the press wagged its tongue about was a woman. One affectionate correspondence Hunter saved, for instance, was from someone who signed the name "Flicka," which means "girl" in Swedish.[43] These letters may provide a hint about her sexuality or affectional orientation.

Two of the most well-known early blues singers, Ma Rainey and Bessie Smith, made no secret of their sexual relationships with women and male lovers. If same-sex relationships were part of what rendered Rainey and Smith unacceptable models of womanhood according to middle-class rhetoric, then it is understandable why Hunter, if similarly inclined, may have desired to keep her romantic life private. One public nod Hunter may have given to speculations about her sexuality is her cover of "Tain't Nobody's Biz-ness," a song popularized by Smith that contains a reference to sexual associations with women.

Black lesbian feminists have forcefully voiced the importance of reclaiming the histories of lesbians of color and understanding their significance in black history. By arguing against the marginal place they hold in historiography, these women push scholars to reconsider the lives of those who have intentionally lived in the shadows or were rendered invisible by society. Ma Rainey's bold assertions of same-sex desire in her music serve as a means by which to foreground and reclaim a history of black women who have rejected heteronormative sexual values. Although some LGBT rights activists and scholars have claimed that Hunter's life is evidence of a far-reaching lesbian presence in history, particularly African American history, historians must also be careful about placing present labels on past actors. As concepts of homosexuality, as Siobhan Somerville posits, were constructed and refined during the same time that understandings of race and ethnicity were also changing, it is important to keep in mind how Hunter envisioned and presented herself.[44] To be sure, identity runs deeper than a superficial label, especially one that does not always reflect the complexity or reality of one's existence.

The choices Hunter made about how she carried herself as a woman in the public eye reveal much about the sexual politics of her time. Sociologist Patricia Hill Collins notes that black sexual politics is "a set of ideas and social practices shaped by gender, race, and sexuality that frame Black men and women's treatment of one another as well as how African Americans are perceived and treated by others."[45] The controversial stance of blues women suggests that no one could commodify their bodies but them. Their sound could be sold, but no one owned their bodies, not even their middle-class counterparts who sought to regulate a particular ideology of morality and maternity. Because the oppression of sexual minorities is based partly on the high value placed on normative femininity in relation to masculinity, understanding the history of how blues women resisted the dominant narrative of gender expression may help to construct new methods of resisting restrictive gender roles for both women and men.

Hunter's skillful manipulation of gender expressions may enhance our current understanding of what it meant to embody competing ideas of gender while keeping a separation between public and private life. Her decision to save notes from her French lessons while leaving almost no trace of her intimate relationships, for instance, reveals the way she prioritized education as well as how she perceived sexual politics. Instead of allowing the sexual politics of her time to limit her options, she disregarded them by playfully embracing a blues aesthetic *and* staunchly defending the significance of middle-class values. By publicly embodying more than one style of womanhood, Hunter intentionally blurred the lines of gendered performances.

The issue of sexual orientation complicates the historiographic discourse on African American women's history. The early historiography sought to correct omissions and misinformation about black women. Historians who sought to write against the cultural stereotype that black women were immoral did not give much attention to indications of nonnormative sexuality. However, if we are to have a fuller understanding of what it meant to be a black woman during the twentieth century, it is imperative that we include those who did not fit neatly into existing heteronormative categories. Hunter's life is useful in this regard. Incorporating her story with those that have been investigated by historians working in the past ten years enriches the historiography of African American women.

Cultural expectations are only part of what determines success. Alberta Hunter's experiences throughout the twentieth century demonstrate that perception is equally important. She never considered herself to be hindered by where she came from or by what she was expected to become as an African American woman. As she neared the end of her life, she continued to emphasize that "women should make up their minds to do something and then do it and not get scared. A woman can do anything if she's got stamina and courage."[46] Hunter's attitude and actions defied expectations of what a woman born into a southern working-class black family at the end of the nineteenth century could accomplish. Alberta Hunter was her own kind of woman.

Notes

1. *Alberta Hunter: My Castle's Rockin',* dir. Stuart Goldman (New York: V.I.E.W. Video, 1992), DVD.

2. Frank C. Taylor and Gerald Cook, *Alberta Hunter: A Celebration in Blues* (New York: McGraw-Hill, 1987), 193. To date this is the only book-length biographical treatment of Hunter's life.

3. Glenda Elizabeth Gilmore, *Gender and Jim Crow: Women and the Politics of White Supremacy in North Carolina, 1896–1920* (Chapel Hill, N.C.: University of North Carolina Press, 1996), xviii–xix.

4. Differentiating between dominant and popular is key here. The middle-class voice is labeled dominant because it set the tone for sweeping agendas. However, the blues singers are designated as popular because they more easily captivated the masses, the same people the middle class sought to define and uplift without an intimate understanding of their daily experiences. Additionally, blues, as a musical genre, was able to more easily draw the attention of average citizens, both black and white, than rhetorical appeals to moral uplift.

5. Stephanie J. Shaw, *What a Woman Ought to Be and to Do: Black Professional Women Workers during the Jim Crow Era* (Chicago: University of Chicago Press, 1996), 14–15.

6. Michelle R. Scott, *Blues Empress in Black Chattanooga: Bessie Smith and the Emerging Urban South* (Chicago: University of Illinois Press, 2008), 2.

7. Shirley Wilson Logan, *"We Are Coming": The Persuasive Discourse of Nineteenth-Century Black Women* (Carbondale, Ill.: Southern Illinois University Press, 1999), 99.

8. Ibid., 5.

9. Patricia Hill Collins, *Black Feminist Thought: Knowledge, Consciousness, and the Politics of Empowerment* (New York: Routledge, 2000), 105–106.

10. Evelyn Brooks Higginbotham, *Righteous Discontent: The Women's Movement in the Black Church, 1880–1920* (Cambridge, Mass.: Harvard University Press, 1993), 196.

11. Angela Davis, *Blues Legacies and Black Feminism: Gertrude "Ma" Rainey, Bessie Smith, and Billie Holiday* (New York: Vintage Books, 1984), xvii.

12. Ibid., xiii.

13. "Delayed Certificate of Birth," Tennessee Department of Public Health, Nashville, Tennessee, August 7, 1964.

14. Michelle R. Scott, "Alberta Hunter: 'She Had the World in a Jug, with the Stopper in Her Hand,'" in *Tennessee Women: Their Lives and Times,* ed. Sarah Wilkerson Freeman and Beverly Greene Bond (Athens: University of Georgia Press, 2009), 99–101.

15. Newspaper clipping, January 17, 1942, Box 15, Folder 1, Alberta Hunter Papers, Schomburg Center for Research in Black Culture, New York, New York.

16. Lynn Gilbert and Gaylen Moore, "Alberta Hunter," in *Particular Passions: Talks with Women Who Have Shaped Our Times* (New York: Clarkson N. Potter, Inc., 1981), 249.

17. Taylor and Cook, *Alberta Hunter,* 42.

18. Ibid., 43.

19. Ibid.

20. *Willard Townsend vs. Alberta Townsend,* divorce no. 386819, Superior Court of Cook County, March 23, 1923.

21. Eric Arnesen, "Willard Townsend: Black Workers, Civil Rights, and the Labor Movement," in *Portraits of African American Life since 1865,* ed. Nina Mjagkij (Wilmington, Del.: SR Books, 2003), 148.

22. Taylor and Cook, *Alberta Hunter,* 42–43.

23. Ibid., 193. This incident took place in the winter of 1952.

24. Undated pages that appear to be from a notebook, Box 1, Folder 8, Alberta Hunter Papers.

25. Taylor and Cook, *Alberta Hunter,* 172.

26. Interview in *DownBeat,* n.d., 60, clipping, Box 16, Folder 1, Alberta Hunter Papers.

27. Taylor and Cook, *Alberta Hunter,* 38.

28. Ibid., 42–43.

29. Lillian Faderman, *Odd Girls and Twilight Lovers: A History of Lesbian Life in Twentieth-Century America* (New York: Columbia University Press, 1991), 2.

30. Deborah Gray White, *Too Heavy a Load: Black Women in Defense of Themselves, 1894–1994* (New York: Norton, 1999), 88.

31. Civil rights organizer Ella Baker, for example, refused to leave behind any personal effects that could be used to personally attack her as a means of weakening the cause she championed. See Barbara Ransby, *Ella Baker and the Black Freedom Movement: A Radical Democratic Vision* (Chapel Hill, N.C.: University of North Carolina Press, 2003), 7.

32. Darlene Clark Hine, "Rape and the Inner Lives of Black Women: Thoughts on the Culture of Dissemblance," in Darlene Clark Hine, *Hine Sight: Black Women and the Re-Construction of American History* (Brooklyn, NY: Carlson, 1994), 41.

33. Ibid., 37.

34. Taylor and Cook, *Alberta Hunter,* 13–14.

35. Alberta Hunter, "Two-Fisted (Double Jointed Rough and Ready Man)," *Down-hearted Blues: Live at the Cookery,* CD, Rockbeat Records, August 2011.

36. A. B. Christa Schwarz, *Gay Voices of the Harlem Renaissance* (Bloomington: Indiana University Press, 2003), 15.

37. Rochella Thorpe, "'A house where queers go': African American Lesbian Nightlife in Detroit 1940–1975," in *Inventing Lesbian Cultures* (Boston: Beacon Press, 1996), 50–51.

38. Ibid., 44.

39. Undated notes, Box 1, Folder 8,

40. Taylor and Cook, *Alberta Hunter,* 105.

41. Schwarz, *Gay Voices of the Harlem Renaissance,* 18–19.

42. Marvel Cooke, "Alberta Hunter Is No Cinderella, But Her Story Is Just About as Romantic," *New York Amsterdam News,* November 5, 1938, 21.

43. Taylor and Cook, *Alberta Hunter,* 42.

44. Siobhan B. Somerville, *Queering the Color Line: Race and the Invention of Homosexuality in American Culture* (Durham, N.C.: Duke University Press, 2000), 13–14.

45. Patricia Hill Collins, *Black Sexual Politics: African Americans, Gender, and the New Racism* (New York: Routledge, 2004), 349.

46. *Vogue,* September 1982, 140, quoted in Taylor and Cook, *Alberta Hunter,* 266.

CHAPTER 8

The P-Word Exchange

REPRESENTING BLACK FEMALE SEXUALITY IN CONTEMPORARY URBAN FICTION

Cherise A. Pollard

Black women's urban fiction engages with the history of negative and dehumanizing representations of black women both past and present. Both Sister Souljah's *The Coldest Winter Ever* (1999) and Sapphire's *Push* (1996) were published during a time when hip-hop music, especially gangsta rap, was becoming influential in American popular culture. As early urban hip-hop novels, both Sapphire's and Sister Souljah's works grapple with the exploitative messages that hip-hop music and videos were giving the black community at the end of the twentieth century. Set in the New York metropolitan area, the locus of the emergence of East Coast hip-hop culture, both of these germinal texts give readers an opportunity to understand the cultural politics of representing black female sexualities in contemporary popular fiction.

Authors of urban fiction strive to achieve a level of authenticity that lends credence to both the story and the storyteller.[1] Pressure to depict a version of authentic urban experience necessarily translates into a reification of ghetto stereotypes such as gang violence, drug culture, poverty, materialism, broken homes, hypersexuality, and an alleged abuse of the welfare system. Of course, this commercialized notion of authenticity is highly problematic because it is fueled by market-driven expectations of readers that are informed by hip-hop culture (a mode of expression that is itself shaped by racism and sexism).[2] Aside from street violence and the romanticization of drug culture, one of the most compelling elements of urban fiction is the depiction of black female sexuality in the context of hip-hop culture's misogynistic sexual economy. The novels by Sister Souljah and Sapphire have captured the popular cultural imagination precisely because of their unflinching descriptions of young black female sexuality. These novels are publicly categorized as supposedly raw and real because of the authors' strategic use of explicit language and graphic descriptions of sex and violence as they venture to depict the purported gritty realities of ghetto life.[3] Using the vernacular is key to creating an urban story that will be perceived as realistic and authentic. One of the most intriguing aspects of the use of explicit language in the depiction of sex and sexuality in this genre is the use of the word "pussy."

This essay examines the ways that black female sexuality is figured in contemporary urban fiction through the depiction of black female characters' articulations of their relationship to and/or their deployment of their genitalia, most commonly referred to as the pussy, or, as I refer to it, the "p-word." In the context of contemporary black urban fiction, the word pussy resonates on multiple levels, most of which are negative. In the highly masculinized context of urban culture, the p-word operates as a noun, a verb, an adjective, and an adverb. In contemporary culture, men still invoke the word pussy to objectify women. At other times, men use it to emasculate and dehumanize other men. Could naming and claiming the p-word under hip-hop's objectifying gaze be empowering? Sister Souljah and Sapphire use the word strategically to critique the contemporary sexual politics of hip-hop culture. Analysis of their use of this word reveals that both of their works feature a didactic element that challenges readers to confront the misogyny that drives the p-word exchange.

Using the word necessarily subverts the patriarchal gaze, bringing to mind, as Audre Lorde asserts, the pornographic rather than the erotic. In "The Uses of the Erotic," Lorde argues that the pornographic is defined by the patriarchal exploitation of women's generative psychic and sexual power: "Pornography is a direct denial of the power of the erotic, for it represents the suppression of true feeling. Pornography emphasizes sensation without feeling."[4] Troubling the relation between the erotic and the pornographic is central to my analysis of these texts. For when these characters attempt to negotiate erotic discourse, they only succeed in engaging the pornographic to deleterious effects. My analysis of the politics of sexual representation in these novels problematizes the distinction between the two categories, thus illuminating the implications of the use of the p-word. On the surface, the word has erotic connotations that pique our interest as readers, particularly when it is used in a highly sexualized context. I use "p-word" in an attempt to defamiliarize the term and, in doing so, to problematize it in a way that calls the cultural and sexual politics implicit in its naming and claiming into question.

The phrase "p-word exchange" attempts to account for the transactional dynamic that undergirds sexual encounters in the context of hip-hop culture and urban fiction. As T. Denean Sharpley-Whiting argues, there is a strong connection between the implicitly "transactional nature" of contemporary urban heterosexual relationships and the more explicitly sexual economy of strip clubs, pornographic videos, and hip-hop culture.[5] That is, in the context of urban hip-hop culture, objectified black female bodies are dehumanized until they become tender, the vehicle through which valuable goods are exchanged. This is the core of the sexual and social dynamic that I call the p-word exchange: the explicit interplay between sex, money, and power that has formed within the landscape of hip-hop culture. My use of the term p-word exchange is also meant to not only highlight the propensity for slippage into the pornographic through the use of vernacular, but also expose the politics of strategically indulging in the graphic nature of depictions of sexual encounters (whether they are transparently abusive or not). Of course, Sister Souljah's Winter and Sapphire's Precious are conceptualizing sex and sexuality from two seemingly oppositional perspectives: Precious is a victim of a lifetime of sexual abuse at the hands of her parents, while Winter engages in sexual activity willingly. Regardless of their position, it is clear that both of these young black girls have been victimized by a hypermasculinized, misogynistic urban hip-hop culture that expects them to offer their bodies to men without question.

My examination of patterns of representation of black female sexuality is grounded in the provocative cultural critique of bell hooks. In her groundbreaking essay "Selling Hot Pussy," hooks surveys the field of nineteenth- and twentieth-century representations of black women's bodies and sexuality. hooks concludes that black feminists must critique the troubling history of sexual objectification and exploitation in order "to create radical black female subjectivity."[6] She argues, "We must no longer shy away from the critical project of openly interrogating and exploring representations of black female sexuality as they appear everywhere, especially in popular culture."[7] My work continues the project that hooks asserts must be accomplished to shift the bounds of representation of black female sexuality in popular culture. This kind of analysis can at times force critics to enter uncomfortable territory, where they must confront silences that usually surround discourses of black female sexuality.[8] Explicit, sexually charged language is not often the focus of rigorous academic inquiry, but it should be. Breaking through these silences is exactly what critics must do in order to, as hooks posits, "openly interrogate and explore representations of black female sexuality," particularly in urban fiction.

Both Souljah and Sapphire are aware of the impact of poverty, drug culture, and hypersexuality on young black women in their communities. Their unflinching depictions of social dynamics and sexual relationships in their works reveals a writerly sensitivity to the impact of misogyny in urban or hip-hop culture that lends credence to the graphic language and patterns of representation that emerge in the texts. This can be seen in the first chapter of Sister Souljah's memoir, No Disrespect (1994), in which she directly confronts the influence that institutionalized racism, misogyny, and fatherlessness have on families that are barely surviving in the ghetto. For Souljah, the problem is multifaceted. Yet the primary symptom of this painful dynamic is mothers who are, to use her terminology, "whores." In the first sentence of the first chapter, entitled "Mother," Souljah throws down the rhetorical gauntlet: "In the projects, somebody can call your mother a one-legged whore who does nasty tricks for men for five dollars and she will still be the most important and influential person in your child-hood."[9] For a book entitled *No Disrespect*, this is an ironic rhetorical move, one that might alienate the very readers she is attempting to reach. Backtracking a little, Souljah attempts to soften her use of the term with a workable, less offen-sive definition: "Now, don't be alarmed by the word 'whore.' It can be applied to anyone who engages in an activity that they don't believe in, but they don't gain from, don't want to participate in, feel violated by, but are forced to do by the limitations of their own mind, the limitations of society, or both in order to survive. A whore can use the mind, body, or spirit as a source of small or large income."[10] Her redefinition of the word whore gives readers insight into why women are compelled to participate in dynamics as deleterious as the p-word exchange: it is part of the grander scheme of survival. Souljah maps the desires and the trauma that poor black women face as they negotiate social, cultural, and political economies driven by a series of exploitative exchanges. Taking the word whore out of its traditional sexualized point of reference, Souljah succeeds in exposing the ways that power, patriarchy, and poverty contribute to black wom-en's exploitation. In Souljah's work, the term takes on a kind of revolutionary resonance: these women use every survival tactic available to them.

Moving from one end of the gritty urban spectrum, the ghetto, with its prob-lematic economic landscape in *No Disrespect*, to the opposing exploitative drug economy in her first novel, *The Coldest Winter Ever*, Souljah tells the story of Win-ter Santiaga, the beautiful daughter of a drug lord, raised by materialistic parents who encourage her to indulge to excess in consumerism. Winter's mother teaches her as a young girl that a woman's value is based solely on her physical appear-ance. By the time she is seven, Winter learns that in the social economy of the ghetto, beautiful women do not have to work and are supported by men with money. For Winter and her mother, shopping is a sport. They dress well and have "the best of the best," but only because Santiaga is at the top of his game. Referring to herself as a "bad bitch," Winter's mother is an example of a high-class "whore" who is raising her daughter to follow in her footsteps. Here it is important to keep Souljah's revision of the term whore in *No Disrespect* in mind. Winter's mother is teaching her the rules of exchange in the urban social economy. The "bad bitch," the binary opposite of the "whore," is at the top of the food chain. That is, she knows the rules of this exchange so well that she thinks that she wrote them herself, and, more importantly, she actually believes that they are effective. Winter tells us that "one thing I learned from my mother is that a bad bitch gets what she wants if she works her shit right."[11] Winter's mother's value is superficial. For the Santiaga women and their counterparts, being a "bad bitch" entails attracting the sexiest, richest, most powerful men available in the drug game: "The money man is the guy who knows how to provide, knows how to bring home the goodness and bless his woman with everything she wants. Or the money man might not be ringing any bells sexually, but if he has ends . . . the bad bitch will moan like this nigga is the original Casanova. . . . Now Moms must have been a bad bitch because she had it both ways."[12] It is clear that Winter understands that the role of women is to manipulate men by playing into this objectifying social dynamic. Considered a princess and a prize, Winter sees that relationships between men and women are based on an exchange of money and even bodily fluids, but not emotions, especially not trust or love.

Given Winter's mother's downward spiral from prized possession (drug king-pin's wife) to damaged goods (she was shot in the face in a drive-by) and finally to dead crackhead, Souljah's message to her readers is that being a "bad bitch" is an untenable position for black women in this urban environment. The lure of material excess and access to masculine power blinds women like Winter and her mother from seeing the bigger problem: they are no different from the women who are perpetually victimized at the bottom of this sexual economy. That is, the "bad bitch" is so deeply entrenched in an exploitative dynamic (a series of increasingly physically and psychically damaging exchanges) that she cannot see that she, too, is being consumed by the very system from which she assumes she benefits.

Sapphire's fictive engagement with this urban cultural dilemma, *Push*, focuses on Clarice Precious Jones, a girl who negotiates a different yet eerily similar set of gritty realities. A victim of the welfare system, educational system, rise of drugs in the black community, and of sexual assault in a fragmented family, Precious struggles to survive as a functionally illiterate, pregnant preteen. When the novel first opens, readers learn that Precious is a twelve-year-old mother of a daughter with Down syndrome whom she affectionately calls Little Mongo. Both her daughter and the son she is carrying are her biological father's children. Through a series of horrifying flashbacks, readers get glimpses into the trauma of sexual abuse that Precious has endured since she was a baby. Thinking about her first pregnancy, Precious explains that her life has been defined by sexual abuse: "I've been knowing a man put his dick in you, gush white stuff in your booty you could get pregnant. I'm 12 now, I been knowing about that since I was five or six, maybe I always been known about pussy and dick. I can't remember not knowing. No, I can't remember a time I did not know. But thas all I knowed."[13] Telling Precious Jones's story gives Sapphire the opportunity to critique these social issues from the victim's perspective. Marginalized by society and silenced within her community, Precious is a character that has literally fallen through the cracks in the system. She cannot read or write on her grade level, but she knows more about sex than any young girl should. She speaks so graphically about the acts of rape that she endured that it is hard to imagine that she is a child. Her use of graphic language marks the deep level of trauma that she consciously associates with her body and her sexuality. Precious's middle name is ironic because she lost not only her virginity but her innocence, what mainstream society might call her preciousness, at a young age. By giving Precious a voice, Sapphire is able to claim humanity for her through her articulation of painful experiences. As a child, she is forced to assume the position of an adult woman in a society that neither respects nor protects the self-esteem and sexuality of black women.

In both Sapphire's and Souljah's novels, the young female protagonists' actions are motivated by their agency in relation to the p-word and its value in the text's sexual economy. In *The Coldest Winter Ever*, the p-word is at times personified as an insatiable creature with a mind of its own. In this pattern of representation, the woman whose body houses it has almost no control over it. Winter is obsessed with one of her father's men, Midnight, whom she describes as the ultimate black man. Midnight is a tall, athletic, and dark-skinned brother. He's five years older than Winter, but he does not consider her a viable love interest because of her drug lord father, her age, her superficiality, and her wholesale adoption of hip-hop materiality. Winter attempts to seduce Midnight several times, but each time Midnight refuses her advances.

The first time they are in a club, Winter practically forces herself on him: "I was standing so close to him that one more inch and I could've slid my tongue down his throat. He looked at me unaffected, completely unmoved and non-emotional. My emotions were wilding. My nipples were up and the muscles in my pussy were beating like a heart."[14] It is worth noting that Winter's actions are driven by desires that emanate from her genitals. Likening her feelings to that of a wild animal, Winter anthropomorphizes her p-word, giving it power over her entire self. Yet the disinterested, logical Midnight refuses to participate in hip-hop's sexual economy. He sees how young girls position themselves within the social dynamic and he denounces this positioning. In the club, he tells Winter that she is "just like all these bitches in here."[15] At another point, after Winter's mother has been shot in the face and Midnight has been ordered to protect them in a hotel in New Jersey, she decides to forget her worries by attempting to have sex with Midnight. She offers herself to him: "I started playing games with my legs, repositioning them, opening them slowly, closing them slowly. I was making it possible for him to see the hairs on my pussy, if he only wanted to. When I got excited enough my juices would start to flow, releasing the scent of a willing pussy, definitely something he wouldn't be able to fight."[16] But he does fight it. He calls her a "little girl," which infuriates Winter because she is trying to be the "bad bitch" her mother trained her to become.

Winter turns herself into everything that she thinks a man would or should want: a hypersexual, available young woman. She is largely emblematic of black woman in hip-hop who are always already objectified. Notice that Winter anthropomorphizes the p-word again, giving it power and control beyond her body and herself. Midnight is immune to the willing p-word because he sees the big picture from two angles: the first is that Winter is the boss's daughter, the second is that he has witnessed firsthand the degrading ways that women position themselves as objects in hip-hop's sexual economy. Instead of handling her business in the bedroom with a future money man, Winter is handled in a fatherly fashion. She counters his rejection by stripping in front of him. When he picks up the remote control instead of dropping his pants, Winter suggests that he might be gay, which is not the case; he just has principles, the most important of which is survival, as having sex with the boss's daughter is counterintuitive to any goal that he might have that includes staying alive.

As the novel progresses, we learn that Midnight is a friend of the motivational speaker Sister Souljah—someone Winter despises because she preaches against drug dealing and other social ills in the urban community—and that he, Midnight, does not listen to hip-hop music. Later, we find out that Midnight is a highly religious man who was born and raised for part of his life in an African country, and that he has a different orientation toward black women than most African American men do. By the end of the novel, at Winter's mother's funeral, we find out that Midnight has left the drug game, moved to Maryland, married, and adopted Winter's youngest twin sisters. Thus, he rescues them from the street life that claimed Winter, her father, and her mother. This kind of male role model is rarely seen in hip-hop music, videos, or film. He is definitely not the kind of father figure that Precious Jones confronts in *Push*.

In *Push*, Precious is angry with herself because her body experiences pleasure when it is sexually abused by her father, Carl, who misinterprets her body's automatic arousal. "I feel so stupid sometimes. So ugly, worth nuffin'. I could just sit here," Precious asserts, "wif my muver every day wif the shades drawed, watching TV, eat, watch TV, eat."[17] Precious's mother's role in the abuse dynamic is sexual because not only does she let Carl abuse her daughter, but she also fondles and forces Precious to perform cunnilingus; psychological, as she verbally abuses Precious; and physical since she beats Precious and forces her to binge eat. Her mother actively encourages Precious's degraded condition because she benefits from it. She allows Carl to wallow in his depravity so that he will stay in the relationship. Precious is victimized by a set of exchanges that her mother puts in motion by giving her baby daughter to her husband for sex. In the pit of despair, Precious remembers: "Carl come over fuck us'es. . . . Call me name butterball big mama two ton of fun. I hate to hear him talk more than I hate fuck. Sometimes fuck feel good."[18] Precious has no control over either the family dynamic or her body. Because she feels pleasure sometimes, she is not sure how to interpret this situation.

Her pregnancies make matters even worse. Even though Precious's body is that of a child's, it functions as though it is a woman's. The first time she is pregnant, it is literally inconceivable to her that she could be carrying her father's baby, her sibling. The second time is equally tragic because now she knows exactly how it happened and why it is wrong. Precious says what she thinks about her father: "He stink, the white shit drip off his dick. Lick it lick it. I HATE that. But then I feel the hot sauce hot cha cha feeling when he be fucking me. I get so confused. I HATE him. But my pussy be popping. He say that, 'big mama her pussy is popping!' I HATE myself and I feel good."[19] She articulates the tension between her anger toward her father and her disappointment in her own body. Several times she uses the word "hate" in capital letters to describe how she feels about the situation. The lack of control is confusing and frustrating to her.

Precious is never treated as though her parents, teachers, or classmates consider her to be worthy of her name. As she attempts to tell her story of abuse and survival, Precious begins to understand that she has been raped by her father and that her mother is an incompetent welfare queen. While this is shocking enough for most readers to consider, we are also faced with the realization that her mother was complicit in her ongoing sexual abuse and that she blamed Precious for the entire dynamic. Precious reveals that the first time she was pregnant, her mother beat her mercilessly when she went into labor and later blames Precious for her husband's desertion, saying that she stole her man. Precious remembers her mother's abusive behavior: "I ax my muver for money to get my hair done, clothes. . . . She used to give me money; now every time I ask for money say I took her husband, her man. Her man? Please! Thas my motherfuckin' fahver! I hear her tell someone on phone I am heifer, take her husband, I'm fast. What it take for my mother to see me? Sometimes I wish I was not alive. But I don't know how to die."[20] Her mother dehumanizes Precious by calling her names like "heifer," and she refuses to acknowledge both the abuse and her daughter's victimization. Precious's mother wants to claim the role of victim instead.

The common narrative for a man's desertion of his family is that he leaves for another woman. Conceptualizing Precious as a woman rather than as a girl allows her mother to ignore the abuse and her complicit actions. Precious's desire to be seen is ultimately driven by a wish to be acknowledged as a child who has suffered greatly. Thinking about the difference between her first and second pregnancies, she cannot ignore her mother's silent acceptance of Carl's behavior: "This time I know Mama know. . . . She bring him to me. I ain' crazy, that stinky hoe give me to him. . . . Got to where he just come into my room any ole time, not jus' night. Climb on me. He slapped my ass, You wide as the Mississippi, don't tell me a little bit of dick hurt you heifer. Git usta it, he laff, you *is* usta it. I fall back on bed, he fall right on top of me."[21] Carl's sexual abuse dehumanizes Precious both in speech and action. He is treating her as if she is neither a girl nor his daughter. In the breakdown of the familial relation between father and daughter, Precious is reduced to the status of a thing—the heifer. His actions cause Precious's contentious conceptualizations of herself as "pussy." That is, before she becomes aware that she is a victim, she thinks of herself as merely a receptacle for his perverse desire. Throughout the novel, Precious struggles to define herself as a whole person, in spite of the sexual abuse and the sexually transmitted disease that her father gave her when she was a young girl. Her acquisition of literacy releases Precious from the bounds of objectification by empowering her to reject the abusive dynamics in which she was raised, while embracing herself as the beautiful young woman she has always been. This is where the significance of her first name, Clarice, becomes relevant. As Precious acquires critical distance on her situation, she begins to see the implications of her past abuse clearly. In many ways, Precious's triumph is that of finding fulfillment as an educated woman and mother who transcends sexual assault and the larger abusive sexual economy. In both of these texts, the sexual economy is fueled by a highly misogynistic hip-hop culture that objectifies black women and girls.

In these texts, the p-word is a lure, something that compels future lovers, mostly male, to do whatever they have to (buy, steal, or kill) to impress the woman who owns the p-word. In this dynamic, the woman believes that she is in full control of her p-word and of the social and sexual situation. Yet in these novels, there is no point where this equal, empowering exchange happens. There are several moments when Winter attempts to profit from the exchange by offering sex or participating in a sexual act, but she never gains from the encounter. In one infamous moment, Boom, a black male in the hip-hop industry, tells Winter point blank that if she wants to go to Pizzeria Uno's, she must have sex with him: "Uno's is pussy. . . . So what's up, you going to give me some pussy or are we going to McDonald's?"[22] This is a moment where a clear exchange of sex for goods is articulated. That is, Winter knows exactly what she is getting into if she chooses Uno's over McDonald's. They do go to Uno's, and later they have sex that Winter finds unsatisfying. She tells us, "I pushed his head down further so he could eat my pussy. . . . I heard him trying to spit the pussy hairs caught in his teeth out. When he found the inside of me he was licking all the wrong places."[23] Despite all of his good looks and sexual bravado, he cannot perform sexually. Because she was ready to participate in an equal exchange of talents, Winter is disappointed. In an angry outburst, she exclaims, "Good hair, dimples, all that, you just a little dick nigga."[24] Obviously, this is a moment when the p-word exchange fails miserably. The woman gets nothing, at least nothing substantial, from this transaction but a meal. Boom does not even know how to perform oral sex and on top of that is not well endowed. Although he performs a certain type of black masculinity that has been forged in hip-hop culture, Boom does not fit the ideal.

This scene shows readers that the discourse surrounding hip-hop sexualities hypes black masculinity to an unrealistic point. In this sense, it could be considered bankrupt, especially when it comes to black women's sexual satisfaction. Put another way, even as hip-hop discourse objectifies black women and fragments their bodies by reducing them to the p-word it is clear that women like Winter do not gain true or lasting pleasure from participating in the p-word exchange. There is a disjuncture between Winter's deployment of her sexual power (her attempts to position herself as p-word in the urban sexual economy) and the actual social control that is beyond her reach. For Souljah, hip-hop's drug culture does not offer Winter an unproblematized way to profit from either her beauty or her sexuality.

For Sapphire, hip-hop culture offers Precious a form of release from her abusive situation. In *Push*, Precious understands that hip-hop can offer black women some form of appreciation outside the sexual dynamic. Precious's desire to be valued in a hip-hop context emerges when she remembers doubling during a particularly heinous sexual encounter with her father. She fantasizes about being a hip-hop dancer at the Apollo. For an overweight black girl, this daydream is particularly powerful: "Then I changed stations, change *bodies*, I be dancing in videos! In movies! I be breaking, fly, jus' a dancing! Umm hmm heating up the stage at the Apollo for Doug E. Fresh or Al B. Shure. They love me! Say I'm one of the best dancers ain' no doubt of or about that!"[25] Here, she is beautiful, talented, envied, and desired. Finding pleasure and respect in her hip-hop dance fantasy, Precious reveals her awareness of the economies of desire in the black urban community. Also, it is worth noting that she says that she "changes bodies"— with "bodies" italicized in the text—which is emblematic of Precious's desire to escape her abusive situation or her physical body, the site of sexualized trauma. In this moment, Precious imagines that she is hypervisible and physically talented, but not sexually so. Her entire nimble body is seen and appreciated by the audience.

This dream sequence highlights Precious's constant awareness that the p-word is an open wound that must be guarded. Yet often it is not guarded because the sexual economy does not offer the possibility for its recuperation. A key element of this pattern is physical and sexual abuse. For Precious, the p-word is a site of disease and dysfunction. She is constantly aware of and embarrassed by the smells that emanate from her mother's genitals. That is also the first thing that she notices about women she does not like regardless of race. Precious has good reason to consider the p-word to be a site of trauma because she has been sexually abused since infancy. Toward the end of *Push*, in a therapy session with a counselor at the halfway house where Precious lives with her son, her mother admits to giving Precious as a baby to her father sexually. Even then, she calls her a "freak."[26] Devalued almost from birth as a sexual object but valued as currency in the sexual economy of her parents' relationship, Precious does not get a chance to develop a sense of self-esteem until she meets Miss Rain, the literacy instructor, who is unlike any of the teachers that Precious has encountered earlier. Miss Rain liberates and empowers Precious to see her inherent human value apart from the abuse dynamic. Miss Rain opens the way for Precious to struggle against both her traumatic past and her mother's present abusive behavior.

Sexualized by the time she is a kindergartener, Precious's experiences of trauma crowd out anything she learns in school. Precious remembers: "Daddy put his pee-pee smelling thing in my mouth, my pussy, but never hold me. I see me, first grade, pink dress dirty sperm stuffs on it. No one comb my hair."[27] Abused at home and ignored at school, she is lost in the educational and social systems. Even after she has given birth to her father's child while she is at the age of twelve, no one, not even her mother, seems to care. As a dark-skinned, obese girl, she is invisible. While it is true that her race and her physicality render her hypervisible, one must consider that Precious struggles to survive in a racist and sexist society that denies her essential humanity, protection, and beauty. Even though her body cannot be ignored, Precious's rights to freedom and educational equality have been refused because society has not claimed her. Reflecting on the fact that neither her mother nor her father acknowledges her humanity, Precious thinks, "My fahver don't see me really. If he did he would know I was like a white girl, a *real* person, inside. He would not climb on from forever and stick his dick in me and get my insides on fire, bleed, I bleed, then he slap me. Can't he see I am a girl for flowers and thin straw legs and a place in the picture. I've been out of the picture so long I am used to it. But that don't mean it don't hurt."[28] Precious knows exactly who is considered a "real person" in this society and who is not. She has the sense that white girls are protected from the kind of violation that she endured. She understands, too, that girls should be appreciated as fragile and pretty—and, most importantly, that they should be visible and seen. But being seen is not just about being perceived on the physical level; it is also about being understood as fragile and being sheltered from harm.

Sapphire's depiction of the physical and psychological implications of the dehumanization and objectification of young black women in black urban/hip-hop culture resonates on multiple levels. It is clear that Precious's abuse continues throughout her life precisely because she has no value in the urban sexual economy: "Sometimes I pass by store window and some body fat dark skin, old looking, someone like my muver look back at me. . . . Who I see? I stand in time some time, look at my body, it stretch marks, ripples. I tried to hide myself, then I tried to show myself."[29] Although she has little actual formal education, Precious is distinctly aware of the interpersonal and cultural politics that shape her life.

Echoing Pecola Breedlove's anguish in Toni Morrison's *The Bluest Eye*, Precious understands that if she were white she would be visible. Yet unlike Pecola, Precious is Afrocentric and so distrustful of white people that she would not want to be white. She also knows that inside she is no different from white girls who are loved and, more importantly, protected by their families and society. She loves Louis Farrakhan and considers him to be a real man, in contrast to her father: "Crackers is the cause of everything bad. And why my father ack like he do. He has forgot he is the Original Man! So he fuck me, fuck me, beat me, have a chile by me. When he see I'm pregnant for the first time he disappear. I think for years, for long time I know that much."[30] Precious knows implicitly that there is a connection between the abuse she suffers and her father's status as a black man in a racist society. For Precious, racism has caused her father to forget his true male identity, unlike her hero Farrakhan, whom she considers an honorable man. Placing herself in the continuum of systematized racism, victimization and disempowerment provides Precious with a framework to conceptualize her experience in this cycle of abuse, but she does not use this line of reasoning to excuse her father from his guilt or responsibility. By having Precious develop this awakening consciousness as she develops her self-esteem and literacy, Sapphire is sowing seeds of recognition in her reader's own political consciousness.

By the end of *Push* and *The Coldest Winter Ever*, both female protagonists have moved beyond hypersexualized identities. Under the tutelage of female characters who are either named after or are strikingly similar to their authors (Sister Souljah inserts herself into the narrative as a celibate inspirational speaker who works in the community, and Sapphire appears in *Push* as Miss Blue Rain, Precious's literacy instructor), both Winter and Precious come to better understand the meaning and value of their lives. Although Precious is struggling with the realization that her father infected her with the HIV virus, she recognizes that she has a chance to live outside of the shadows of abuse. As *The Coldest Winter Ever* closes, Winter is serving a mandatory fifteen year prison sentence. Her manipulative boyfriend, Bullet, abandoned her in a rental car with enough illegal drugs and guns to lead to her arrest. Despite her incarceration, Winter sees the connection between her superficial, materialistic, hypersexualized life and her complicity in her own downfall. Both Winter's and Precious's development of inner strength and self-confidence is achieved after long battles against oppressive social, cultural, and economic forces. As they move toward this awareness, both characters do not engage in sexual activity and they stop using the p-word, which is an interesting development in both texts. It speaks to the strategic use of the word in these urban novels and prompts contemporary critics to consider the ways that black female sexualities are deployed by authors in order to advance political agendas, cultural commentary, and social awareness.

Analysis of the complexities of sexual representation in these foundational black women's urban fictional texts exposes the problematic issues, such as misogyny, sexual exploitation, and violence against women, that have long permeated hip-hop culture. Both Sapphire and Souljah create hybrid texts that merge elements of hip-hop culture with traditional literary forms, specifically those of the black feminist literary tradition, to develop this new genre. Both authors work with and against the depiction of black women's sexuality in urban hip-hop culture. Given the protagonists' ages (both are in their early teens when the novels begin and are nearing adulthood when they end), the highly sexualized content of these texts is shocking. Yet it is exactly this tension between the characters' ages, the texts' sexual content, and the graphic nature of urban life that makes them such compelling cautionary tales. Because the p-word is such a loaded term—and because those who use it often do not realize the political implications of using it and may, at times, interpret its use in the text as a moment when a character is being "real"—when authors such as Sapphire and Sister Souljah use it, they attempt to awaken the consciousness of their readers. Both novels expose the ways urban cultural codes devalue young black girls. In the process of addressing long-standing cultural and community problems, both authors connect to their readers through shocking depictions of traumatic experiences that compel readers to engage with the political project of developing feminist critical self-awareness.

NOTES

1. David Wright argues that the appeal of urban fiction is rooted in its unflinching representations of street life. David Wright, "Streetwise Urban Fiction," *Library Journal* 131, no. 12 (2006): 42–45

2. S. Craig Watkins suggests that both hip-hop–inspired music and literature were motivated by the desire of artists and writers to tell their authentic stories. S. Craig Watkins, *Hip Hop Matters: Politics, Pop Culture, and the Struggle for the Soul of the Movement* (Boston: Beacon Press, 2005), 236.

3. Urban fiction offers an interesting mixture of escapist fantasy and unflinching economic, cultural, and social realities. Since Sister Souljah's publication of *The Coldest Winter Ever* (New York: Pocket Star Books, 1999), the genre has become incredibly popular, garnering a diverse readership. Ibid., 235.

4. Audre Lorde, "Uses of the Erotic: The Erotic as Power," in Audre Lorde, *Sister Outsider* (Berkeley: Crossing Press, 2007), 54.

5. T. Denean Sharpley-Whiting, *Pimps Up, Ho's Down: Hip-Hop's Hold on Young Black Women* (New York: New York University Press, 2007), 122–123.

6. bell hooks, "Selling Hot Pussy," in bell hooks, *Black Looks: Race and Representation* (Boston: South End Press, 1992), 128.

7. Ibid.

8. For a more rigorous discussion of the problematics of confronting the issue of silence surrounding black female sexuality in academic discourse, see Evelynn Hammonds, "Black (W)holes and the Geometry of Black Female Sexuality," in *African American Literary Theory*, ed. Winston Napier (New York: New York University Press, 2000), 482–497.

9. Sister Souljah, *No Disrespect* (New York: Vintage Books, 1996), 3.

10. Ibid.

11. Souljah, *The Coldest Winter Ever*, 11.

12. Ibid., 5.

13. Sapphire, *Push* (New York: Vintage Books, 1996), 12.

14. Souljah, *The Coldest Winter Ever*, 30.

15. Ibid., 30.

16. Ibid., 55.

17. Sapphire, *Push*, 35.

18. Ibid.

19. Ibid., 58.

20. Ibid., 32.

21. Ibid., 24.

22. Souljah, *The Coldest Winter Ever,* 281.

23. Ibid., 281.

24. Ibid., 282.

25. Sapphire, *Push,* 24.

26. Souljah, *The Coldest Winter Ever,* 135–136.

27. Ibid., 39.

28. Ibid., 32.

29. Ibid.

30. Ibid., 34.

PART III

RESISTING ERASURE

CHAPTER 9

"Ou libéré?"

Sexual Abuse and Resistance in Edwidge Danticat's *Breath, Eyes, Memory*

Sandra C. Duvivier

[Haitian women's] narratives of sexual violations were rendered invisible as the state exercised its power to obscure violations against women by dismissing their testimonies as nonsensical or inconsequential to the political life of Haitian society.
—*Donette A. Francis*[1]

Haitian women's accounts of sexual abuse have been largely suppressed as Haiti's efforts to (re)build the nation—amid corrupt governmental leadership and Western (neo)colonial interventions—have taken precedence over and, at times, sanctioned it. In response, Haitian women have emerged and galvanized, challenging sexual abuse and violence while simultaneously providing a space where the voices of silenced women might be heard. In *Breath, Eyes, Memory* (1994), Haitian American writer-activist Edwidge Danticat provides a literary means to not only expose Haitian female sexual subjugation, thereby delineating the ways that patriarchal and gendered practices marginalize girls and women, but also highlight Haitian women's attempts to challenge it and extricate themselves from its ramifications. Thus, in alignment with Haitian women feminist activists, whose work demonstrates their steadfast refusal to acquiesce to female victimization, Danticat also illuminates Haitian female agency.

This essay concerns itself with Danticat's portrayals of sexualized violence and Haitian women's responses to such abuse. In so doing, it also examines Haitian women's attempts to extricate and empower themselves. It is not my intention to present these women as having completely transcended abuse and its ramifications, or to depict their means of extrication as only revolutionary or subversive. Rather, it is to show how these women exhibit agency and find ways to resist their victimization in very dire situations. In examining Danticat's depiction of sexual abuse and Haitian women's responses to it, I delineate the relationship between state- and family-sanctioned practices in Haiti, especially in relation to gender, sexuality, class, and color. I also analyze the ways these practices marginalize Danticat's protagonists, the Cacos, particularly Martine. Finally, I examine the Caco women's responses to their marginalization.

SANCTIONED BY THE STATE: HAITI AND THE POLITICS OF GENDER, SEXUALITY, CLASS, AND COLOR

Haiti's historically precarious relationship to Europe and the United States has shaped its internal politics. Having revolted successfully against the French government, and thus gaining independence from slavery in 1804, Haitians have faced the ramifications of being the first black independent republic in the Western hemisphere. For example, France forced Haiti to pay an independence debt that in today's currency would be valued well into the billions. To pay off this debt, Haitians were forced to borrow money from European creditors, thus entering a cycle of debt that impoverished the state. The United States, threatened by the effects of the Haitian Revolution on its enslaved population, issued an embargo against the newly established country and refused to recognize it as an independent nation until 1862. The United States later controlled Haiti politically and socioeconomically during its occupation of the island (1915–1934) and forced many Haitians to work under slave-like conditions. These (neo)colonial interventions compromised the country's autonomy as a postcolonial nation-state and largely depleted the country's economy.

As a result of colonial ideologies and socioeconomic domination, political rivalry ensued between blacks and the mixed-race elites with largely French ancestry. Because of problematic colonial politics favoring whiteness in its various forms, the mixed-race elites tended to dominate the political, educational, and cultural milieu of the country. It was out of this context that François "Papa Doc" Duvalier emerged as a seemingly viable candidate for presidency. Emboldened by *Négritude,* the black consciousness movement among the black francophone community in the 1920s and 1930s that denounced French colonialism and racism generally, Haitians elected Papa Doc because of his strategic alignment with Haiti's black masses. However, instead of benefiting the masses, his presidency proved menacing for the Haitian population and exacerbated the patriarchal politics that have informed Haiti socioeconomically, politically, and culturally ever since the country's inception.

Breath, Eyes, Memory is set during the reign of the Duvaliers, primarily during the tenure of Jean-Claude "Baby Doc" Duvalier (1971–1986), though it presents the dictatorship of his father, President-for-Life François "Papa Doc" Duvalier (1957–1971), in flashback to contextualize Martine's sexual abuse in relation to state politics. In order to enforce his dictatorship, François Duvalier created the police force, the Tonton Macoutes, to instill terror among the population and to capture or assassinate those who openly criticized his rule. While the Macoutes were considerably less brutal than they were during Papa Doc's reign and did not have a similar record of mass assassinations under Jean-Claude Duvalier's presidency—which he assumed upon his father's death in 1971—they still continued to terrorize the population until they were disbanded in 1986, when serious political opposition forced the younger Duvalier into exile.[2]

Unlike Haiti's previous state politics, which afforded women protection under the law as political innocents, the Duvalier regime, particularly the reign of the elder president for life, subjected them to torture and violence largely through the Macoutes. These officers subjected women who were related to dissenters or who voiced dissent themselves about the government to sexualized violence. The Duvalierist state subverted previous gender politics concerning women and their protection under the state.[3] Implicit in their former protection was their inferiority, which had previously rendered them incapable of being subjected to the same forms of punishment as men. However, during the Duvaliers' dictatorship, women were subjected to the same treatment as, if not worse than, their male counterparts. As Michel-Rolph Trouillot asserts, "Duvalierist violence eliminated the gender distinction that, until then, had ensured preferential treatment for women. . . . Many women were attacked because a husband or male relative was out of reach—in exile or in a foreign embassy. The Duvalierist preference for the sexual 'conquest' of females associated with the political opposition, from torture-rape to acquaintance-rape to marriage, infused the politicization of gender with violence. Womanhood, which had traditionally afforded partial protection from the state, now became a disadvantage."[4]

The father-son regime sanctioned sexualized violence against women and control of women's sexuality as a means of asserting state power and squelching internal opposition to the regime. Women were no longer protected as they had been prior to the Duvalier regime, but various tenets of sexism and patriarchy that undergirded these former state politics regarding women have very much remained. Haitian women have been symbolic indicators of the state and markers of national boundaries but they have been largely excluded from the liberty and autonomy that characterize the dominant narratives framing the national myth.[5] Instead, the state has exercised control over and possession of women's sexuality.[6]

While the government had sanctioned sexualized and gendered violence against women, some families—serving as microcosms of larger Haitian society—also engaged in practices that sexually violated girls and women. Danticat explores these practices through the subject of female virginity tests, particularly of the characters Martine and Sophie—and, to a lesser degree, Martine's sister Atie—in her novel. Virginity tests, which have been conducted by families to ensure their family honor, provide a seemingly viable means for women and families to advance socioeconomically through marriage. Virginity is seen as capital, especially for families who have limited options for socioeconomic mobility. These tests exemplify a privileging of female virginity in Haiti and rigid sexual politics—due, in large part, to Christian-influenced religious ideologies of female chastity before marriage, gender politics, class, and responses to representations of black (especially female) bodies as hypersexualized.

Some Haitian women, particularly those who are poor and working class, define their bodies as a financially profitable resource.[7] These women, who view marriage and/or conjugal union as a potential avenue to higher socioeconomic/class standing, use their sexuality as an instrument of labor or as a commodity that can reap beneficial rewards, including the acquisition of land. Because marriage provides a viable opportunity to advance one's status, many families perceive female sexuality, particularly virginity, as a financial asset. These families place a premium on female virginity because entire families benefit when a woman marries into a higher socioeconomic stratum. This creates an environment for certain practices, such as virginity testing, that control female sexuality, repress female sexual autonomy, and perpetuate/contribute to Haiti's extant patriarchal politics.[8]

Though virginity tests are a patriarchal practice, those who conduct them are not always men. Many mothers, who often themselves have experienced testing and its traumatic effects, nevertheless test their daughters, thereby evidencing their internalization and perpetuation of a practice that regulates female sexuality. As a marker of honor, virginity represents currency, and many mothers insist that their daughters preserve their sexual purity given its relationship to socioeconomic advancement that is otherwise not readily available to them. These families lack class status in terms of money and education, yet still possess it in terms of an untarnished family reputation, a significant asset. Conversely, young daughters who are not virgins have little chance for this advancement, and the community often holds them and their families in contempt.

Internalizing State Politics: Violation, Limited Mobility, and Family "Legacy"

Danticat's naming her female protagonists' family "Caco," and their precarious relationship to the state and global political economy, alludes to Haiti's rural poor Caco rebels who vehemently protested the U.S. occupation. The revolutionary implications of the name are not lost in the novel, as the Caco women find ways to challenge the system: Martine by fleeing to the United States; and Sophie by defiantly challenging her mother Martine, after she begins conducting virginity tests on Sophie and later finding a healthier means to disengage her family from their legacy of sociosexual/economic marginalization. Despite the

Caco rebels' revolutionary and subversive activities, especially on behalf of those from rural and economically disadvantaged backgrounds, they also violated girls and women. Haitian girls and women faced the threat of rape from both these rebels and American soldiers. As Donette A. Francis argues, the "Caco name . . . signifies the complicated space Haitian women occupy in both narratives of local resistance and narratives of American imperialism."[9]

Martine, like the Caco rebels, is a member of the masses whose access to mobility is limited. She is a member of neither the traditional elite nor of the burgeoning middle class. Instead, she is a dark-skinned woman from a lower socioeconomic background who performs tasks that reflect her status: she works in the cane fields, where, in the absence of protection, she is raped, allegedly by a Macoute officer, who, as she later tells her daughter, "grabbed me from the side of the road, pulled me into a cane field, and put you in my body."[10] To provide Martine with distance from the location of her abuse (and further evidencing the politics of color and class), her mother Ifé sends her to the neighboring town of Croix-des-Rosets to work for a wealthy "mulatto" family as a *restavèk* (meaning "stay with" in Haitian Creole). A *restavèk* is usually a poor rural Haitian child or teenager (most often a girl) who lives with and labors for an economically stable person or family in a more urban, industrialized environment. Martine's employment in the sugarcane fields, the site of her sexualized violence, alludes to her victimization by Haiti's internal politics and the global political economy that marginalizes and exploits Haitian workers.[11]

Because these gendered, socioeconomic, and color politics operate in Haiti, it is a site of sociosexual marginalization for Martine, who is subjected to rape and virginity testing—both of which are attributable in part to her lower socioeconomic standing. For instance, Martine's earliest encounter with sexual violation was her testing, which was done to preserve her chastity and provide her with a husband. Yet this practice stops once adolescent Martine is raped and becomes pregnant. Because of the alleged status of Martine's rapist, the crime goes unpunished. Martine must live not only as a victim of state-sponsored sexualized violence but with the thought of her attacker moving freely through Haiti and possibly raping her again without consequence. In a society where sexuality is intrinsically gendered and related to class, this rape and its ensuing pregnancy have another damaging repercussion for Martine: marriage is no longer a viable avenue by which she might improve her socioeconomic status.[12] Martine's pregnancy and her later status as a mother are both visible markers that she is no longer a virgin.

Part of Martine's previous compliance with the sanctioning/regulation of female sexuality includes her passing virginity tests, which Ifé conducts. To Martine, these tests are comparable to rape. She refers to both the testing and her rape as the "two greatest pains" of her life that "are very much related" (170). Martine, though traumatized, escapes further tests ironically because of her rape: "'The one good thing about my being raped was that it made the *testing* stop. The testing and the rape. I live both every day'" (170). Even though the tests stop, the ramifications are not lost on Martine. She both internalizes and becomes indoctrinated by the gender politics that sanction the practice and even becomes culpable herself for sexual violation as she later subjects her daughter Sophie to these virginity tests.

Breath, Eyes, Memory opens in Croix-des-Rosets, Haiti, with Martine physically absent: she has emigrated from Haiti to the United States. In fact, Martine's presence in Croix-des-Rosets is often defined by both her physical absence and appearance in other forms: memories, recollections, photographs, and voice recordings on the cassettes she sends to her family back in Haiti. Martine is now in the United States, having gotten her visa with the assistance of the family who employed her as a *restavèk*. Though not in classic political exile or escape from political tyranny, Martine takes flight from the sociopolitical and sexual oppression of poor Haitian women and in that sense she is in self-imposed exile. She exhibits agency in her attempts to resist marginalization and distance herself from the site of her rape and testing. Unbearable aspects of home lead to her flight from Haiti, and the United States comes to serve as a new, if not surrogate, home.

(Dis)Continuing the Legacy: Migration, Sexualized Violence, and Extrication

The United States is also a site of sexual abuse for Martine and for her daughter Sophie, who migrates there at the age of twelve, once Martine tests her. While living in the United States allows Martine to eventually extricate herself from the poverty and substandard living that, in part, warranted her virginity testing, it does not help to heal or liberate her from sexual abuse. There, she is still vulnerable to the haunting memories of her rape, which are exacerbated by not only Sophie's presence, but also by Martine's sexual encounters with her partner Marc. Instead of finding a healthy distance from and means to cope with her socioeconomic and sexual marginalization in the United States, Martine carries with her the internalized notions of propriety and socioeconomic mobility imposed upon her in Haiti. She engages in destructive behavior, such as skin bleaching, and, despite her own precarious relationship to sexualized violence, she performs virginity tests on her daughter, Sophie.

Martine's internalization of her marginalization informs her perception of her sexual encounters with Marc. The significance of Martine's relationship with Marc lies not only in their sexual encounters—which Martine engages in to please and placate him, although she relives memories of her rape with each encounter—but also in the fact that it would not have been possible in Haiti. Haitian-born Marc is from a higher socioeconomic background than Martine. By her own admission, Martine asserts that in Haiti, "it would not be possible for someone like Marc to love someone like me. He is from a very upstanding family.

His grandfather was a French man" (59). Her remarks bear witness to the limited possibilities for Haiti's poor, while further highlighting Haiti's color-caste system: at least one of Marc's parents is mixed race. Moreover, they attest to the ways the United States liberates her from the class and color politics that would prevent their relationship from happening in Haiti.

Nevertheless, Martine's internalization of these politics diminishes the potential for the United States to function as a site of healing from her sexual violation. Instead of serving as a fulfilling partner with whom she engages in a healthy relationship, Marc becomes a signifier of her rape with each sexual encounter they share. When Martine participates in sexual activities with Marc, she often engages in what she refers to as "doubling": envisioning good memories to distract herself from feeling violated or reliving her rape. Paralleling her rape, Martine also becomes pregnant by Marc, and thus her pregnancy further triggers her already recurring nightmares of her rape. The unborn baby appears in these nightmares and elsewhere in Martine's mind as an abusive figure: "'Everywhere I go, I hear it. I hear him saying things to me. You *tintin, malpròp.* He calls me a filthy whore. I never want to see this child's face'" (217). Because he is the father of the unborn baby and the person with whom Martine performs what she sees as obligatory sexual duties, Marc's presence exacerbates and reinscribes Martine's sexual abuse.

In imagining this unborn child referring to it using female-specific derogatory names associated with sex and impropriety, Martine's feelings of immorality based on her sexual history surface with this pregnancy. Both her rape and relationship with Marc reveal her lack of agency and the supposed immorality of her having sex, whether consensual or not, before marriage. Martine is plagued by these feelings, as her pregnancies exist outside marriage and signify, in her mind, her impropriety. Martine responds to her internalization of these politics with self-destructive behavior. For instance, she purchases a cream "that promised to make her skin lighter" (51). Toward the novel's end, Sophie describes Martine's skin as "unusually light, a pale mocha, three or four shades lighter than any of [my family's complexion]" (159).

Danticat's narration implies that Martine bleaches her skin in response to both Haiti's hierarchical divisions based on class and color and her sexual abuse. Yet it does not constitute a healthy way for Martine to cope with the color/class hierarchy that left her vulnerable to her traumatic rape and testings. Her bleaching illustrates not only her internalization of colonialist politics regarding skin color, but also her further devaluation and abuse of her body, as both her rapist and Haiti's state politics had done to her. Her destructive behavior does not end with her bleaching. Her violent nightmares often cause her to awake from slumber and perform violent self-inflicted acts, including attempted stabbings (especially upon learning of her pregnancy) that ultimately end with her tragic death.

There is an important connection between the increase of Martine's violent nightmares and Sophie's arrival in the United States to reunite with her mother.

Sophie, a product of this rape, resembles her rapist father, thus becoming a direct reminder of Martine's rape. Moreover, Sophie is barely younger than Martine was at the time of her rape. To make matters worse for Martine, she never even saw her rapist, who thus could be any man—familiar or unfamiliar—she encounters in native La Nouvelle Dame Marie, which contributes heavily to her inability to be healed. She does not confront her rapist. Leaving Haiti does not free her from the effects of her violation, and she remains controlled by the incident.

Martine's internalization of the sexual, gendered, and economic systems that have victimized her informs how she raises Sophie. Martine chooses a profession for her daughter to study, dictates that Sophie remain a virgin until marriage, and mandates that Sophie date someone who is materially comfortable. However, Sophie begins to express a sense of self and individuality. Although she outwardly complies with Martine's rigid rules, she secretly cultivates a relationship with Joseph, an older man she later marries. Upon learning of this relationship, Martine begins testing Sophie.

Martine first tests Sophie after the eighteen-year-old returns in the early morning hours from a clandestine meeting with Joseph, which, to Martine, signifies Sophie's improper conduct and possible sexual engagement. Her testing of Sophie also illuminates the degree to which she has not transcended her socio-sexual marginalization in Haiti. Sophie is living a materially comfortable existence in the United States, where she is receiving a so-called proper education. Furthermore, because Joseph is very stable financially, she has the prospect of marriage into a higher socioeconomic stratum. All of these factors render testing for marriage unnecessary. That Martine tests her daughter anyway illustrates her own need to come to terms with issues concerning her legitimacy and propriety by imposing them on her daughter.

During the initial testing, in order to distract Sophie from what she realizes is a dehumanizing and violating occurrence, Martine equates their relationship with that of the *marassas,* important twin spirits in vodun whose close relationship rendered them inseparable. She states, "They were the same person, duplicated in two. They looked the same, talked the same, walked the same. When they laughed, they even laughed the same and when they cried, their tears were identical. . . . You and I we could be like *Marassas*" (84–85). Though she is not inseparable from her mother, Sophie becomes Martine's *marassa* as she inherits her mother's legacy of sexual violation. Beyond their interactions as mother and daughter, their lives are now interconnected in their sexual victimization and oppression under the same patriarchal system. In fact, both Martine and Sophie have nightmares, "double" whenever they feel violated, engage in consensual obligatory sex with their partners, and inflict bodily harm on themselves.

Sophie's initial response to her testing exacerbates rather than allows her to transcend the sexual abuse: she sexually violates herself. In an attempt to liberate herself from her weekly testings, a virginal Sophie inserts a pestle into her vagina:

"My flesh ripped apart as I pressed the pestle into it. I could see the blood slowly dripping onto the bed sheet. I took the pestle and bloody sheet and stuffed them into a bag. It was gone, the veil that always held my mother's finger back every time she *tested* me" (88). The significance of Sophie's act lies in the irony of this forging of freedom and the desperate measures victims of these virginity tests take to avoid or end this practice.[13] Danticat emphasizes the seriousness of a practice that would cause its subjects to take such extreme measures to avoid it.

Just as Martine relives her testing and rape, Sophie's sexual violation continues to plague her throughout the text. Because she engages in obligatory sexual duties with her husband Joseph, whom she marries after she fails her virginity test (after the pestle incident) and can no longer live with Martine, he becomes a reminder of her sexual violation. Sophie responds to her sexual activities with him in a number of ways, including fleeing to Haiti without notifying him and by doubling, as her mother had taught her to do: "He reached over and pulled my body towards his. I closed my eyes and thought of the *Marassa*, the doubling. I was lying there on that bed and my clothes were being peeled off my body, but really I was somewhere else" (200). Sophie's description of her sexual activities with Joseph, who is not an abusive husband, reveals that she perceives these encounters as sexually violating. Sex with Joseph, who was once a source of happiness and self-discovery, is now a source of her nightmares, along with her memories of her testings.

In response to her sexual abuse, Sophie becomes sex-phobic and develops bulimia, often binging and purging after her sexual encounters with Joseph. Her bulimia is a coping mechanism she develops to deal with the physically and psychologically damaging consequences of sexual abuse and discomfort.[14] Sophie binges and purges in an attempt to exert autonomy over her body, which was previously controlled by her mother and is now, according to nationalist discourses on the role of women, arguably Joseph's property. However, her attempts cause her to further abuse her already harmed body, which, according to Sophie, she now hates.

Nevertheless, Sophie's relationship with Joseph allows her to find healthier ways to combat the traumatic effects of her sexual abuse. She moves with him to Rhode Island and gains distance from the site of her abuse. With Joseph's encouragement, Sophie sees a therapist and joins a sexual phobia group. When she does this, her narrative of sexual abuse diverges from that of her mother, who refuses any type of professional assistance. While Martine's actions allow the rapist to control her, Sophie takes measures to break the cycle of sexual violation, which she may, as the narration implies, very well pass on to her baby daughter Brigitte. In fact, Brigitte, even as an infant, begins to exhibit sleeping patterns similar to those of her mother and grandmother, both of whom lose sleep because of nightmares related to their traumatic experiences.

Martine's illusion that the rapist is ubiquitously present, particularly as evidenced in her unborn baby, causes her to resort to stabbing her stomach to not only extricate herself from his powerful grip but also abort her baby. In wrapping herself in sheets before she stabs her stomach seventeen times, she predicts that she will die soon, thus revealing the premeditated nature of this self-imposed abortion. For Martine, who had labeled herself as being one step ahead of the mental institution, committing suicide by stabbing herself is a viable alternative to a life afflicted by sexual violation.

At the end of the novel, Sophie returns to Haiti for Martine's funeral and visits the cane fields where her mother was raped. This is significant, as it enables her to confront the physical site of Martine's rape. The cane, a phallic symbol with patriarchal implications, exemplifies not only Martine's rape and sexual abuse but also the sociosexual victimization and suffering of the generations of women in Sophie's family. It emblematizes the detrimental effects of the global political economy on women, whose bodies are commodified as they serve as low-wage workers in the fields. In addition, because of the nation's attempts to secure and maximize its international commerce with more-industrialized nations, it has not paid significant attention to conditions in the fields, often leaving the laborers vulnerable to attack or even sickness based on unhealthy conditions.

Following her therapist's advice, and in the presence of Ifé and Atie, Sophie runs to the fields and begins to beat the cane stalks as a means of extricating herself from her family legacy of socioeconomic, political, and sexual marginalization:

> From where she was standing, my grandmother shouted . . . "*Ou libéré?*" Are you free? . . .
>
> From the thick of the cane fields, I tried my best to tell her, but the words would not roll off my tongue. . . .
>
> My grandmother quickly pressed her fingers over my lips.
>
> "Now," she said, "you will know how to answer." (233–234)

Although Danticat does not depict Sophie's future, which results in an ambiguous conclusion, Sophie's attack on the cane opens up an avenue for her and her descendants to heal from the sexual and economic domination that has victimized generations of women in her family. And so, much like the Caco rebels' legacy of challenging hegemony, Sophie's cutting of the cane is also a revolutionary act of possible liberation for her family.

It is important for both grandmother Ifé and aunt Atie to be present during Sophie's attack of the cane because although they have had to carry their own burdens associated with their status, they can be witnesses to a possible healing for Sophie and, by extension, themselves. Both Ifé and Atie, like Martine, have been hurt by abiding by the rules and passing the tests yet they have not reaped the benefits of marriage or material security. Ifé's husband dies young and she raises her daughters in poverty; and because Atie is a poor, uneducated, rural "daughter of the hills" by her own admission, she is rejected by her only love, Donald Augustin, and left husbandless. However, in defiance of a patriarchal system that has marginalized her—and much to Ifé's disapproval—Atie cultivates a same-sex relationship with Louise. Nevertheless, Louise immigrates to the United States without informing Atie, leaving her chagrined. As a result, the tests these women have endured have been fruitless since their respectability does not provide them with the legitimacy, status, and long-term loving relationships they seek.

In *Breath, Eyes, Memory,* resistance is complex and should not be viewed through a narrow lens. While it is subversive and seemingly transcendent, at other times it is precarious. Although Martine does not heal from the trauma of sexual abuse and internalizes the marginalizing politics that victimize her, she exhibits agency by providing Sophie with the foundation that renders it possible for her to find healthier ways to transcend sexual trauma and break the cycle that has plagued her family for generations. But her resistance is precarious, as evidenced by her attempts to extricate herself from sexual abuse by stabbing her own stomach. Her death emblematizes, then, a possible demise or death of the legacy of sexual abuse and its ramifications for the Cacos and their future descendants. Thus, Sophie may not only find more successful ways to deal with the trauma of sexual abuse but also, very importantly, may develop a healthy, empowering sexuality and pass a new legacy of self-actualization and empowerment to Brigitte and other future Caco women.

NOTES

1. Donette A. Francis, "'Silences Too Horrific to Disturb': Writing Sexual Histories in Edwidge Danticat's *Breath, Eyes, Memory,*" *Research in African Literatures* 35, no. 2 (2004): 79.

2. Though the reigns of François and Jean-Claude Duvalier differed and should not be conflated as monolithic, there were considerable continuities between the two. During both regimes, the poor remained destitute and the government privileged the interests of middle- and upper-class and business-owning Haitians. Second, with the help of the Tontons Macoutes, both governments silenced opposition and victimized both male and female dissenters (until mass revolts in the mid-1980s). Finally, the country's national and international reputation worsened during both regimes. See Michel-Rolph Trouillot, *Haiti, State against Nation: The Origins and Legacy of Duvalierism* (New York: Monthly Review Press, 1990); Elizabeth Abbott, *Haiti: The Duvaliers and Their Legacy* (New York: Simon and Schuster, 1991); David Nicholls, "Haiti: The Rise and Fall of Duvalierism," *Third World Quarterly* 8, no. 4 (1986): 1239–1252; and Mets Lundahl, "History as an Obstacle to Change: The Case of Haiti," *Journal of Interamerican Studies and World Affairs* 31, nos. 1–2 (1989): 1–21

3. In fact, the state perceived women as being in the same category as children and the elderly. For a detailed discussion of Haiti's gender politics, see Carolle Charles, "Gender and Politics in Contemporary Haiti: The Duvalierist State, Transnationalism, and the Emergence of a New Feminism (1980–1990)," *Feminist Studies* 21, no. 1 (1994): 135–164.

4. Trouillot, *Haiti, State against Nation,* 167.

5. Anne McClintock, *Imperial Leather: Race, Gender, and Sexuality in the Colonial Contest* (New York: Routledge, 1995), 354. McClintock discusses women generally in relation to

nationalism, but because of the applicability of her observations, I apply them to Haitian women specifically.

6. Because these violations against women were state-sanctioned, reporting them would have had adverse effects. Women who reported sexual and other crimes against themselves and their family members faced the risk of being terrorized, perhaps murdered, as they were perceived as expressing discontentment with or protesting the government. Not only did the state fail to protect women, it also possibly subjected them to further politicized and sexualized violence by exposing their violations. See Beverly Bell, *Walking on Fire: Haitian Women's Stories of Survival and Resistance* (Ithaca, N.Y.: Cornell University Press, 1991), 33–34.

7. See Carole Charles, "Popular Imageries of Gender and Sexuality: Poor and Working-Class Haitian Women's Discourses on the Use of Their Bodies," in *The Culture of Gender and Sexuality in the Caribbean,* ed. Linden Lewis (Gainesville: University Press of Florida, 2003), 169–189; and Sandra C. Duvivier, "'My Body Is My Piece of Land': Female Sexuality, Family, and Capital in Caribbean Texts," *Callaloo* 31, no. 4 (2008): 1104–1121.

8. Haitians are not a monolithic people, and not every Haitian family practices testing.

9. Francis, "'Silences Too Horrific to Disturb,'" 77.

10. Edwidge Danticat, *Breath, Eyes, Memory* (New York: Vintage, 1998), 61. All subsequent references to *Breath, Eyes, Memory* will be cited in the text.

11. As a major cash crop in Haiti during slavery and after emancipation, sugar has remained an important global export. The country depends on sugar, and the low-waged workers who produce it, to secure foreign capital.

12. Much like the politics of color in Haiti, politics concerning virginity and marriage are by no means absolute. Many Haitian women of various complexions and socioeconomic backgrounds who are not virgins and have children are still able to marry. In other instances, unmarried women engage in sexual activities with men for property and other provisions. See Ira P. Leventhal, "Labor, Sexuality and the Conjugal Contract in Rural Haiti," in *Haiti— Today and Tomorrow: An Interdisciplinary Study,* ed. Charles R. Foster and Albert Valdman (Lanham, Md.: University Press of America, 1984), 15–33.

13. Girls and women sometimes resort to extreme lengths to avoid virginity tests. For instance, when several Turkish schoolgirls attempted to commit suicide by drinking rat poison rather than take such tests, the Turkish government responded by rescinding the law that allowed the tests. See "Turkey Scraps Virginity Tests," *BBC News,* February 28, 2002, http://news.bbc.co.uk/2/hi/europe/1845784.stm.

14. Francis, "'Silences Too Horrific to Disturb,'" 84.

CHAPTER 10

Rape Fantasies and Other Assaults

BLACK WOMEN'S SEXUALITY AND RACIAL REDEMPTION ON FILM

Erin D. Chapman

Since the advent of the millennium, award-winning popular films such as *Crash* and *Monster's Ball* have been hailed as powerful representations of a popular perception of racial politics, interracial relations, and social opportunity encapsulated by the label "post-racial." Films such as these advance the notion that American society has overcome its history of structural racism and that any racial and economic social inequality that persists is personal—individually expressed and eliminated through interpersonal communication and individual effort.[1] Thus, Roger Ebert praised *Crash* for demonstrating "how racism works not only top down but sideways, and how in different situations, we are all capable of behaving shamefully."[2] In other words, the film is to be congratulated for its conflation of structural racism with individual prejudice and the resulting denial of the ongoing operation of white supremacy as a formation central to U.S. society. In a similar vein, *Los Angeles Times* critic Kevin Thomas labels *Monster's Ball* "a fable of absolution and redemption" in which "the burden of the past, both immediate and distant" ensnares the characters. "Yet they have the chance, especially by sticking together, of letting go of [that] wrenching past and starting life anew."[3] It is up to the characters to unburden themselves of racism and its effects. Themes of postracial personal responsibility and redemption suffuse these dramas. And in this fictional postracial world, men overcome racism through sexualized encounters with black women who facilitate their redemption.

Crash and *Monster's Ball* both rely on pernicious racial and sexual mythologies that permeate our culture. They are two of a host of films and television series that might be termed rape fantasies in their use of black women's sexuality and depictions of sexual assault to titillate viewers and promote themes of facile racial harmony without adequately addressing the significance of sexual assault and exploitation or attending to the complexity of black women's subjectivity.[4] While *Crash* and *Monster's Ball* seem to bravely and adequately confront the difficult terrain of interracial sexual congress, the racialized sexual exploitation of women, and sexual assaults on black women's bodies, they actually rarely focus on black women themselves and fail to present their perspectives on these issues. Rather, the filmic plots reveal themselves as rape fantasies. Rape fantasy films elide black women's injury and oppression as their focus remains or moves onto the subjectivity of other characters, principally black and white men and therefore the communication of cultural themes and social messages explicating those men's experiences and advocating the alleviation of their pain. As these films direct viewers away from African American women's perspectives, they utilize the hypervisibility of black women's sexuality and thus deepen its inscrutability except as it serves men's desires, needs, and redemption. In the postracial millennium, filmic racial redemption is a dream white and black men realize through black women's sexual oppression. In the sections that follow, I will first define the rape fantasy and then show how each film uses it to achieve a masculinist racial redemption.

The Rape Fantasy: Women's Representations, Seduction, and Rape-Lynch Discourse on Film

Steeped in U.S. culture's abiding investment in the mythology of the rape-lynch discourse and the insidious discourse of seduction, these films are rape fantasies in that they function as fantasies of racial progress accomplished through white and black men's engagement with black women's sexuality and at the expense of black women.[5] A rape fantasy does not necessarily include a filmic depiction of a rape. More important than the image of sexual assault is the use of black women's sexuality in the plot and themes of the film to rehabilitate and redeem men and to absolve the larger society of the racist-sexist oppression black women endure. Rape fantasy films expose black women's sexuality in a variety of familiar tropes that obscure the complexity of black women's subjectivity and obfuscate their oppression. These films rarely advance black women's self-determined sexual subjectivities. Rape fantasy films are excellent examples of Evelynn Hammonds's admonition that the "visibility [of black women's sexuality], in and of itself, does not erase a history of silence nor does it challenge the structure of power and domination—symbolic and material—that determines what can and cannot be seen" or understood about black women.[6]

Black women characters in filmic rape fantasies are not without agency. Indeed, their agency and power are central as they accomplish the redemption of the male characters. Black women characters' agency and sexual subjectivity, however, do not serve black women's interests. These films neither illuminate the shape and history of black women's oppression nor envision a politics that would liberate black women as well as black men and the larger society.

Instead, rape fantasy films rely on the seduction of the viewer into ignoring or belittling the sexual abuse and/or sexual exploitation of black women's bodies and women's injury and pain. This seduction is accomplished both by refocusing viewers' attention on men characters as "real" victims of oppression and by the dissemblance of dominance in abusive relationships through the deployment of sentimental images of reciprocity, romance, consent, and affection. Through this refocus and dissemblance, the abuse and exploitation of the black woman's body is "licensed within the scope of the humane and the tolerable" and made digestible, even normal and right, for the viewer.[7] At a minimum, pain and injury are simplistically resolved away in the course of the plot through the relentless obfuscation of the perpetrator's power and domination and the victim's consent, acceptance, and forgiveness. At their worst, rape fantasies can be precisely what the term implies—plots and images through which sexual violence is presented as erotic and desired by both the on-screen victim and, ultimately, the viewing audience. Whether the film includes an image of sexual assault or not, however, a rape fantasy makes use of black women's sexuality to forward black and white men's redemption in accordance with a masculinist vision of postracial harmony in the twenty-first century.

In her assessment of Western society's visual lexicon of rape, cultural critic Ariella Azoulay finds that while "there is an unwritten prohibition on showing 'real' images of rape [to the general public], 'staged' rape images are freely shown on porn sites."[8] Although sexual assault affects one-third of the world's women at some point in their lives, we do not have the benefit of documentary images as a means of understanding its nature and consequences.[9] Instead, Western society is much more comfortable with the fictional representation of sexual violence against women, and such assaults are overwhelmingly staged as pornography in hetero-patriarchal terms.

Western popular culture prefers the fictional staging of rape as pornography because images of actual rape would serve as powerful testaments "to a flaw in the citizen status of rape victims," making it impossible to ignore the pervasiveness of misogyny and the ongoing consequences of patriarchy.[10] At the same time, sexual representations of women in popular visual culture, including advertisements, filmic sex scenes, pornography, music videos, and other media, confirm and reinforce the devaluation of women.

Azoulay does not conflate all visual representations of women's sexuality with images of rape. She is clear that most visual representations of female sexuality "are not images of rape." However, she does identify "a continuity extending from these [fictional, popular] images to the missing images of rape. This is so because rape is the ultimate fulfillment of woman's being for a man." Women are made available through popular sexual images to serve men and their manhood, their

sexual dominance and male privilege, rather than themselves or their womanhood.[11] There is a line of continuity linking the misogyny expressed through rape
and pornographic rape fantasies and the popular depiction of women's sexuality.
Whether the woman is depicted as object, subject, agent, or currency, images of her
sexual assault and sexual exploitation facilitate men's agendas rather than her own.

Of course, black women do not require a sexualized popular cultural representation to dehumanize and hypersexualize their subjectivity. Black women
are "always-already sexual" and always-already abandoned by the law, refused
the subjectivity of the human.[12] Their sexualized representations in visual popular culture are not as distinct from their subjectivities in society as nonblack
women's are. Overwhelmingly represented as either hypersexual or inhumanly
strong, black women are rarely understood as victims of sexual assault, since
sex with black women either presumes or does not require their consent and
the sexual assault and sexual exploitation of them is dismissed as less than truly
injurious. Race magnifies the line of misogynist continuity linking rape to popular representations of black women's sexuality. Black women's vulnerability and
oppression are exacerbated by their representations in films that ostensibly work
to critique and reject racism but accomplish this through the use of black wom-
en's sexuality as means for men's redemption.

The discourse of seduction is central to the rape fantasy. According to cultural
theorist Saidiya Hartman, this discourse obscures power and dominance as it
invests victims with supposed emotional and lascivious power over perpetrators.
"Seduction erects a family romance—in this case, the elaboration of a racial and
sexual fantasy in which domination is transposed into the bonds of mutual affection, subjection idealized as the pathway to equality, and perfect subordination
declared the means of ensuring great happiness and harmony."[13] This is the heart
of the rape fantasy—the racial family romance eliding violence, exploitation, domination, and the happiness and harmony achieved at the expense of black women's
humanity and through society's willful ignorance of their pain and oppression.

In the films, *Crash* and *Monster's Ball*, that concern me here, the filmmakers use seductive actions and language to obscure the power of male characters
relative to black women characters and to thus reposition the dominated as the
dominant. However, seduction also functions in these films between the film
itself and the viewing audience. The directors use filmic sentimentality—beatific
images, music, beautiful faces, and emotional dialogue—to create a poignant
tone that penetrates the viewers' discomfort with the domination and sexual
violence or exploitation perpetrated by men characters on black women characters.[14] These films seduce viewers into empathy with struggling men characters
despite, or even through, their violation and exploitation of black women's bodies. Identifying and empathizing with these male protagonists, audiences wish
for their eventual success. Thus, even representations of the rape of black women
become conduits for harmonious racial redemption but never earn the redress

of those women's suffering. Sexual abuse becomes a fantasy of familial—and national—affection, reciprocity, and redemption.

In addition to relying on seduction, the filmmakers also draw upon U.S. society's rape-lynch discourse to propel their narratives of redemption. According to the traditional rape-lynch discourse as it was articulated in the post-Reconstruction South and built upon the prior discourse of seduction, white women are the only recognized or potential victims of sexual assault. And the assailants of these white women are always, according to the myth, black men. Based in racist convictions of black women's unchaste immorality and black men's brutal bestiality, the rape-lynch discourse worked to justify the lynchings of black people and the razing of black communities and obscured the real aim of the lynchings, which was white supremacist patriarchal terrorism to prevent and discourage African American political, economic, and social advancement.[15]

Even as the rape-lynch discourse began to be popularized through newspapers, novels, plays, and films like the 1915 *The Birth of a Nation,* African American anti-lynching activists such as Ida B. Wells and Mary Church Terrell began to invert it. Such activists not only asserted that black men's rape of white women was unproven and often not even the accusation that prompted a lynching but they also inverted the discourse to argue that, in actuality, black women were the true victims of widespread interracial rape. White men were raping black women because they saw them as sexually licentious and recognized them as unprotected and therefore available. White men also raped black women as an aspect of the terrorizing of black communities in the effort to maintain white supremacy. Furthermore, white men assaulted black women with impunity. The law seldom recognized or punished such crimes, and black communities could only rarely prevent or punish such assaults. Lynching and rape actually went hand in hand as violent tools for maintaining economic, political, and social white supremacy.

However, the inverted rape-lynch discourse Ida B. Wells and other African American activists articulated never became part of the national popular lexicon, although it was accepted by many African Americans and their liberal white allies. And, among African Americans and liberal whites both discourses were masculinized. As historian Darlene Clark Hine noted in 1989,

> Until quite recently . . . when historians talked of rape . . . they bemoaned the damage this act did to the Black male's sense of esteem and respect. He was powerless to protect his woman from white rapists. Few scholars probed the effect that rape, the threat of rape, and domestic violence had on the psychic development of female victims. In the late nineteenth and early twentieth centuries, as Carby has indicated, lynching, not rape, became the most powerful and compelling symbol of Black oppression.[16]

As such, lynching was increasingly understood as a crime aimed at the emasculation of black men and the curtailment of their sexual prerogatives rather than as a means of disciplining the political and economic development of black communities and of limiting the opportunities of black women as well as men.

The combined pervasive power of the rape-lynch and seduction discourses has left a legacy of black female dehumanization. Especially when black women are the victims of sexual assault or exploitation, these discourses deny them pain, humanity, and justice. Rather than to explore black women's experiences or to view the world and its events from black women's perspectives, the point of stories of racialized sexual terrorism or exploitation is to portray men's pain and perspectives and to emphasize black male humanity by causing the viewer to empathize with his emasculation and, in turn, to desire the reversal of that emasculation. The character and destiny of white men are also increasingly explored through representations of black women's sexuality and sexual abuse. Such portrayals ask whether white men—historically the perpetrators of racial oppression and racialized sexual violence—can redeem themselves and earn forgiveness, thus re-earning their exalted status as dominant leaders of a postracial, democratic society. The directors of *Crash* and *Monster's Ball* have created filmic versions of a postracial fantasy of black and white men's redemption through the exploitation of black women's sexuality.

Unpacking the workings of the repeated rape fantasy in these films allows us to see what our reliance on the seduction and rape-lynch discourses so often obscures: black women's ongoing subordination, injury, and dehumanization, even through films that intend to critique racism and its broad social effects. Thus it is that ostensibly racially progressive films such as *Crash* and *Monster's Ball* can seem to advance U.S. racial redemption while relying upon the subordination and denial of black women's oppression.

THE GENDER POLITICS OF RACIAL REDEMPTION IN *CRASH*

One of the many interwoven plots of *Crash* proceeds from the sexual assault of an African American woman character, Christine Thayer.[17] Early in the film, a white police officer, John Ryan, stops Christine and her husband Cameron, a black man, on their way home from a party, and he vents his personal frustrations and sense of inadequacy by verbally and physically assaulting them. Officer Ryan demands that Cameron Thayer get out of his car and stand on the curb to be questioned and searched. Ryan intends to humiliate Cameron and possibly injure him. Seeing this intention and objecting to Ryan's abuse of power, Christine exits the car and demands that Ryan release her husband. Instead, Christine finds herself the object of Officer Ryan's unjust scrutiny. Stating he must search her person for a weapon, he proceeds to forcibly handle Christine's body as she stands prone, hands on the car in the traditional position of a criminal submitting to state authority. The scene culminates with Ryan's sexual assault of Christine as the officer uses his finger to forcibly penetrate her genitalia while his partner and her husband watch in impotent horror. All four of these characters spend the rest of the film working through the personal repercussions of this assault.

Through the scenes involving these characters and others connected to them, *Crash* explores questions of rape, race, and redemption, inverting the discourse of the brutal black male attacker and the delicate white female victim. It purports to right the wrongs perpetrated by the traditional rape-lynch discourse but does so by rehabilitating the humanity of white and black male figures and subsuming black women's subjectivity to this masculinist project of white-black racial redemption.

In the aftermath of their encounter with the police, we find the Thayer couple at home arguing about the import of the assault. As they trade barbed accusations of racial ignorance and lack of so-called black experience, we learn that these characters are privileged members of the black middle class. We also learn that Christine does not believe their lives were in danger. "They were gonna shoot us on Ventura Boulevard? Right," she quips incredulously. Cameron answers, "They were cops, for God's sake. They had guns." She accuses him of "shucking and jiving" in allowing the officer to "finger fuck" his wife. As he storms from the room and slams the door, she triumphs, "Yeah, that's right—a little anger. It's a bit late, but it's nice to see!"

The fictional Christine Thayer expects her husband's protection. She does not consider the encounter with the policeman to have been potentially life-threatening but focuses instead on questions of humiliation and public embarrassment. Her husband clearly believes he has narrowly averted a vital crisis. He was willing to sacrifice his pride to save his life.

There are two problems with this plot line in the film. First, Christine Thayer seems a wholly fantastical, postracial character. In what world does a black woman, a black Angelino no less—no matter her background—not understand her life and that of her husband to be in danger when they are in the hands of an angry policeman? Second, the plot reduces the sexual assault of Christine Thayer to a humiliation rather than a violent, physical, and psychological violation. Neither of the Thayers understands the sexual assault in this way, however. This, too, is fantastical, a fantastic belittlement of the injuries involved in sexual assault.

The film's theme of racial redemption relies on the idea that Christine Thayer has not really been injured, that only her pride was at stake. In the course of the plot, she later learns, as her husband already knows, to value her life over her pride. Through scenes of Cameron's racial frustrations on the job and another encounter between him and the LAPD, the film also shows that the sexual assault of his wife is injurious to Cameron Thayer's very idea of himself, his manhood, his sense of control over his life and fate. Given that rape-lynch discourse serves as the organizing principle of representations of black sexuality and sexual violence against black people in our culture, we do not understand sexual violence perpetrated on black female bodies without reference to black men and their subjugation, which is posited as greater than black women's. Black women, like Christine Thayer, are merely raped, so the logic goes, while black men are tortured, mutilated, castrated, burned, and, finally, murdered—emasculated and eliminated. The rape of black women is not understood in these terms of torture, terror, and utter dehumanization. Thus, although he suffered none of the above physical harms, the injury in the encounter with Officer Ryan was to Cameron Thayer, not Christine, and to both characters' understanding of his—that is, Cameron's—worth. They are estranged from one another as a result of the threat to his masculinity.[18]

These characters' perceptions of the injustice they have experienced set up their twin crashes as the film begins to conclude. Cameron Thayer comes to risk his life in order to protect another black person (but a young black man, not his wife, and not a woman) in the face of another encounter with armed white policemen. He proves to himself that he can stand firm in the face of white authority and defies the notorious Los Angeles Police Department in doing so, thereby redeeming his sense of empowered masculinity.[19]

Christine Thayer comes to a situation in which her life itself—not merely her honor—is at risk and she must forgive her assailant in order to allow him to save her life. This culminating scene is perhaps more disturbing than the sexual assault scene earlier in the film. Here, Christine is again forced into intimacy with Officer Ryan. This time, however, this forced intimacy is shrouded in seduction. Christine's car has overturned in the middle of the street, and another car—presumably the one that collided with hers—is disabled and on fire several yards away. Upon discovering the crash site, Officer Ryan and his new partner run to assist the victims.

Inside her car, Christine hangs upside down, suspended by her seatbelt and apparently trapped. Without recognizing her, Ryan pushes himself into the car and begins his attempt to free Thayer's body. She turns, recognizes him, and immediately rejects his assistance, screaming "Not you!" and demanding that "somebody, anybody else" be called. Surprised, abashed, annoyed, and eventually angered, Officer Ryan screams into her face, "Lady I'm not gonna fucking hurt you" and proceeds in his attempts to loosen the seat belt. Crying, screaming, and nearly incoherent, she continues to object to his nearness, to receiving his attention and help. Finally, he stops and looks into her eyes. "Okay, okay," he concedes, "I'm not going to touch you." Holding her gaze, he explains that no one else is available to help and that gasoline is pooling nearby. Christine suddenly understands that her life is in danger. She must submit to Ryan's proximity and assistance.

In their further communications, Officer Ryan asks permission from Thayer for each move he makes regarding her body and position. Meanwhile, she whimpers, "Are you gonna get me out?" and he assures her that he will. Looking into one another's eyes and nearly entwined in each other's arms as the plaintive orchestra music swells and a lone woman's voice melodiously sings, actors Thandie Newton and Matt Dillon form a picture of trusting intimacy and common cause. Here, the import of the scene moves well beyond the cooperation required to free Christine from her overturned vehicle. Rather, the image offers a portrait of a plaintively submissive black woman who nevertheless wields the power to forgive and a formerly oppressive white man humbly receiving that intimate forgiveness, thus earning his racial redemption.[20]

As the pooling gasoline finally ignites, threatening the characters' lives, Officer Ryan's partner runs to extricate him from the overturned car, leaving Christine trapped within. Unwilling to sacrifice Christine's life, Ryan throws off his partner's restraining hands and plunges back into the car to grab her arms. As his partner and another officer pull Ryan from the car by the legs, he drags Christine with him, thus saving her from a torturous death by fire.

Through this scene, director Paul Haggis succeeds in enacting two seductions. With her tears, outrage, weakness, and need for rescue, Christine Thayer tames and seduces Officer Ryan, the perpetrator of rape, into a sensual, beatific, humble intimacy with her, his victim. The dominant and domineering Officer Ryan is reduced to a supplicant requesting permission to aid the pitiable, weeping Thayer. In granting this permission, Christine yields her indignation and outrage, submitting to Ryan's machinations on her behalf and thus granting him redemption, which was purportedly always in her power. Then, too, the music and the arresting images of the beautiful faces so near to touching seduce viewers into forgiving and redeeming Officer Ryan as he acts heroically and selflessly to save Christine's life.

Free of her exploding car, a traumatized Christine clings to Officer Ryan and cries. As emergency technicians lead her away, she turns to look again at her rescuer and her eyes linger on him, expressing surprise, perhaps even longing. This lingering gaze bespeaks the aftermath of both the forced and the redemptive intimacies between Christine and Ryan. After all that has passed between them, she seems simply grateful.[21]

It is only after Christine and her husband Cameron have learned their separate lessons that they can come back together in any accord. She calls him. After a pause to consider his reaction, he answers and says, "I love you." She smiles gratefully into the phone. We are assured of their shared understanding and reunion. She has now experienced a situation that required her to swallow her pride to save her life and so she understands his actions in their previous encounter with Officer Ryan. On the other hand, he did not need to understand her position, as, according to the rape fantasy's logic, he was always at greater risk, but he has redeemed his sense of masculine power to the extent that he can face her expectation that he act as her protector.

This plot line in *Crash* thus recreates a time-worn and oft-recurring trope of the sublimation of black women's subjectivity to a greater, masculinist good. In this facile representation of racial redemption, black women's oppression goes unrecognized for the sake of harmony. Through the denial of this black woman's pain—the reduction of violent assault to humiliation and the balancing of that purportedly small humiliation against the greater issue of black male life or death—viewers are allowed a reprieve. We are not required to condemn the principal white male character, Officer Ryan, nor must we endure any lingering suspicion of violent racist oppression as a tenet of contemporary social reality that is sanctioned by the state and carried out by its law enforcers. Instead, racism is personal—perpetrated and experienced by individuals—and can therefore be addressed, forgiven, and even eliminated at the personal level, through the rape fantasy.

Demystifying Seduction in *Monster's Ball*

In light of Haggis's dismissal of sexual assault in *Crash*, Marc Forster's *Monster's Ball* might seem a refreshingly honest look at the exigencies of interracial sex, love, and race politics.[22] However, although the film concludes with a focus on Leticia's decision to pursue her relationship with Hank and so seems to express her perspective at least as equitably as it does his, it is a rape fantasy utilizing a black woman to tell the story of a white man's personal redemption through interracial sexual congress.[23]

Dead and void inside, Hank finds in his improbable relationship with Leticia an emotional and sexual connection that reinvigorates him and finally redeems his life from emotional isolation and despondency and thus also redeems him from his abusive racial dominance over black lives. Although his initial interactions with Leticia motivate Hank to recognize the humanity in the black people around him, including the black children he habitually ran off his property with a shotgun, and to condemn his father's white supremacy, he also learns to value his own humanity and connection with other humans, ostensibly regardless of their color. While Hank's character undergoes a profound transformation in the course of the film, Leticia's arc is nearly flat. Even as she encounters tragedy after tragedy, gratefully accepts Hank's helping hand and affection, and then chooses to remain with him despite the ongoing inequality of their social positions, her character remains the same two-dimensional type—a black woman with no specific individual history, distinctive characteristics, or community.[24] Although neither realizes it, Leticia and Hank are connected from the moment the film begins through her husband's incarceration on the death row where Hank works as a corrections officer. They subsequently encounter one another a few times without noticing each other until her son is hit by a car and Hank stops to help. In the wake of the fatal car crash, the two strike up a casual, friendly acquaintanceship that at first seems pleasant but inconsequential.

The central scene of *Monster's Ball* is the sex scene that occurs a few days after the death of Leticia's son. When Hank drives her home, Leticia asks him in. She gets drunk and talks out her random thoughts and woes. She shows him the pictures her husband and son drew before their deaths and explains that her husband was executed. From this Hank learns that, as a death row corrections officer, he has played a crucial role in her life, but he does not reveal this. Hank seems more and more bewildered by Leticia's rambling, one-sided conversation. Finally, he admits, "I'm not sure . . . I'm not sure what you want me to do." She responds, suddenly lascivious and drooling, "I want, you know, I want you to make me feel better. I want you to make me feel good. I just want you to make me feel good." Fairly growling out these sexual invitations and demands, she pulls down the strap of her tank top and pulls out her breast, offering it to him. She then puts one leg across his lap, attempting a pitiful, tear-drenched, drunken seduction. "Can you make me feel good?" she demands. She pulls out both breasts, spreads her legs wide, and slides from the couch to the floor, demanding and begging all the while that he make her "feel good." These actions and words are anything but sexy as actress Halle Berry twists her body and contorts her features to express Leticia's rock-bottom desperation and misery.

Shocked but willing, Hank initially penetrates her from behind, the position viewers have come to recognize as the one he and his son habitually used with a prostitute they both frequented. But Hank's sex with Leticia differs markedly from the perfunctory experiences he had with Vera, a blonde white woman. Having stripped completely naked and shed all their inhibitions along with their clothes, Hank and Leticia fairly gorge themselves on sexual congress. They engage in all the apparently available positions, but for much of the scene, Hank lays facing upward on the floor between the couch and the coffee table while Leticia rides him. At the end, as she lies prone upon his chest, he says, "I needed you." She replies, "I needed you. I needed you so much. I needed you so much." He says, "I haven't felt anything in so long."

As mentioned above, director Marc Forster includes scenes in which Hank and his son avail themselves of the services of a blonde prostitute. These scenes not only establish the equal numbness of the father and son as they both have sex with the same woman in the same perfunctory way but also provide a contrast to the central sex scene. In *Monster's Ball*, sex with a prostitute is impersonal, brief, and entirely unremarkable. Forster manages, with lighting and camera angles, to exhibit Vera's nudity without inspiring our carnal interest, instead eliciting pity, disappointment, and boredom from both the actors and the audience. Thus, the central sex scene between Hank and Leticia is emphatically not an instance of prostitution, not impersonal, but is instead passionate, decadent, and explosive—a real combustion of bodies and sensual heat. Yet this scene is entirely devoid of the typical Hollywood ambience of romance.

Clearly, the filmmakers intend to forestall criticism of this scene as exploitative of Leticia's and Berry's sexuality. At the same time, by rejecting any hint of romance, they challenge the conventions of Hollywood filmmaking in order to heighten viewers' discomfort. In this way, they force us to confront the characters' opposing social positions and the discursive baggage accompanying interracial sex between a white man who has spent his working life exercising the state's oppressive power of life and death over black people and a poor, tragically beleaguered black woman whose life and well-being are continually shaped by that power. The filmmakers fully understand what is at stake in this scene and intend to push us past it, past our reading of white-black sex through the inverted rape-lynch discourse.

Furthermore, the filmmakers directly address viewers' expectation of white male sexual exploitation and dehumanization of black female bodies through the scene in which Leticia meets Hank's father, Buck. After some awkward introductory conversation, Buck remarks, "In my prime, I had a thing for nigger juice myself. Hank just like his daddy. Ain't a man til he split dark oak." These are the thoughts that the inverted rape-lynch discourse teaches us to suspect Hank has about his encounter with Leticia but clearly does not, and these insults represent the sort of disrespect Leticia should expect from Hank but clearly did not. We are not encouraged to ponder these characters' inexplicable innocence of racialized sexual tropes. Nevertheless, this discourse hangs over the couple's relationship. They must overcome it in order to interact respectfully and make emotional contact as simple humans. Having raised this problem, though, *Monster's Ball* quickly subsumes it. The audience is treated to scenes in which Hank expels Buck from his house to the care of a black-administered nursing home where Hank hopes he will "die in peace" without the ability to poison his son's life any longer.

As with *Crash,* the postracial politics of the film posit racism as personal and therefore make overcoming racial disparities incumbent upon the individual characters.[25] This is an aspect of the rape fantasy *Monster's Ball* advances. Leticia is to set aside the monumental losses—poverty, the loss of her house, the deaths of her husband and son, and emotional and physical pain—that the racist carceral state, represented by Hank, has visited on her life. Hank's determination to quit his job and reject his avidly white supremacist father, both of which are motivated by his sexual experience with Leticia, are shown to be enough to absolve him of the personal sin of racism. And he has suffered his father's debilitating criticism as well as his son's suicide. To the extent that the film acknowledges the structural oppression of the state and its institutions, we are to understand their impact on Leticia and Hank to have been equivalent and Hank to have relinquished any privileges it has offered him.

Because the filmmakers so directly confront the rape-lynch discourse, the rape fantasy embedded in *Monster's Ball* is more insidious than that in *Crash.* Like *Crash, Monster's Ball* utilizes a black woman's sexuality and character to explore other characters' experiences and the advancement of those characters' subjectivity. In the course of the film, viewers learn nothing of Leticia's life or background beyond the male family members that connect her to Hank. Her inner life is left unexplored. Beyond the general racial loyalties and antiracist politics with which we endow her because of cultural assumptions about southern black women, we know nothing of her fears, hopes, and motives. We witness Leticia endure tragedy after tragedy—the execution of her husband, the murder of her son, her eviction from her house, and finally her realization that her new love was her husband's executioner. The film exploits her poverty, oppression, and pain as we watch her drink, cry, scream, beg, and orgasm in desperate misery. Yet neither the dialogue she speaks nor the imagery of the scenes in which she appears allows us to learn her particular story. She does not seem to have one. She undergoes no change as the film progresses, except to accept the salvation Hank comes to offer. Leticia is just a black woman, flat, generic, oppressed, and tragic, with no specific life story or personality. As such, she is subordinated to serve as the primary means through which Hank transforms to embody the film's grand narrative of redemption and the object of the audience's voyeuristic gaze as she fucks her way through her pain.

In *Monster's Ball,* seduction discourse works through the clear articulation and then apparent critique and rejection of the rape-lynch discourse as the only lens through which to understand black women's sexuality. Leticia is not raped or coerced through the sex she has with Hank. But she does seduce Hank and that seduction advances his redemption and humanity.

On one level, the film's seduction works through filmic sentimentality. Inter-cut with the unromantic images of Hank and Leticia in the midst of sex are sentimental clips showing a brown-skinned, feminine hand, presumably Leticia's, reaching into a bird cage and trying to catch the bird, which eludes capture, its wings flapping desperately as it flies around the cage. By the end of the sex scene, the bird is caught and held secure in the dark hand. In offering her body and demanding sexual release, Leticia has reached for and caught both her own fulfillment, her own "good feeling," and Hank's elusive heart. As a result, he who has not "felt anything in so long," relearns affection and intimacy, which he can then offer her as salvation from poverty and loneliness.

The film's seduction also works on another level, however. Reading the sex scene through Hartman's theory of seduction reveals that a scene that might be viewed as radically refreshing and transcendent of racial and sexual convention is actually based in long-standing racial mythologies, the same mythologies that undergird our cultural investment in rape-lynch discourse. Hartman writes,

> As a theory of power, seduction contends that there is an ostensible equal-ity between the dominant and dominated. The dominated acquire power based upon the identification of force and feeling [and through the strength of weakness]. . . . The artifice of weakness not only provides seduction with its power but also defines its essential character, for the enactment of weak-ness and the "impenetrable obscurity" of femininity and blackness harbor a conspiracy of power . . . power comes to be defined not by domination but by the manipulations of the dominated.[26]

The central sex scene in *Monster's Ball* is actually a seduction scene in which the oppressed and pain-riddled Leticia speaks from her degraded position, using her pitiable weakness to manipulate and command Hank's sexual attentions. Her licentious bodily contortions and the revelation of her breasts as offerings in exchange for sexual release are signs of her degraded yet empowered manipulations. Hank's attraction to this drunken, wretched woman evidences his adherence to the conventions of racialized sexuality by which black women are constructed as "will-less, abject, insatiate, and pained," ever ready for copulation. His penetration of her under these circumstances is thus a violation, the fruition of the original fantasy of the master-slave relation.[27] Through seduction discourse, the central sex scene turns the power relation between Hank and Leticia on its head. The film transforms Leticia's pain and weakness into manipulative, seductive power and obscures Hank's dominance even as he penetrates her. The act is not an actual rape, but it does conform in every way to the rape fantasy. Afterward, in the course of the filmic plot, as Hank reaches for Leticia and exiles his father, he triumphs over the rape-lynch discourse and wins his redemption. Ultimately, he, not Leticia, is the one who is empowered and transformed through participation in their sexual congress.

In addition to the seduction enacted between the two characters, the central sex scene also functions to seduce the audience. In this instance, we are seduced not through beatific, sentimental images but through our voyeuristic desire to see the taboo act in explicit detail. The scene is shot much like a pornographic film in that the camera is placed level with the actors and often close up so that the viewer seems to be participating in the sexual acts. Other shots are also level but from another room, seeming to peek around furniture and through a doorway so that the viewer becomes a concealed voyeur participating from a distance. These camera angles coupled with Halle Berry's hedonistic display of bared breasts, open legs, and writhing body serve to denigrate the actress. While Leticia may emerge from this scene satisfied, trusting, and in love with Hank, Berry comes away as a naked body exploited by the director and consumed by us, the filmgoers. Indeed, a perusal of contemporary Internet sites reveals that this sex scene in *Monster's Ball* is infamous as a "hot," pornographic romp in fantasy and wanton sensuality devoid of any larger political purpose or social commentary. The film allows viewers to experience the culture-wide fantasy of the master's rape of the slave girl in explicit, pornographic visual detail.

Exploiting Halle Berry's sexuality and Leticia's oppression and pain, relying on the deeply embedded cultural myths of black female licentiousness and fascination with exotic black female eroticism, and seeming to address black women's fulfillment while actually utilizing a black woman character as the arbiter of white male redemption, *Monster's Ball* joins *Crash* as a millennial filmic rape fantasy. These films proffer the false hope of the postrace narrative, a twenty-first-century racial transcendence through interracial intimacy, the empowerment of black manhood, and white redemption from racism while justifying ongoing white social domination. As we continue to invest in a masculinist rape-lynch discourse and in racist-misogynist seduction narratives as guides through our consideration of black sexuality and racial politics, we are constantly led away from black women's subjectivity, perspectives, and exploration of the possibilities for their advancement and fulfillment.

As a culture, we have not risked picturing the sexual assault and exploitation of black women beyond the bounds of some version of the rape fantasy. We refuse to picture that rape in full realization of its personally painful consequences and its sociocultural implications of interracial and intraracial sexual oppression through ongoing structural white supremacist patriarchy. As with Thomas Jefferson's rape of Sally Hemings, we must either deny it or refashion it as a love story, a rape fantasy of seduction and taboo romance.[28] Likewise, we rarely address or "picture" black men's sexual oppression of black women. Rather than acknowledge and work to dismantle the structure of white supremacist patriarchy itself, we prefer to forward the dream, or fantasy, of black patriarchal aspiration by which black men achieve the same privileges of patriarchy white men have always enjoyed. The rape of black women as actual violation and injury is invisible just as black women's sexuality remains unfathomable and thus continually vulnerable and violable.

NOTES

I thank Kimberly Juanita Brown, Gayle Wald, and the late Jesse James Scott for their thoughts and readings as I revised this article.

1. For more on "postracial" discourses, also called "post–Civil Rights" discourses, as they affect representations of black women in popular culture and U.S. politics, see Kimberly Springer, "Divas, Evil Black Bitches, and Bitter Black Women: African American Women in Post-Feminist and Post-Civil Rights Popular Culture," *Interrogating Post-Feminism: Gender and the Politics of Popular Culture*, edited by Yvonne Tasker and Diane Negra (Durham, N.C.: Duke University Press, 2007), 249–276; and Patricia Hill Collins, *Black Sexual Politics: African Americans, Gender, and the New Racism* (New York: Routledge, 2004).

2. Roger Ebert, "The Fury of the 'Crash'-Lash," RogerEbert.com, March 6, 2006, http://rogerebert.suntimes.com/apps/pbcs.dll/article?AID=/20060306/OSCARS/603070301, accessed January 8, 2012.

3. Kevin Thomas, "'Monster's Ball' Follows a Riveting Dance with Demons," *Los Angeles Times*, December 26, 2001, http://articles.latimes.com/2001/dec/26/entertainment/et-thomas26, accessed January 15, 2013.

4. Such films and television series include *Hustle & Flow, A Time to Kill, Law and Order*, especially the spinoff *Law and Order: Special Victims Unit*, and the various incarnations of *CSI*.

5. "Rape-lynch discourse" is a term derived from Crystal Feimster's work on women, lynching, and anti-lynching politics in the United States. See Crystal Feimster, "Ladies

and Lynching: The Gendered Discourse of Mob Violence in the New South, 1880–1930"
(PhD diss., Princeton University, 2000); and Crystal Feimster, *Southern Horrors: Women
and the Politics of Rape and Lynching* (Cambridge, Mass.: Harvard University Press, 2009).
"Seduction discourse" is a term derived from Saidiya Hartman's work on the continuities
in the social and cultural modes of racializing, sexualizing, and dehumanizing African
Americans during slavery and after legal emancipation in the United States. See Saidiya
V. Hartman, *Scenes of Subjection: Terror, Slavery, and Self-Making in Nineteenth-Century
America* (New York: Oxford University Press, 1997).

6. Evelynn M. Hammonds, "Toward a Genealogy of Black Female Sexuality: The Problematic of Silence," in *Feminist Genealogies, Colonial Legacies, Democratic Futures*, edited
by M. Jacqui Alexander and Chandra Talpade Mohanty (New York: Routledge, 1997), 180.

7. Hartman, *Scenes of Subjection*, 86.

8. Ariella Azoulay, *The Civil Contract of Photography* (New York: Zone Books, 2008),
276.

9. Ibid., 241. Azoulay notes that one of every three women will experience some form
of sexual assault, and one of every four women will experience rape defined as forcible
vaginal penetration. For my purposes here, rape, sexual assault, and sexual exploitation
are coterminous.

10. Ibid., 269.

11. Ibid., 264–265, 267.

12. Ann duCille defines the term "always-already sexual" in her article "Blues Notes on
Black Sexuality: Sex and the Texts of Jessie Fauset and Nella Larsen," *Journal of the History
of Sexuality* 3, no. 3 (1993): 418–444. Critical race scholars and Afro-pessimist theorists have
established the inability of black people to access the subjectivity of the citizen/human.
See, for example, Richard Delgado and Jean Stefancic, eds., *The Derrick Bell Reader* (New
York: New York University Press, 2005); Charles Mills, *The Racial Contract* (Ithaca, N.Y.:
Cornell University Press, 1997); Charles Mills, *Blackness Visible: Essays on Philosophy and
Race* (Ithaca, N.Y.: Cornell University Press, 1998); Toni Morrison, *Playing in the Dark:
Whiteness and the Literary Imagination* (New York: Vintage Books, 1993); Frank B. Wilder-
son III, *Red, White & Black: Cinema and the Structure of U.S. Antagonisms* (Durham, N.C.:
Duke University Press, 2010); and Hartman, *Scenes of Subjection*.

13. Hartman, *Scenes of Subjection*, 89.

14. These films might be considered a subset of the "stories" Rebecca Wanzo identifies
as taking "narrative refuge in a sentimental logic that treats interpersonal intimacy as a
salve for the failures of institutional redress." In this subset, that interpersonal intimacy
apparently also works to redeem the perpetrator of the oppression/crimes that require
redress. Wanzo, *The Suffering Will Not Be Televised: African American Women and Sentimental Political Storytelling* (Albany: State University of New York Press, 2009), 114.

15. For more on the convergence of race, lynching, rape, and terror in African American
women's historiography, see Patricia Schechter, *Ida B. Wells-Barnett and American Reform,
1880–1930* (Chapel Hill: University of North Carolina Press, 2001); Paula Giddings, *Ida, A
Sword among Lions: Ida B. Wells and the Campaign against Lynching* (New York: Harper
Collins, 2008); Feimster, *Southern Horrors*; and Danielle L. McGuire, *At the Dark End of
the Street: Black Women, Rape, and Resistance—a New History of the Civil Rights Movement from Rosa Parks to the Rise of Black Power* (New York: Alfred A. Knopf, 2010).

16. Darlene Clark Hine, "Rape and the Inner Lives of Black Women in the Middle West:
Preliminary Thoughts on the Culture of Dissemblance," in *Unequal Sisters: A Multicultural Reader in U.S. Women's History*, 2nd ed., ed. Vicki L. Ruiz and Ellen Carol DuBois

(New York: Routledge, 1994), 345. Hine refers to Hazel Carby, *Reconstructing Womanhood: The Emergence of the Afro-American Woman Novelist* (New York: Oxford University Press, 1987), 39.

17. *Crash*, dir. Paul Haggis, (Los Angeles: Yari Film Group and Los Angeles: DEJ Productions, 2004). *Crash* won three Academy of Motion Picture Arts and Sciences Awards in 2005, including Best Picture.

18. Rebecca Wanzo acknowledges the masculinism of *Crash*'s depiction of the impact of racialized sexual assault but does not critique it as such. She simultaneously suggests an equality between the Thayers' experience of the assault on Christine's body and asserts that its primary impact was through Cameron's inability to prevent or redress it. See Wanzo, *The Suffering Will Not Be Televised*, 142.

19. In contrast to my reading, Wanzo emphasizes that "actor Terrence Howard communicates Cameron Thayer's resentment that he accept help from the very source of his suffering [although it is Officer Ryan's partner, who was a bystander to the original assault, with whom Cameron interacts in this second encounter]. Intimacy is forced on him: the performance of intimacy is, in fact, the only way in which he can be saved." This description of the encounter seems more directly applicable to Christine's second encounter with the police, in the person of Officer Ryan himself, than it is to Cameron's. Wanzo, *The Suffering Will Not Be Televised*, 142.

20. Although focusing purely on theorizing the film's emphasis on "touch," Tarja Laine supports my reading of this second encounter between Christine Thayer and Office Ryan. "By making herself untouchable, Christine calls upon Ryan to admit to his racist attitudes or to change them. Furthermore, only by first turning into something untouchable does Christine now become capable of returning the touch. This is an instant of reciprocal touch that leads to Ryan's conscious self-perception." Like Haggis, Laine posits Christine Thayer and Officer Ryan as equally empowered subjects capable of reciprocal touch, thus sublimating the actuality of racism-sexism as a structure of oppression rather than a question of interpersonal understanding. Likewise, Christine is endowed with the power to "touch" Ryan into redemption from his racism. Laine, "'It's the Sense of Touch': Skin in the Making of Cinematic Consciousness," *Discourse* 29, no. 1 (Winter 2007): 40–41.

21. Wanzo notes that Christine has been "put in a position where she can only be grateful—she has no other affective possibilities." Wanzo, *The Suffering Will Not Be Televised*, 142.

22. *Monster's Ball*, dir. Marc Forster (New York: Lee Daniels Entertainment, 2002). Halle Berry won the 2002 Academy Award for Best Actress for her performance in *Monster's Ball*, and the film received multiple Academy Award, Golden Globe, and other nominations and awards.

23. Numerous critics understand *Monster's Ball* as a narrative of white male redemption. See Judith Franco, "'The More You Look, the Less You Really Know': The Redemption of White Masculinity in Contemporary American and French Cinema," *Cinema Journal* 47, no. 3 (Spring 2008): 29–47; Mia Mask, "Monster's Ball," *Film Quarterly* 58, no. 1 (Fall 2004): 44–55; and Aimee Carrillo Rowe, "Feeling in the Dark: Empathy, Whiteness, and Miscege-Nation in *Monster's Ball*," *Hypatia* 22, no. 2 (Spring 2007): 122–142. In contrast, Sharon Holland rejects the redemption interpretation. See Holland, "Death in Black and White: A Reading of Marc Forster's *Monster's Ball*," *Signs* 31, no. 3 (Spring 2006): 809.

24. Those who identify white male redemption as a primary theme in the film also recognize the absence of sufficient depth of character development in Leticia. They attribute this to both the filmmakers' negligence and Halle Berry's poor acting.

25. Mask and Holland disagree with my assertion. Although their arguments are distinct, both argue that *Monster's Ball* confronts and explicates the ongoing power and effects of structural racism as it operates through the prison-industrial complex. See Mask, "Monster's Ball"; and Holland, "Death in Black and White."

26. Hartman, *Scenes of Subjection*, 88–89.

27. Ibid., 87.

28. Kimberly Juanita Brown, "Black Rapture: Sally Hemings, Chica da Silva, and the Slave Body of Sexual Supremacy," *Women's Studies Quarterly* 35, nos. 1–2 (Spring/Summer 2007): 45–66. *Jefferson in Paris* (1995) and *Sally Hemings: An American Scandal* (2000) are examples of filmic love stories—or rape fantasies—that have been made of Jefferson's sexual relationship with Hemings.

CHAPTER 11

"Embrace the Narrative of the Whole"

COMPLICATING BLACK FEMALE SEXUALITY IN CONTEMPORARY FICTION

Johanna X. K. Garvey

The erotic is a resource within each of us that lies in a deeply female and spiritu-al plane, firmly rooted in the power of our unexpressed or unrecognized feelings.
—*Audre Lorde*

In this essay, I explore representations of Black female sexuality and same-sex desire in selected works of fiction by African American women published from 1997 to 2005. These include Suzan-Lori Parks's *Getting Mother's Body* (2003), Shay Youngblood's *Soul Kiss* (1997), Marci Blackman's *Po Man's Child* (1999), and Martha Southgate's *Third Girl from the Left* (2005). These texts explore Black women's experiences from multiple perspectives, often featuring young women with "missing" mothers who seek models of agency and empowerment. Confronting patriarchal societal norms of female sexuality and pernicious stereo-types of Black women, these young female protagonists resist masculine control, social regulation and restriction, and pathologizing labels. Struggling with abuse, rape, and self-inflicted harm, they interrogate the dictates of heteronormativ-ity and develop healing "uses of the erotic." While none of these texts depicts a black queer and/or lesbian community that might contextualize their experience, the texts illustrate the role of women who demonstrate "a power that cannot be denied" and show young Black women how to "embrace the narrative of the whole," which moves toward an affirmation of their humanity and wholeness.[1] To this end, these contemporary texts by Black women present new visions of family and belonging while challenging normative models of citizenship and, in most cases, deliverance from suffering, numbness, and self-negation.

The chronological and geographical range of these novels shows that the contestation of Black female sexualities has occurred across decades and in multiple locations in the United States; it is national in scope. In the four contemporary novels discussed here, the historical backdrop places Black women in a larger context and makes African American lives central to U.S. history. Incorporating historical events and various forms of cultural production by Black Americans into their texts, these authors illuminate the extent to which Black women's lives are integral to national narratives, identity, and citizenship.[2] As Candice Jenkins argues, Black women have been "'scripted out of narratives of American national belonging' because of their alleged sexual and domestic characters—their intimate lives."[3]

Against a backdrop of twentieth-century events that include the destruction of a Black community in Tulsa, Oklahoma, in 1921, the Civil Rights Movement and its aftermath, the era of blaxploitation films in the 1970s and more, these narratives unfold in diverse locations: Texas and Arizona in 1963, the summer of Martin Luther King's "I Have a Dream" speech (*Getting Mother's Body*); Georgia in the years from the 1968 assassination of Martin Luther King Jr. through the mid-1970s (*Soul Kiss*); Ohio from 1970 to 1991 (*Po Man's Child*); Oklahoma and Los Angeles, especially the 1950s to the 1990s (*Third Girl from the Left*). This historical scaffolding provides a deep history and reminds us of lasting traumas at the core of nationhood—rooted, in part, in the Middle Passage and slavery, particularly as they have marked the bodies and impacted the psyches of African American women.

The female characters neither deny nor relinquish blackness and femaleness but rather embrace their identities in the face of racialization, sexism, racism, and homophobia. In her argument for understanding the erotic as power, Audre Lorde states that it is the "nurturer or nursemaid of all our deepest knowledge" and that it illuminates our responsibility "not to settle for the convenient, the shoddy, the conventionally expected, nor the merely safe."[4] In these texts, Black women mentor and guide both girls and women, modeling identities that embrace the erotic for Black women who love, especially those who love Black women.[5]

The erotic Lorde calls for is conspicuously lacking in the opening scene of Suzan-Lori Parks's *Getting Mother's Body,* as the sixteen-year-old protagonist Billy Beede has sex in the car of a man named Snipes, by whom she is already pregnant. The two times they have had sex are characterized more by discomfort, distance, and prevarication for both of them than as an opportunity for Billy to embrace and claim her sexuality. Parks's novel, written in a style that reflects her primary work as a playwright, takes place in Lincoln, Texas, in the early 1960s, following the journey of sixteen-year-old Billy Beede across Texas and into Arizona in search of riches that may lie buried with her mother, Willa Mae. The abbreviated, script-like narration—which is divided into short sections told from different perspectives of the family, other characters who interact with Billy, and by Willa Mae's disembodied voice most often singing blues songs—does not offer extended psychological or emotional analysis. Readers must infer much from the spoken words and inner monologues of Billy and the others.[6] Billy is the first of several Black female characters discussed here who have experienced trauma: in her case, the horrific death of her mother, Willa Mae, from a self-induced abortion. As Dill Smiles, Willa Mae's transgender lesbian lover, recounts, "Billy was standing in the corner of the room like a little dark ghost. Willa Mae was dying in a bed of blood. She'd tried to get rid of her second baby and botched it."[7] This maternal loss when Billy was only ten compounds the confusion and lack of grounding that an unstable, roaming existence with her promiscuous and frequently jailed mother had already caused in the young girl. Not surprisingly, Billy longs for a more purportedly normative shape to her life: a wedding and married life with Snipes.

The overwhelming desire for respectability and the putative norm that marriage represents propels women in these texts into relationships that undermine the power of the erotic and instead lead to harm, numbness, or other forms of trauma and spiritual illness. Parks's text bears out what Lorde laments: "fear that we cannot grow beyond whatever distortions we may find within ourselves keeps us docile and loyal and obedient, externally defined."[8] Billy's naïveté about sex, coupled with her yearning for a seemingly safe identity as wife and mother, prevent her from hearing the deceptiveness of Snipes's words to her. Her shame at being visibly pregnant with no ring and her conviction that marriage will bestow propriety lead her to see a wedding dress as the symbol of acceptance and belonging (a version of what Candice M. Jenkins terms the "salvific wish").[9] With dress in hand, she boards a bus to the town where she expects to reunite with Snipes: "My dress is laying there [in its box] quiet and soft. . . . When Snipes sees this dress he won't believe it. I bet lovemaking feels like lovemaking once [you're] married."[10] Unfortunately, Billy arrives at Snipes's home to find he already has a wife and children, so she impulsively sets fire to the dress and, on her return journey, decides to get an abortion. This new desire to abort the fetus shows yet again that Billy has internalized a normative assumption that pregnancy demands marriage; otherwise, she cannot envision motherhood and is desperate to get rid of the baby. Without enough money to pay the abortionist and unable to sell the singed wedding dress or to return it for a refund, she concocts a plan to travel to her mother's grave in Arizona and retrieve the treasure she believes is buried with Willa Mae. The dead mother's body would thus provide a means of salvation, erasing the need for marriage as the achievement of a salvific wish for acceptance and approval of the daughter's sexuality.

Despite her Aunt June's attempts to nurture her following her mother's death, Billy has grown into adolescence without viable models of female sexuality and eroticism—thus, her belief that marriage will solve her problems and provide the love and support for which she yearns. The trauma she suffered at age ten and her outsider status in her relatives' home (where she sleeps under a counter and lacks affective connection) cause Billy to respond from a place of uncertainty and instability, even as she seeks firm grounding and belonging. She has not yet learned to love and to value herself, so as a substitute she has grasped at what feels like nurturing through sexual intimacy with Snipes. After she learns that he is married, however, she sees no other path to deliverance than removing the sign of her transgression. I use the term "deliverance" as liberation, a freedom to love and to be visible as an authentic Black female self, especially (though not only) to other Black women. The movement ideally is from the self-as-other to a loved self and an embrace of the erotic. Such a deliverance, which is also a birthing and a coming to voice, would counter pernicious stereotypes and norms, thus confounding assumptions, challenging prejudices, and enacting the power to transform.

The novels under discussion demonstrate the potential for same-gender loving between Black women to model a new paradigm for a younger generation traumatized by the "norms" and biases of the dominant culture, which they have also internalized. In fact, the four texts examined here illustrate the radical possibilities of Black women's desire and sexuality, which they insert into American cultural history and national constructions of identity, thereby refusing silence, shame, erasure and instead embracing the erotic in its multifaceted fluidity. Parks incorporates same-sex intimacy and desire in the novel through Dill Smiles, a transgender character who identifies and presents herself as a man. In the schema Mignon Moore developed in her sociological study of the "invisible families" Black lesbians create, Dill might be termed a "straight-up gay woman" who, in terms of gender presentation, identifies as a man and is attracted to women who present as female, so that they resemble a heterosexual pair.[11] When establishing a relationship with Willa Mae, Dill accepted that she also slept with men, including the one who later fathered Billy. As one of the men in the barbershop says to Dill, "'You Billy Beede's father figure. . . . You ought to go visit Snipes.'"[12] Dill denies being the girl's father and inside is "glad North is suggesting that I could father anything."[13] The depiction of Dill's relationship with Billy, then, complicates Black female sexuality while simultaneously challenging the heteronormative thrust of the narrative.

To say that Dill is passing as a man would both simplify the complexities of her gender and sexuality and reify the dichotomies that her attitudes, actions, and self-presentation blur.[14] Dill lives as a man and engages primarily with the male community for reasons that are left unclear. Without any community of gay women or even one other lesbian to bond and interact with in Lincoln, Texas, she may have turned to those with whom she most strongly identifies: straight men. Yet her secrecy about her sex does not ultimately serve her but instead potentially influences Billy's turn to heteronormativity as perceived salvation. Dill has a gun that the men refer to frequently and that she brandishes when defending Willa Mae's grave in Arizona, a weapon indicative of her inner fears and need for self-protection in order to defend her gender-bending performance. She consistently presents as masculine: she runs a pig farm, drives a pick-up truck, wears men's clothing, and intimidates the men in town. At the same time, she claims to accept her lesbian identity and sexuality: "They call me bulldagger, dyke, lezzy, what-have-you. I like my overalls and my work boots. Let them say what they want. It don't bother me none."[15] That confident embrace of her sexuality sounds remarkable for a context in which a Black lesbian might lead a life of secrecy and silence. And Dill does make the men revise the accepted, rigid ways of thinking about gender identity, as revealed in their inner monologues and spoken words. Their acceptance of her within their male-bonded space affirms her potential for full transformation.

However, as the past emerges more clearly over the course of the narrative, Dill's apparent confidence is belied by her self-conscious policing of her transgendered performance and an intense discomfort, as evidenced in her unspoken thoughts that reveal even occasional self-hatred. As Dill tells her own story, she explains that Willa Mae came back to Lincoln to live with her brother (Roosevelt), but "she ended up living with me instead. Me and her was like husband and wife, almost. When Billy was born, it was me, Dill Smiles, who took care of Willa Mae and her bastard child both."[16] That arrangement, a not-so-invisible family, worked even when Willa Mae took male lovers, until she "outed" Dill as a woman. At that point, the men in town apparently did not know that Dill was a biological woman, though readers receive information about that earlier period from Dill, not from the men of the community. Dill performs her gender-bending in the barbershop, a male preserve where she seems to feel at home, bantering with the men and engaging in their conversation about the upcoming March on Washington, the Civil Rights Movement, justice, President Kennedy, and the need for every black man to have a gun. Dill momentarily shares in their brotherhood, but then she drifts into the memory of how Willa Mae betrayed her in front of these same men:

> They all remember or remember being told how Willa Mae went and bellowed through the streets that I weren't no man. . . . At first it just came down to a woman's word against a man's word. Her word against mine. All the men in the world have been called non-men at some time or another by their women. But, as time went on, I did get the looks and there were whispers. . . . Over the years they all put two and two together. But it remains unspoken. . . . For most of the people in Lincoln, the way I carry myself and the work I do and the clothes I got and the money I earn keeps their respect.[17]

The men in the barber shop both refer to her as a "man" and jokingly call her "a violent hell of a bitch,"[18] words that on one level indicate the fluidity of her gender and sexuality. Nevertheless, that nonnormative identity is precarious, most crucially in Dill's own self-image. She is haunted by Willa Mae's revelation and lives in a form of secrecy and invisibility instead of embracing herself and challenging the dichotomous roles permitted by conventional standards. Her gun shores up her performance of masculinity and creates a connection to the male community, but its safety operates on an external level, hiding the insecurities that her inner thoughts reveal. There is a hollowness to Dill's self-presentation, even a disassociation that signals her ongoing need for deliverance from a prison-house of prescriptions for gender and sexuality.

Dill also evinces self-loathing in inner dialogue when she assumes that "white boys" have stolen her truck (when in fact Billy has taken it for her trek to Arizona). Imagining the words and thoughts of the (wrongly) presumed thieves, Dill expresses the shame and fear caused by the racism and homophobia of the larger world. As noted earlier, the narrative form compels readers to examine the characters' unvoiced words more carefully, as they are the primary means by which Parks incorporates psychological analysis into the text. When Dill imagines a conversation between drunken white men, she reveals the extent to which she has allowed external attitudes and prejudices to influence her sense of herself: "*It's just a nigger's truck. A nigger who's doing well for herself. A bulldagger nigger who got a sow with thirteen new nigger-sow piglets. Woulda stole the piggies but the nigger-lezzy Smiles sleeps with a shotgun. Oh, but you should seen what nigger-lezzy Smiles used to sleep with.*"[19] This extremely disturbing passage, part of the longest interior monologue of Dill's in the novel, continues as she "hears" the imagined men's desire for Willa Mae and their assumptions about a Black woman's promiscuity. The dialogic sequence, profoundly shocking because it comes from Dill's mind, reveals the inner insecurities she feels about her assertion of Black masculinity, especially when set against the racist, homophobic white masculinity. A chaotic rant, the passage projects both her fears and the trauma caused by Willa Mae's betrayal.

Another form of haunting occurs through Willa Mae's voice, especially in the passages that elucidate her side of the relationship with Dill. We learn that she herself initially thought Dill was biologically male: "The first few months I was with Dill I thought she was a man in the most regular sense of the word which is to say I thought she had a man's privates."[20] Willa Mae's experience has trained her to think of gender in terms of biological sex, and she apparently has had no prior sexual relations with a woman. She likely would not have looked at Dill as a sexual partner had she realized immediately that Dill was female.

Willa Mae further states that there "ain't nothing normal when it comes to Men and Relations," so it took a while for her to figure out that Dill was a woman. Their relationship challenged normative expectations, at least temporarily. As Dill indicates, Willa Mae respected her "enough to say that the first baby [Billy] she was carrying might be mines."[21] The second pregnancy, however, by the same man, combined with a growing lack of respect, destroyed the so-called marriage and sent Willa Mae to Arizona and the abortion that killed her. The power of the erotic that had potential to thrive between Dill and Willa Mae is defeated by the investment in norms that can result from fear and shame. Dill appears to be caught in a state of melancholia throughout the narrative until her confrontation with Billy and Laz (the son of the undertaker in Lincoln) at Willa Mae's grave, when she brandishes a gun in her attempt to prevent them from digging up her bones.

While the goal of that exhumation is to find the treasure, its deeper significance lies in the exposure of Dill's buried trauma and the shame she still carries as a mournful weight. We have already witnessed how the noxious attitudes Dill has unconsciously absorbed release their toxins into her mind as she tries to account for the theft of one marker of her masculinity, the pickup truck. She has attempted to (re)claim her masculine selfhood in the journey she makes to Arizona and Willa Mae's grave. Twenty-year-old Laz, who accompanies her, driving his hearse, repeatedly considers her "a man," even asking her "'What's it like, being a man?'" He continues, "Dill is more of a man than I am. She's had Willa Mae and she's had herself. That's two women more than I've had."[22] He asks her advice concerning women and sex and comments at one point that she "pees standing up."[23] Significantly, Dill serves as a role model not to Billy, who is so in need of an alternative to the available script for a young Black woman in 1960s rural Texas, but to Lazarus, a naïve Black man who anxiously seeks to perform masculinity in order to be respected and to find an appropriate female mate. Dill clings to her chosen persona to the very end and is ultimately erased from the narrative, her grief never assuaged, her identity bound up with her former role as Willa Mae's husband. As she lies down on the gravesite, Dill imagines her mother watching and thinking, "There's my daughter topping her woman one last time. . . . I [Dill] am a man, but an old old man, and Willa Mae, six feet underneath the top of the ground, unfolds her hands from where I laid them crosst her chest and, with a smile, takes me in her arms."[24] These last words directly from Dill leave her both content and depleted, an emptying out of the character that is disappointing and sad.

The conclusion of the novel performs a recuperation, through Billy, of a heteronormative script as she rides back to Lincoln with Laz and her pregnant belly, her mother's body, and the diamond ring that she found buried with Willa Mae. Tellingly, what Dill has fingered so often in her pocket was a fake ring that Willa Mae exchanged for the real one. So what Dill has held onto so tightly, frozen in desperation and a desire to belong, is a simulacrum of heterosexual marriage. And Dill is left with memories of what was the love of her lifetime in a narrative that explores, accepts, and seems to value her transgressive sexuality yet that denies her a full voice or a truly transformative power of the erotic. Does she serve as a model for Billy, who if anything has considered her a rival for Willa Mae's attention and love? I would argue not, as the final sentences flash forward to Billy married to Laz, with her two-year-old child (not aborted) and a second baby on the way. I would like to consider Dill a trickster who, in L. H. Stallings's terminology, might serve as "a figurative model to create discourses of desire for the representation of Black women's genders and sexual desires."[25] But Dill has not transformed or delivered Billy through her model of same-sex desire, perhaps because shame and fear undermine her self-presentation and self-definition, thus disempowering her to an extent. Dill troubles the heteronormative model that governs attitudes in 1960s small-town Texas, as evoked by Parks, but hers is a failed attempt at subversion and her voice is silenced by the narrative's ultimate drive toward the containment and solidification of normative roles and behavior. This character can be considered an eruption of the erotic that is suppressed, quieted, smoothed over, and almost erased at the end by Billy's dubious achievement of a life that affirms heteronormativity.

While *Getting Mother's Body* begins with a sex scene in the front seat of a car, follows Billy Beede's desire to get married, and concludes tidily with marital bliss and financial well-being, in Shay Youngblood's *Soul Kiss*, maternal abandonment is slowly counterbalanced by same-gender-loving "othermothers" in the adolescent life of the protagonist Mariah. Her mother, Coral, cannot sustain the responsibility of raising a daughter, in part due to alcohol and drug abuse, and disappears after leaving Mariah with two aunts in Georgia. The shock of this separation initially causes severe trauma for a daughter who experienced intense merging with her mother while young: sharing baths, fondling her mother's naked body, and exchanging soul kisses on the mouth. "I felt so close to her, as if my skin were hers and we were one brown body. She didn't seem to mind my curious fingers touching and soaping every curve and mystery of her body. There were no boundaries, no place I could not explore."[26] Such bonding might seem to offer a version of the erotic as healthy and nurturing, but in fact it has set Mariah up for anxiety and betrayal when her mother abruptly abdicates her role. Instead of having formed the basis for a strong sense of self and the ability to relate to another person from that space, Mariah's emotional development has been stunted; she has no context within which to understand her identity as female and as black because her mother has not only too fully absorbed Mariah into her own body, but also severed that connection.

They also shared words: Coral would leave slips of paper for Mariah, a word a day, as a means of connection. In the face of abandonment, her mother's silence, and a confusion about her own embodiment, Mariah treasures language, learning to express her longing and desires in words she tastes and holds on her tongue. She gradually develops a new language that can encompass "a narrative of the whole," an inclusive and expansive understanding of the erotic. Initially, however, Mariah confronts silence and repression surrounding lesbian sexuality when her physical attraction to a female friend, Joy, causes that girl's mother to react with homophobic outrage: "'It's an abomination before God,' Joy's mother declares and makes us pray together on our knees on the dirty kitchen floor."[27] Then she marches Mariah home and tells Aunt Merleen that she caught the two girls kissing, blaming Mariah's "wicked ways." Merleen shifts the focus from sexuality to class, dismissing the girl's mother and telling Mariah not to play with the "project children," then turning the episode into a secret from Aunt Faith, enforcing a code of silence surrounding same-sex desire.

Resisting such policing, Mariah challenges gender norms again when she refuses to wear girly clothes to church or school. Fortunately, Aunt Merleen supports Mariah's choice and brings her the clothing that she desires: overalls, a boy's flannel shirt, and high-top sneakers. Mariah's new life does not unfold as a dream, however, because she longs for both her mother and the father she has never met. The unbearable pain of separation, intensified by months of waiting for her mother to return, creates the urge to inflict self-harm: she burns her bed, bangs her head repeatedly against a wall, and wishes to set herself on fire. The aunts—who are cousins, not sisters—provide a home and a family, but Mariah does not appreciate that love and stability until she has experienced more trauma. Youngblood illustrates the debilitating effects of secrecy and silence and the necessity of the deliverance that can come with disclosure and honesty, specifically concerning Black female sexuality and same-gender loving.

The two aunts nurture the growing girl and model a life partnership, though Mariah does not recognize the nature of their relationship until she returns for Aunt Merleen's funeral. On a bus bound for Los Angeles, she comes to understand that beyond offering her sustenance and shelter, "they have mothered me with a kind of love that I grew to know was solid as the faith of the congregation at the Macedonia Baptist church."[28] Unmarried and childless, they have made a life together grounded in love. At Merleen's gravesite, Faith converses with her spirit in "conversations that explain all the years that held them together like the pages of a book." Faith tells Merleen, "'We didn't have to hide, nor hurry up our love. It seem to swell and grow every season.'" And Mariah notes that "seeing their life from the inside makes me believe it is possible to live in the rich shelter of longtime love."[29] Maintaining a face of public propriety, they have conducted their love in private with a kind of silence, no communal acknowledgment, no lesbian-affirming or women-centered community offering them a safe haven and connection in the small-town life of Georgia in the 1960s. On the contrary, a hostile dominant culture has firmly imposed this silence and invisibility upon them, and they have accepted this lack of public recognition of their relationship.

Thus, Mariah was not only unaware of the true nature of their positive same-sex loving relationship, hidden in plain sight, but she also has no available role models for alternative sexuality as she grows up and enters adolescence. Instead, she expresses her desires and addresses her physical and emotional longings to a cello that she names "Rosemary," a creative version of an othermother or a female companion. When she sleeps with a male baseball player passing through town, fourteen-year-old Mariah has a first sexual experience that she neither understands nor owns. Rather, she imagines that it will bring her a perfect baby daughter who will love her. Thus, she is not much affected when the baseball player moves on. She suffers trauma, however, en route to find her missing artist father in Los Angeles, when an older white man from Texas lures her into his car with the offer of a restaurant meal and instead drives to a deserted field and rapes her. "I want to scrape the surface of my skin with a knife, peeling away all the places he has touched me. Not just on the outside where his fingers have crawled like lice but inside of me where I can feel something cold, hard, and broken. I don't ever want to be touched again."[30] Experiencing trauma, she imagines murdering him in multiple violent ways as the memory lodges in her bones; she also realizes that "[her] body is a ripe field of history."[31] Notably, she has not taken "Rosemary" with her on the cross-country bus and has no means of contacting her aunts back in Georgia, thus suffering a reenactment of the maternal abandonment that has marked her passage toward womanhood. As these texts illustrate, deliverance in the form of sexual healing comes not in solitude but in connection with others, and the narrative indeed embraces the whole community of women, not just the individual character.

Alone without female community or Black women to model self-love or the power of the erotic in healing ways, Mariah tries to educate herself. The narrative offers multiple lessons in masculinist heterosexuality through this young Black woman's encounters with her father who does not observe appropriate paternal boundaries, paints her naked, and conflates her with her mother Coral. "All summer long I am naked for my father," Mariah says of her posing for his artworks.[32] She experiences her body as an object—aestheticized, manipulated, assessed— the threat of bodily accessibility that Black women have experienced from slavery onward. Mariah needs an othermother or female figure who can guide her to a different consciousness of her body and her sexuality and lead her in that way toward deliverance.

While Lorde presents a vision of the erotic—essentialized to a degree—that includes all women, the texts under discussion vividly underscore the importance of Black women in each other's lives. As these texts illustrate, deliverance in the form of sexual healing comes not in solitude but in connection with others, and the narrative indeed embraces the whole community of women, not just the individual character. The young women in these narratives observe and relate most deeply to mothers, aunts, and othermothers who are African American, and as a result, sexual healing comes most directly from their relationships with these women. Both Mariah and her father are attracted to her teacher, Mrs. Oyama, an incestuous triangulation that further confuses Mariah and impedes her ability to claim her own sexuality. Moreover, in Los Angeles, she has no Black women in her life. When she has a nightmare in which her father climbs into her bed with an erection, she realizes that she must be the parent and save both him and herself.

Significantly, none of the three men she interacts with sexually is African American: the baseball player is Dominican, her father is Mexican, and her rapist is a violent white Texan. Her isolation exacerbates the effects of trauma, and Mariah remains silent about these experiences, divulging them only to her beloved "Rosemary": "I want to open her up, hold her close, and let her heal me. Later when we are alone, I will take medicine from her body, wrap us both in sweet, blue music and dreams."[33] The first steps may be solitary, but they involve expressive release in some form. Mariah's music, like her creative use of words, begins to utter, to speak, her pain, and in that process she delivers herself.

Healing requires testimony and sharing, voicing trauma and finding witnesses to experiences of abuse and violence. In her nurturing Aunt Faith, Mariah finds support and the potential for healing. When Mariah discovers the nature of Faith's relationship with Merleen, she reacts without surprise; rather, she finds their relationship "natural" and "right." Mariah also reconnects with childhood friends, especially Tree, who might serve as another model, a Black woman who is comfortable in her own body and in a fluid gender identity. When Mariah first sees her again, she thinks that Tree is "a tall, skinny boy wearing a blue baseball cap, a red-and-cream-colored varsity jacket, and jeans. . . . I check to make sure all the doors are locked and feel for the hammer Aunt Merleen always kept under the seat in case of emergencies."[34] Tree admits that sometimes she wishes she were a boy, but when Mariah visits, she notices that Tree "is wearing a blue mechanic's uniform that is too big for her [and] pink frosted nail polish on her toes."[35] She provides Mariah with an example of the ability to adopt a range of traits and behaviors that trouble strict categories of gender and sexuality.

Youngblood has said of Mariah that she has the potential to avoid categorization as either straight or lesbian: "I'm not saying that Mariah is not a lesbian, I'm not saying that she's not heterosexual. . . . By the end of the book, I wanted her to be hopeful that there was good, big, honest love for her in the world and that there are all kinds of possibilities for love. I believe that our sexuality is very fluid and is on a continuum."[36] To be capable of such love, she must begin the process of healing, which at first terrifies her: "Words begin to drip from the ceiling onto my head. Big words, heavy sentences, and pages from old newspapers fall onto my face and melt away like rain, I become afraid to leave the house. . . . I become afraid of everything."[37] On her return to Georgia, Aunt Faith forces her to drink water and then guides her into the bathtub, initiating a ritual of healing that encourages Mariah to start speaking: "words begin to spill out of my mouth like snakes. Words fly from my throat like birds. I spit out every detail like poison. I leave out nothing."[38] After beginning a process of healing with the support of her aunt, Mariah is ready for the fluid possibilities Youngblood envisions for her.

Black female sexuality faces different challenges from the beginning of Marci Blackman's *Po Man's Child*. It opens with 27-year-old protagonist Po checking herself into a psychiatric hospital after sadomasochism with her white girlfriend

Mary leaves Po with knife wounds on her arms and a staggering numbness in her mind. The opening scene enacts a deadly game of truth-telling. The story that Mary demands from Po concerns her parents—the true family history— but Mary clearly refuses to hear the deeper truths. That narrative reaches back to slavery, a history that Mary rejects, unable to hear, know, or understand it as relevant to her relationship with Po. "[Mary] can't tag along on this quest I'm on, she says. If she does then she'll be there with me. It's a trip she's just not ready to take."[39] That journey would take them back through generations of Po's ances- tors to an enslaved man named George, whose story hangs like a shadow over the family in the second half of the twentieth century. That founding narrative holds Po captive as long as she submits to the shame and self-negation it instills in her.

Though haunted by "the curse of Uncle George," Po's genealogy also grounds itself in generations of women, in particular her Aunt Florida, who frame the novel. As Po lies in the hospital, she recalls her room, the setting of the scene with Mary: "Aunt Florida is angry and it's not a good sign. Yesterday the picture of her that adorns my mantle—the one with the cigar in her mouth, and the nickel-sized tar black eyes that glare at you no matter where you stand in the room—tipped over three times."[40] From the opening paragraph, Aunt Florida's presence reminds Po that the pain and numbness she experiences repeat self-destructive patterns inherited from historical traumas. "And as Aunt Florida used to say, the truth has a way of forcing its way out even when you try your damnedest to stop it."[41] Tellingly, as the scene of violence peaks in Mary's brutal strike with a hunting knife, Po sees that the candles have blown out and Aunt Florida's picture is face down. Struc- turally, the ringing phone that brings news of her father's death functions like the alarm clock at the start of *Native Son:* a wake-up call to explore the historical roots of the present, face those traumas, and write a different narrative. The present moment, a week in Ohio in 1991 when Po's father dies as she lies bleeding in her apartment, is interwoven with memories from the 1970s and 1980s, two decades weighed down by "dreams deferred."

The scene between Po and Mary and their interactions in Po's hospital room demonstrate not the erotic but sexualized abuses of power that invoke slavery. Indeed, reflecting on their behavior in bed, Po has drawn comparisons to Mor- rison's *Beloved,* herself as Sethe and Mary as Schoolteacher. "A chokecherry tree. That's what I told Mary I wanted her to put on my back. Over the years, the numbness had gotten worse. Guess I figured since I couldn't feel anything as it was, there might as well be a reason."[42] She continues: "I wasn't in this for retribu- tion; I got involved with Mary for one reason only: like Uncle George, I believed I needed her to help me feel."[43] Instead of this model of relation, "the curse of Uncle George," Po needs to internalize the models offered by her Great-Grandma Shirley and especially her (now-deceased) Aunt Florida.

The curse of Uncle George, which Aunt Florida relates to Po, helps explain Po's numbness (which is reiterated in many of her family members, including her two siblings and her father's suicidal brother). This enslaved ancestor's story—the curse—is one of self-mutilation and essentially "outdoing the abuser." "What made folks look at Uncle George sideways, she said, was that every time he ran away and got caught, the lashing he gave himself was worse than any the overseer could have imagined."[44] He escaped slavery five times and was caught five times, and each time he "found some way to mutilate himself even further," inflicting self-punishment until his final choice of suicide. From Aunt Florida, a woman who lived with another woman for years in a loving relationship, Po learns a different kind of freedom, one that "embrace[s] the narrative of the whole." Great-Grandma Shirley is comparable to Morrison's Baby Suggs: "She devoted her whole life to carrying on the resistance that had been passed down to her. Resistance in the form of love, self love, empowering love. . . . Pure, all-encompassing love that asked for nothing in return. . . . 'You got to relearn how to love yourselves,' Shirley would say. 'Cause ain't nobody else gonna do it for ya.'"[45] Unlike Uncle George, whose forms of resistance replicated the violence of slavery, the women in Po's family offer models of resistance and/as healing, affording protection both psychologically and spiritually and ultimately showing her the way to deliverance.

These Black women are survivors, Po tells us, whose stories bear witness to trauma and healing. In fact, Aunt Florida's presence serves as a talisman for Po as she performs her quest from the safe space of her room in the hospital, just as in the sadomasochistic scene in which Aunt Florida appears to stop the knife in Mary's hand: "And once in motion it's as though something or someone is trying to resist it. As though if I squinted long enough I could see its tip embedded in the palm of Aunt Florida's blistered, wrinkled, and tired old hand pushing upward to slow its decline."[46] While her aunt's death twenty years earlier catalyzed the numbness already present in Po, her felt presence protects and supports the young woman in her struggle to find freedom as she wrestles with layers of trauma.

Like Mariah's aunts in Youngblood's novel, Aunt Florida offers an example of same-gender loving between two black women in a committed relationship. It is a story of visibility, not secrecy, however, as Florida was promoted in her job at the post office from sorting mail to standing behind the counter, making her the first black woman in such a post. Gooch Johnson came just to witness this landmark, buying one stamp each day at Florida's window. Falling in love, they "decided to share their lives. Immediately, the rumors and insults flew, with folks outright threatening to kill them and the ladies of the neighborhood standing on their stoops and raising their eyebrows whenever the pair walked by. But Aunt Florida and Gooch paid them no mind," living together for thirteen years until Gooch's death.[47]

This model contrasts sharply with the relationship Po has established with Mary, the latter based on Po's need to feel pain and suffer mutilation. The first

time she cut herself, she was seven, and Aunt Florida had just died. That response
to loss and grief shifts by the end, as Po understands that her great-aunt has not
abandoned her but continues to guide and deliver her. In the most recent experience, as she lies on bloodied sheets in her apartment, Po has a conversation
with her great-aunt, who reminds her of her history and provokes her to make a
choice. When Po claims that the family has brought the curse upon itself, Florida
counters, "*On ourselves, huh? She asked incredulously. So let me get this right. You
sayin that Uncle George and his kinfolk kidnapped themselves from Africa, shackled
themselves in chains, sold themselves into bondage, then passed the legacy on down
to us*"?[48] Florida guides Po to the understanding that the curse needs one's belief
in order to persist, that one can choose not to let it continue its haunting but that
one cannot resist in solitude: "*You connected. Fact that you all here makes you so.
And as far as knowin each other goes, patterns torn from the same fabric, no matter
how different, can't help but know each other. Once you remember that, fightin to
sew it back together comes real easy.*"[49]

A crucial part of the healing process involves a shift away from wanting to "stay
dirty" and instead to choose health and wholeness, which Po recognizes even as
she clings to the disease of victimhood. Not until the final page does Po truly hear
Aunt Florida's words and begin to internalize them. In that conversation, Po
listens to Billie Holiday on her stereo and finally understands "that the real
story, the one worth telling, was buried beneath the fabric of suggestion, the
interception of light. . . . It was time to let the shadows walk silent and embrace
the narrative of the whole."[50] Aunt Florida provides a witness for Po, as Aunt
Faith has done for Mariah, and the same-gender-loving older women provide
both models and support for the younger Black women.

A fourth narrative, Martha Southgate's *Third Girl from the Left*, explores Black
women's sexualities and offers an aesthetics of sexuality across three generations
in one family that is haunted by the violent death of Anna Mae, "Mama" to
the first of those women. Mildred witnessed her mother's murder in the Tulsa
race riots of 1921 and lived with both trauma and a hidden sexual pleasure
that she silenced and relinquished for the salvific wish (treated below). Mildred's daughter Angela flees a stultifying life in Tulsa for Los Angeles in the
1970s, dreaming of becoming an actress, discovering she must exchange sex for
work, then experiencing pregnancy and motherhood, even as she also enters a
long-term same-gender-loving relationship that she embraces in silence. Her
daughter, Tamara, goes to New York to become a filmmaker. Her documentary
bookends the narrative, as she uses the camera to tell the stories and unite the
female generations in a process of testimony and witnessing.

In a reversal of the generational roles seen in Youngblood and Blackman,
Tamara resembles Aunt Florida and Aunt Faith in that she not only serves as
guide for her mother and grandmother, but also provides the venue for their
voices and stories to be heard. A short film she made of Angela talking about her

"career" in blaxploitation movies of the 1970s earns Tamara her place in NYU's film school, but it is the postgraduation film she makes of her mother and grandmother that reveals their beauty: "You see that beauty as it finally is even though no one wants to see it as it is in a black woman in America, not a hoochie, not a ho, not a mammy, not a dyke, not a cliché, just a woman. A lot of women. Real women doing what they can, making art where they can make their lives mean something where they can."[51] Significantly, Tamara is heterosexual, raised by two same-gender-loving Black women, and her admiration for her mother includes her full acceptance of Angela's lesbianism, a sexual identity that Angela herself appears unable to embrace openly.

Beautiful, loving black women who own their bodies, hearts, spirits, and minds emerge from a narrative that often depicts their pain and silence, their difficult path to Lorde's vision of the erotic. A combination of childhood trauma and the destructive, inhibiting power of the salvific wish may silence a black woman's sexuality, as illustrated by the life of Mildred. On one level, this character inhabits empty space and stifling desire, denying herself the power of the erotic.[52] Mildred has built her life in response to the rabid whites who invaded Greenwood, the Black section of Tulsa, and burned, killed, and, most horrifically, shot her mother to death as the five-year-old girl froze in terror. After that, "the day was a hole. A hole the size of her dead mother's skyward gaze."[53] Disciplining herself with a trauma survivor's response to a child's utter lack of control in the face of racist violence, Mildred anchors herself in respectability and seeming safety as she marries a pharmacist and mothers three children. She carefully maintains that solid middle-class life, allowing herself only the pleasure of attending movies in the town's theatre, Dreamland, until she falls passionately in love with a new projectionist, William. This affair, in which she discovers sexual pleasure for the first time and the art of Jacob Lawrence that William shares with her, rocks her so-called safe existence and essentially splits her in two: the woman whose ultimate adherence to public propriety causes a denial of the erotic versus an inner, expressive self who turns to art.

Inspired by Lawrence's Migration Series and unknowingly seeking healing through painting, she invades her husband's small workshed and takes it over as a studio: "She didn't know what she was doing. Didn't have a plan. But it felt right. She took off her nightgown so she wouldn't stain it. Piled it onto the stool for padding, sat naked, painting, thinking of nothing but the colors in front of her, the flat, rough wood in her hand. . . . [Her first attempt] didn't look like much. But her heart felt just a little bit less like dust. The taste of ash was gone from the back of her tongue."[54] Even as she denies herself the pleasure and passion of a life with William, she does not remain "colonized," but instead liberates herself through the aesthetic realm of her artwork.[55] She thus exemplifies one way to move toward deliverance, to give birth to a new, creative self who finds release and freedom in artistic expression.

Unfortunately, this resistance to normative prescriptions remains invisible to her daughter Angela, who sees only the surface respectability and rejects that repressive life for one that she perceives as more active and pleasurable. After the text's opening frame of Tamara's film, the first section opens with a scene of sexual predation as Angela is pressured to give a blow job to a white movie producer for consideration for a role in a popular blaxploitation film. Southgate's novel thus presents the exploitation of a black female body, confronting the audience with sex acts that constitute abuse, showing the initial lack of agency of the black woman.

Angela's story, while different from that of Billy, Mariah, or Po, is also punctuated by an arc of resistance and coming to voice: in her case as a lesbian in a long-term relationship and as mother to a daughter. In her partnership with Sheila, though, we also observe what scholar Evelynn Hammonds identifies as a practice of hiding nonnormative gender identity and resisting the identification "lesbian," rendering this refusal of dominant norms and structures of power more potential than revolutionary.[56] The legacies of heterosexism and homophobia makes it extremely difficult for Angela to perceive herself as a lesbian, as both she and Sheila have internalized stereotypes, and even after almost thirty years together, they cannot comfortably call themselves gay.

These texts demonstrate the need for a new language to replace the wounding words Dill absorbs and then ventriloquizes, to speak the love that Faith and Merleen have kept quiet, and to name the relationships established by Aunt Florida and by Angela. According to the terminology Mignon Moore developed to describe same-gender relationships between Black women, Angela and Sheila might be "hetero-identified lesbians," though in contrast to what Moore found in her subjects, we do not see the two characters seek out a lesbian/gay community or become comfortable with referring to themselves in those terms.[57] They first have sex almost by accident and Sheila vociferously refuses to label her sexuality, while Angela has absorbed social and cultural taboos: "Angela had never even heard of two women together like that. She was sure it wasn't allowed back home. But something that had been knotted in her all her life, just below her breastbone, had been untied. And now it was done. She was loose. A loose woman, what her mother always used to fear so."[58]

Angela instinctively knows that this sexual relationship violates the rules by which her mother Mildred has structured her public persona and raised her daughters, while Sheila's response indicates that she has accepted stereotypes of gay women. While Angela and Sheila will not deny or forsake their relationship, they are, nevertheless, negatively affected by these constructions of Black female sexuality. "They never said what they were doing. They just did it. . . . They never said, *This is a family. We are each other's loves. We belong with these other women we've been hearing about, these lesbians.*"[59] Only Tamara—and the third-person narrative voice that calls them "lovers"—moves beyond that silencing and secrecy to an avowal of their lesbianism.

What I am calling a "sexual aesthetics" in Southgate's novel grounds itself firmly in moments that are deeply significant for African American history and culture, such as the Tulsa riots, the blaxploitation era in Hollywood, and the increasing presence of Black filmmakers in the 1990s. This aesthetics performs a claiming of citizenship generally for African Americans and specifically for Black women, as evidenced in Mildred's painting and Tamara's documentary filmmaking.[60] Both women's creations challenge and then fill the "lexical gaps" related to Black women's sexualities, what critic Hortense Spillers describes as "interstices," missing words.[61]

Tamara's film about the generations of women in her family, "Dreamland," serves an iconographic purpose in challenging the dominant culture's stereotypes and symbology, undermining and erasing them and offering a Black female-centered vision. She performs what Spillers calls for in the context of music, which in Southgate's text appears instead in the medium of film: "the black woman must translate the female vocalist's gestures into an apposite structure of terms that will articulate both her kinship to other women and the particular nuances of her own experience."[62]

Tamara's film begins with her own voice: "'My mother raised me in Los Angeles with her lover, who was an actress too. My mother has never called herself a lesbian, even though she's made a life with this woman for nearly thirty years, and they love each other very much. . . . She gave me so little history. She had a hard time with the truth.'"[63] Tamara offers the truth in "Dreamland." And at the heart of that truth, "there's a power here, a power that can't be denied. As you look at our beautiful, beautiful faces, there's no getting around it. There is something there that can't be denied."[64] Indeed, these women have moved from self-denial, repression, shame, and fear to an embrace of the full narrative of their individual and collective lives, delivering themselves and each other from pain and trauma while tapping into the erotic as inner resource.

Collectively, these narratives offer crucial insights into Black female sexuality, revealing trauma located in legacies of U.S. history and ultimately performing a celebration of healing uses of the erotic. In 1950s Oklahoma and 1960s small-town Texas, salvation may still appear to lie in conventional, bourgeois standards, anchored in heterosexual marriage and family. While Dill is not completely successful at integrating and accepting all aspects of herself, she does offer an alternative that might destabilize the assumptions and definitions surrounding gender and sexuality in her adoptive community. Moreover, she has modeled ways to challenge binaries, though lacking the lesbian community and affective connections that might nurture her and allow her to find deliverance.

Even in Los Angeles in the 1980s and 1990s, Angela and Sheila have difficulty accessing the power of the erotic on their own: they need the encouragement and creative vision of Tamara with her camera and insights into their relationship, as well as the knowledge of Mildred's past, to find true deliverance. On the other hand, in both Georgia in the early 1970s and Ohio in the 1990s, young Black women experience sexual liberation and healing through their connection with same-gender-loving aunts who can model for them the healthy and freeing power of the erotic. As seen in the relationships between Mariah and her aunts, Po and Aunt Florida, and especially in the concluding scene in *Third Girl from the Left*, Black women embody creativity and love when they embrace the erotic in themselves and in each other. In these contemporary texts by black women, the protagonists deliver themselves and others from bonds of self-negation and numbing traumas as they celebrate and voice myriad sexualities that demand affirmation. Again in Lorde's powerful, provocative words, the "erotic is the nurturer or nursemaid of all our deepest knowledge."[65]

Notes

1. Martha Southgate, *Third Girl from the Left* (New York: Houghton Mifflin, 2005), 268; Marci Blackman, *Po Man's Child* (San Francisco: Manic D Press, 1999), 234. On the need for a context for Black lesbian characters and the disappearance of communities for Black lesbian writers, see Jewelle Gomez, "But Some of Us Are Brave Lesbians: The Absence of Black Lesbian Fiction," in *Black Queer Studies: A Critical Anthology*, ed. E. Patrick Johnson and Mae G. Henderson (Durham, N.C.: Duke University Press, 2005), 190. The texts I include in this study do not depict such a context or community, though taken together they offer a vision of an imagined community that might begin to fill the gap.

2. See Jafari Allen, "Blackness, Sexuality, and Transnational Desire: Initial Notes toward a New Research Agenda," in *Black Sexualities: Probing Powers, Passions, Practices, and Policies*, ed. Juan Battle and Sandra L. Barnes (New Brunswick, N.J.: Rutgers University Press, 2010), 82–96. Allen also notes that Martin Manalansan "contends that newer work is beginning to recognize sexuality's constitutive role in formation and definition of citizenship and nation" (83).

3. Cited in Mignon R. Moore, *Invisible Families: Gay Identities, Relationships, and Motherhood among Black Women* (Berkeley: University of California Press, 2011), 11.

4. Audre Lorde, "The Uses of the Erotic: The Erotic as Power," in Lorde, *Sister Outsider* (Freedom, Calif.: The Crossing Press, 1984), 57. The erotic helps us overcome fear and stasis and find self-respect, honor, and completeness instead.

5. On the term "same-gender loving," which I employ for some of the relationships discussed here, see Trimiko C. Melancon, "Toward an Aesthetic of Transgression: Ann Allen Shockley's *Loving Her* and the Politics of Same-Gender Loving," *African American Review* 42, nos. 3–4 (2008), esp. 643–646.

6. This novel is told in brief first-person segments by a fairly large cast of characters, speaking of both the present moment and incidents in the past, such that the information we receive is biased and often incomplete. Parks has established a hugely successful career as playwright, so perhaps it is not surprising that her first and only novel employs dramatic elements and techniques in its narrative structure.

7. Suzan-Lori Parks, *Getting Mother's Body* (New York: Random House, 2003), 37.

8. Lorde, "The Uses of the Erotic," 58.

9. On the "salvific wish," see Candice M. Jenkins, *Private Lives, Proper Relations: Regulating Black Intimacy* (Minneapolis: University of Minnesota Press, 2007). She defines this

"wish" as "a black, largely female, and generally middle-class desire—a longing to protect or save black women, and black communities more generally, from narratives of sexual and family pathology, through the embrace of conventional bourgeois propriety in the arenas of sexuality and domesticity" (14).

10. Parks, *Getting Mother's Body*, 57.

11. See Moore, *Invisible Families*, esp. 23–36. She states: "When straight-up gay women form families, their patterns of mate selection are strongly based on gender presentation: they actively seek out gender complementarity in a partner. They seek partners who look feminine, and they also tend to enter motherhood through routes other than heterosexual intercourse, such as adoption or partnering with a woman who already has children" (36).

12. Parks, *Getting Mother's Body*, 89.

13. Ibid., 90.

14. See Laura Wright, "Casting the Bones of Willa Mae Beede: Passing and Performativity in Suzan-Lori Parks's *Getting Mother's Body*," *Tulsa Studies in Women's Literature* 30, no. 1 (2011): 141–157. Wright briefly discusses Dill's sexuality, though she focuses more on Dill's relationship with Willa Mae in the context of the latter's passing for white and what Wright reads as a signifying on Faulkner's *As I Lay Dying*. Drawing upon Judith Halberstam, Wright states that "Dill's masculinity is her identity, not an attempt to mask identity. . . . Despite her status as biologically female, within the context of Parks's novel, Dill's gender identity remains somewhat fluid and unfixed" (153). I am arguing that although Dill has the potential for such an expression of gender fluidity, she remains constricted by shame and trauma, in a state of self-abnegation and melancholia at the end of the novel.

15. Parks, *Getting Mother's Body*, 34.

16. Ibid., 37.

17. Ibid., 89.

18. Ibid., 90.

19. Ibid., 140, italics in original.

20. Ibid., 224.

21. Ibid., 241.

22. Ibid., 155.

23. Ibid., 192.

24. Ibid., 244.

25. L. H. Stallings, *Mutha' Is Half a Word: Intersections of Folklore, Vernacular, Myth, and Queerness in Black Female Culture* (Columbus: Ohio State University Press, 2007), 24. Invoking Audre Lorde as such a trickster, Stallings discusses "unnaming": "Once the categories of gender are dismissed, sexual desire no longer has to properly align with any particular sex. By being unnameable, we can sustain control over the deferment of gender, explore individual sexual desires, and become equipped with a mother tongue to discuss our subjectivity" (79). The character of Dill, however, remains too entrenched in the categories of gender to be able to move to this kind of freedom and empowerment.

26. Shay Youngblood, *Soul Kiss* (New York: Riverhead, 1997), 7.

27. Ibid., 41.

28. Ibid., 106.

29. Ibid., 182–183.

30. Ibid., 113.

31. Ibid., 119. On Black women and a history of rape in the United States, see Patricia Hill Collins, *Black Sexual Politics: African Americans, Gender, and the New Racism* (New York: Routledge, 2006), 224–232.

32. Youngblood, *Soul Kiss*, 161.

33. Ibid., 121.

34. Ibid., 180.

35. Ibid., 184.

36. Debra Riggin Waugh, "Delicious, Forbidden: An Interview with Shay Youngblood," *Lambda Book Report* 6, no. 2 (1997): 7.

37. Youngblood, *Soul Kiss*, 204.

38. Ibid., 206.

39. Blackman, *Po Man's Child*, 15.

40. Ibid., 9.

41. Ibid., 19.

42. Ibid., 82.

43. Ibid., 84.

44. Ibid., 54.

45. Ibid., 224.

46. Ibid., 19.

47. Ibid., 52.

48. Ibid., 212, italics in original.

49. Ibid., 214, italics in original.

50. Ibid., 234.

51. Southgate, *Third Girl from the Left*, 268.

52. See Evelynn M. Hammonds, "Toward a Genealogy of Black Female Sexuality: The Problematic of Silence," in *Feminist Genealogies, Colonial Legacies, Democratic Futures*, ed. M. Jacqui Alexander and Chandra Talpade Mohanty (New York: Routledge, 1997). Hammonds states: "Black women's sexuality is often described in metaphors of speechlessness, space, or vision; as a 'void' or empty space that is simultaneously ever-visible (exposed) and invisible, where black women's bodies are always already colonized" (171).

53. Southgate, *Third Girl from the Left*, 129.

54. Ibid., 176.

55. For an extended analysis of this role of aesthetics, see Caroline Brown, *The Black Female Body in American Literature and Art: Performing Identity* (Hoboken, N.J.: Taylor and Francis, 2011), chapter 5, esp. 171–187.

56. Discussing homophobia shaped in response to racism, Hammonds looks at women who are "outsiders" in Black communities: "If we accept the existence of the 'politics of silence' as an historical legacy shared by all black women, then certain expressions of black female sexuality will be rendered as dangerous, for individuals and for the collectivity" (181).

57. On hetero-identified lesbians, see Moore, *Invisible Families*, 49–53, esp. 53.

58. Southgate, *Third Girl from the Left*, 44.

59. Ibid., 206, italics in original.

60. On the blaxploitation films and their contributions to African American culture and pride, see Isaac Julien's documentary *BaadAsssss Cinema*, which Southgate credits in her "Author's Note."

61. "The absence of distinguishing terms is solidly grounded in the negative aspects of symbol-making. The latter, in turn, are wed to the abuses and uses of history, and how it is perceived. The missing word—the interstice—both as that which allows us to speak about and that which enables us to speak at all—shares, in this case, a common border with another country of symbols—the iconographic." Hortense Spillers, "Interstices: A

Small Drama of Words," in *Pleasure and Danger: Exploring Female Sexuality,* ed. Carole S. Vance (London: Pandora, 1992), 77.

 62. Ibid., 88.

 63. Southgate, *Third Girl from the Left,* 267.

 64. Ibid., 268.

 65. Lorde, "The Uses of the Erotic," 56.

CHAPTER 12

Saving Me through Erasure?

BLACK WOMEN, HIV/AIDS, AND RESPECTABILITY

Ayana K. Weekley

The "down low" has garnered much attention in the past decade of the HIV/AIDS epidemic in the United States.[1] Conversations about men on the down low (DL) have appeared in various media outlets: in the *New York Times,* on the Oprah Winfrey show, and in infamous books such as J. L. King's *On the Down Low: A Journey into the Lives of "Straight" Black Men Who Sleep with Men.* Each of these has illustrated the complicated nature of discourses on the down low: it relates not only to race, gender, sexuality, and HIV/AIDS in black communities but also to understandings of the nexus of sexual identities and sexual behaviors. Furthermore, down-low discourses contain many widely accepted beliefs and assumptions about the HIV/AIDS epidemic, such as, for instance, that bisexual men serve as "bridges" for HIV from gay men to heterosexual women. This claim, however, remains largely unsubstantiated.[2] Because of the complexity of the racialized and gendered claims of DL discourses, they demand a critical analysis.

Drawing on black feminist theories and critiques of the politics of race, gender, and sexuality, this essay examines the 2007 film *Cover* to not only pay critical attention to down-low discourses but also, importantly, argue that we need to be as attentive to black women within these discourses. It is through black women and particular characterizations of black womanhood that down-low discourses and, in turn, DL men have been constructed. I argue that down-low discourses have relied on particular constructions of black womanhood and black female sexuality, largely focusing on married women living within the constraining respectability of black middle-class life.

In both popular and academic discourses, how down-low men define and/or identify themselves or other men as DL is widely varied and context specific. The most general understanding is that men on the DL are "men who have sex with men and women" (MSMW) and do not disclose this behavior to their female partners. Yet this broad definition leaves many questions unanswered. Do men on the down low, for instance, identify as heterosexual, bisexual, gay, or only as DL? Must they have a female partner to be on the DL? Or could they be DL simply by not disclosing some aspect of their sexual behavior, however clandestine, to their friends and family? Clearly, defining the down low raises many questions about the nexus of sexual identity and sexual behavior.

Even though the down-low phenomenon defies easy or simplistic categorization, I want to outline some the key features of down-low discourses. First, the down low has been discussed as both a racialized sexual identity and as a lack of contemporary gay identity. In the mid-2000s, for instance, when DL discourses were at their height, the down-low phenomenon was discussed as primarily, if not exclusively, a black male endeavor. Moreover, the arguments were that black men on the DL were less likely than other men to identify as gay. The DL was discussed both as its own identity and as a way to describe men who did not identify as gay.[3] Second, and perhaps most importantly for the context of my examination in this article, the claim was that black DL men were not only the conduits or bridges for the transmission of HIV from gay or bisexual males to black women, but also were responsible for the disproportionately high rates of black women with HIV in the United States.[4]

The increased concern about HIV transmission from MSMW to women was, in part, a result of the release of new studies that reported at least three important and related findings: first, the rate of HIV in young black men who have sex with men was higher than expected; second, several of the men in the study self-identified as heterosexual; and, third, some men in the study reported having both male and female sexual partners.[5] Questions about what these research findings meant for HIV prevention for young men who have sex with men and what the results meant for women, particularly black women, were at the forefront of discussions about the HIV/AIDS epidemic in the mid-2000s. This is the context for *Cover* and the dynamics to which it was responding in its 2007 release.

To be sure, the down-low phenomenon has been heavily critiqued and, at times, shrouded in myths. In 2009, the Centers for Disease Control and Prevention (CDC) refuted the notion that black men on the DL were transmitting HIV/AIDS to their black female partners.[6] In this essay I analyze down-low discourses that circulated in the early to mid-2000s. Despite the critiques and discrediting of theories about DL men, these discourses continue to circulate and are still a part of the cultural lexicon for discussing black sexualities even in the contemporary moment.

The increased concern for black women in the HIV/AIDS epidemic is critical and noteworthy, in part, because by the mid-2000s, it had long been established that black women and men sustained disproportionately high rates of those with HIV/AIDS in the United States.[7] Feminists such as Evelynn Hammonds have argued that within the larger category of women, black women have been made both invisible and hypervisible in the HIV/AIDS epidemic.[8] Since the early 1980s, feminists have highlighted the inattention to and neglect of women in the discourses around HIV/AIDS, especially since the epidemic was initially defined and understood as a gay man's disease. Women quickly became invisible in both medical and popular discourses about HIV/AIDS.[9] As the epidemic progressed, however, it became clear that women were being diagnosed with HIV/AIDS in significant numbers and that, within those numbers, black women were disproportionately represented. The disparate number of black women living with HIV/AIDS has long been ignored because women generally were marginalized within both medical and popular discourses, including media news coverage of HIV/AIDS. However, black women became hypervisible in the epidemic because they were labeled as particularly dangerous vectors of transmission to black men and children. The explanations that were given for their disproportionate rate were their purported drug use and/or their putatively uncontrollable sexuality.[10]

The construction of black women within the HIV/AIDS epidemic has been far from simple and not without problems as they moved from invisibility to being labeled as conduits for HIV transmission. In the context of the down low, however, black women are framed as the unwitting victims of black men's duplicitous behavior. This framing of black women as victims and black men as threats in down-low discourses is the particular racialized and sexualized morass I explore. To illustrate, in this essay, I provide an analysis of director Bill Duke's film *Cover*, which tells the story of Valerie and Dutch, a married couple beginning a new chapter of their life after their recent move to Philadelphia. While they are portrayed as an ideal couple—Dutch is a successful psychiatrist and Valerie is the good sorority girl, an alumna of Spelman College, and a rising photographer—Dutch is on the down low, unbeknown to Valerie. As the film unfolds, the viewer watches Valerie slowly realize there is a problem in her marriage. Finally, she walks in on her husband and his male friend during a sexual encounter in a hotel room shower. The film then shifts the focus to her ways of dealing with the repercussions of this revelation. The analysis that follows explicates how the women in the film are framed and how the narrative contextualizes their actions in relation to the down low.

Many theorists have written about the various types of black nationalisms that circulate in black U.S. politics and how they shape political discourses. I am specifically interested in black feminist critiques of the ways black nationalisms are deeply gendered discourses that often relegate black women to the margins of black communities while ignoring their contributions or dictating the boundaries of acceptable behaviors.[11] I argue that *Cover* embraces what Wahneema Lubiano identifies as "common sense black nationalisms" that support heteronormative black respectability. As Lubiano argues, black nationalisms, broadly defined, constitute a plethora of beliefs and practices that black Americans have

produced to articulate a past and present in relation to racism and marginalization in the United States. Black nationalisms are ways of producing visions and
politics that not only help unify black Americans but also aid in the creation of
campaigns to petition the nation-state for rights and better conditions. As such,
black nationalisms are closely tied to a politics of respectability that, as black
feminists assert, construct black womanhood based on middle-class ideals of
femininity, religious virtue, and sexual chasteness. The politics of respectability
is deeply gendered in its reliance on the behavior of black women. Like black
nationalisms, respectability politics emphasizes the advancement of African
American communities and the protection of black women from the racist and
sexist violence perpetrated against them.[12]

Lubiano has critiqued black nationalisms and respectabilities, illustrating that
black nationalisms have become widely accepted and are often seductive because
they offer a vision of black community uplift and progress that is both desired and
difficult to refute. However, the path to racial advancement is often paved with
the exclusion of certain subjects, particularly those who thwart visions of heteronormative black communities, including nonconformist women, feminists,
and LGBT people. While my focus is on the women in down-low discourses, it is
important to note that DL men fall outside the boundaries of heteronormative
sexuality and are certainly marginalized in these black nationalist discourses. It is
imperative that we attend to how down-low discourses frame gender and sexuality for both women and men in terms of respectability if we are to resist the
sexist and heteronormative solutions that are often presented for the down low
and the HIV/AIDS epidemic. We need to examine which women are centered in
these discourses and used to galvanize narratives of responsibility and protection
and which women these narratives exclude. On either side of this dichotomy,
black women are constrained by representations of black female respectability
that down-low discourses that malign black down-low men require.

THE FRAMING OF COVER

As the film opens, viewers meet Valerie as she is pulled into a police interrogation room, while also learning that someone has been murdered and Valerie is
the lead suspect. Once in the interrogation room, Valerie recounts her side of the
story. Most of the film is a series of flashbacks as Valerie explains how she came
to be in this room accused of murder. As a murder mystery, it is clear from the
onset of the film that this is a tale of crime and betrayal. The audience is primed
to think of this narrative in terms of guilt and innocence. Who do we think is
innocent? Who is guilty? Is Valerie guilty or was she framed? The introduction
sets up the "who-do-it" murder mystery that structures the entire film.

Cover attempts to disentangle the who, the why, and the how of both the murder and the down-low phenomenon. Even as the film opens by foregrounding a

woman who is central to the narrative, it is black men on the down low who pose the primary problem the film seeks to uncover and resolve. One solution that is discussed several times in the film is getting DL men to "come out." However, getting men to come out or disclose their sexual behaviors is clearly not an easy task, especially since the down-low phenomenon illuminates the complexity of sexual identities and how DL men situate themselves along a continuum of sexualities. While the film does not provide clear answers on this topic, it includes a multiplicity of voices and views that range from the politics of responsibility and intolerance to themes of tolerance, arguing that if we want black men to come out, the black community and society at large must create an environment of acceptance. This is not a message of open acceptance but one of minimum tolerance for the sake of saving black women.[13]

The second solution is encouraging black female respectability as a way to save black women and communities. Women who do not adhere to middle-class respectability make it difficult, if not impossible, to frame black women as victims in down-low discourses. In order to support a framework that simultaneously protects black women from DL men and blames these men for purportedly bringing HIV to black women, the narrative needs the right kind of black women: so-called good women who ascribe to the tenets of black middle-class respectability. Ideally these women are church-going Christian women who not only put God and their families first but also conform to established gender roles that position black men as leaders in their families and communities. These women cannot be promiscuous or adulterous because they should not have any other transparent reason for contracting HIV. *Cover* provides, then, representations of two kinds of women: those enveloped in respectability and identified as the black women who deserve protection, and those who are not redeemable and are ostracized for their indiscretions. Women beyond reproach who exemplify the tenets of respectability are necessary, and indeed requisite, to both animate and reify the claims of down-low discourses.

Valerie

Valerie has moved north to Philadelphia to support Dutch's career, leaving her job and putting her own life and career on hold. She is a God-fearing woman who attends church regularly with her family and immediately gets involved with the women's support group in her new church home. The church is the center of Valerie's life and of the lives of many of the women and men in the film. It is where the women go to discuss partner infidelity, homosexuality, and the down low with other women, and it is where they turn for support and friendship.

Religion is woven throughout the narrative and is a central lens through which Valerie and the other women approach the issues of infidelity. After Valerie uncovers the truth about her husband's deceptive sexual behavior, she cannot understand why this has happened to her, a deeply Christian woman; although she is a devout believer, her faith is shaken, and it is too much for even her to bear. She begins drinking and does not leave her bedroom. When her pastor and his wife visit to provide support and intervention, Valerie asserts,

> I have been everything God asked me to be. I have been a good wife. I have been a good mother. Every Sunday I make sure I'm in somebody's church and I take my family with me. I saved myself for my husband. I saved my body for my husband. I have never ever thought about cheating on him and I did these things not only because I loved Dutch, but because I loved God.

Dutch's secrecy and betrayal are cast as acts that not only betrayed Valerie but that also made her question the entirety of her life, her core beliefs, and her devotion to God. The thing she did not know she should fear and be on watch for—her husband's sexual intimacy with men—blindsided her, rattling her to her core. The down low is thus cast as a consumer of lives: it ends Valerie's marriage and family as she knew it, while momentarily shattering her faith. From her perspective she has done everything right, meaning that she has followed the rules of respectability as outlined by her faith and the church. In part, Valerie is distraught because her adherence to a politics of respectability and organized religion did not save her from this fate. Now she must grapple with that reality.

Living as a "good" woman did not protect Valerie from her husband's infidelity and thus prompts a reflection on the efficacy of a politics of respectability. As black feminists have argued, respectability has rarely served black women well. Respectability did not result in more protection for black women from sexual violence, it did not end stereotypes of black female sexual excess, and it did not lift black women and their families out of poverty.[14] The normative discourse of respectability must be challenged for the ways it has policed black women's behavior.[15] Valerie's experience in *Cover* not only animates these issues but might also be read as a challenge to respectability. However, she is not the only woman affected by the DL in the film. Two other women, Monica and Charlotte, are directly impacted by men on the down low in the film, and their stories are diametrically opposed to Valerie's. I will focus primarily on Monica, however, because, next to Valerie, she receives the most attention in the film about the issue of women with partners on the DL. Analyzing these women's experiences in tandem produces a very different narrative framing, one that illuminates the regulatory discourses governing black women's gendered and sexual choices at work in the film.

Monica

Unlike Valerie, Monica not only knew her husband was on the down low but entered into the arrangement willingly. Her awareness of her husband Kevin's sexual proclivities raises another set of complex questions about the down low. Is her husband really down low? If he is, who is the audience he is deceiving with his behavior since it is not his wife? These attributes and questions make this DL narrative very different from the ones we have most often been presented with in popular discourse. While the audience does not get full insight into Monica's choices about her marriage, we do know she is very aware of his sexual behavior and that she has come to find their arrangement untenable. By the end of the film she has suffered a nervous breakdown and attempted suicide. Why, one might ask, is she framed so differently from Valerie?

Monica serves as a foil to Valerie. She highlights the different choices and compromises they have made. Monica, who has never associated herself with the church or religion (institutionalized or otherwise), has entered into a marriage of convenience, yet she has later become unhappy with the arrangement. She openly seduces Dutch, illustrating the inadequacy of her marriage and her unfulfilled desire. In addition, she does not have children, another way that she has not achieved the heteronormative ideal of the nuclear family. Yet Monica's desire for children and the reality that her arrangement with Kevin will not produce them are reasons for her discontent.

Beyond what she does not have in comparison to Valerie, Monica is punished for her participation in the deception. She is held accountable not only for marrying Kevin (even as she is fully aware of his sexual preference for men) but for also providing him with public "cover" that conceals, and by extension both validates and approves, his sexual behavior outside the heteronormative paradigm. Besides the three men in the film who are on the down low, Monica is the only other person in the film who is fully aware of all their sexual behaviors. However, she says nothing. She does not disclose the men's secrets to Valerie or other women with whom they are sexually involved. She participates in the silence and the secrecy, hence the punitive measures.

In a narrative that is looking for perpetrators—not only of a murder but also the culprits who are responsible for the ruin of black women and families and the spread of HIV/AIDS—Monica is treated as anything but innocent. Her silence and complicity contribute not only to her own pain but also that of all of the women in the film, and she is punished for it. The film implies that if Monica were dedicated to ensuring the well-being of black women, families, and communities, she would not have aided the down-low men or entered into a marriage that concealed down-low behavior. Monica is not a victim of the down low as it has been popularly or customarily constructed, but she is culpable for her assistance with and acquiescence in the down-low behavior of her husband and other men.

The collapse of Monica's personal life and sanity is attributed to her lifestyle choices. Monica, who had more information about her partner than any of the other woman in the film, could have been portrayed as the women with the most stability and choices related to her desires, yet in *Cover* she is ultimately punished the most vehemently. By the close of the film, her relationship is essentially over, she is suicidal and engages in self-harm by cutting herself, and she abuses alcohol and drugs. In fact, after a scene where she shows up—self-medicated, incoherent, and with visible cuts—at Valerie and Dutch's home while wielding a gun (requesting that Valerie pull the trigger), viewers do not see or hear from/about her again. Are we to believe she cannot recover from this? Or that another suicide attempt was successful? The audience is left to guess her fate. All of the factors that contribute to the down low and the spread of HIV, including silence and complicity, must come to a reckoning in *Cover*.

Two women: Valerie and Monica. One woman was not aware of her husband's infidelity and the other was both aware of and complicit in her husband's sexual choices. Why would the woman who has entered into a relationship knowingly with a man on the DL be the one most destroyed by the breakdown of her marriage? This is difficult to understand, unless we view her in contradistinction to Valerie. Valerie is the woman the film's narrative supports, and of the three women in relationships with men on the down low, she survives and her future is the most promising. Even though she witnesses the demise of her marriage, she is HIV free. Near the end of the film, she leaves Dutch, relocates, and moves on to a successful life elsewhere. Monica, on the other hand, has become obsolete (if not dead), while Charlotte has contracted HIV. Moreover, while things may not be momentarily perfect for Valerie, her faith and commitment to being a good woman ultimately sees her through. In this framework Valerie, unlike Monica, is worthy of our attention, sympathy, and anger on her behalf.

Conclusion: Innocent or Guilty, Victim or Culprit?

As a site for examining and analyzing how down-low discourses operated, *Cover* is provocative and unique. The narrative presents many of the common arguments and claims that circulated in popular down-low discourses that emerged in the mid-2000s. As *Cover* illuminates, down-low discourses that seek to save black women and families by appealing to gender and sexual respectabilities participate in a commonsense black nationalism and politics that continue to define the boundaries of community around those who adhere to the tenets of middle-class respectability. Even when it is done in the name of saving black women, the erasure and silencing of so many who either do not desire to conform or will never be able to do so should give us pause. We must be critical of the ways down-low discourses align themselves with ideologies that proscribe normative gendered and sexual behaviors within black families and communities. Alliances that support the marginalization of gay and bisexual identities and behaviors while placing strictures on the type of black women we should work to save are far from benign. Black women and men in the United States of various identities who participate in myriad sexual and nonsexual behaviors that expose them to HIV have been disproportionately affected by HIV/AIDS since the beginning of the epidemic. Prevention and education should remain the focus when discussing the epidemic with all black Americans, regardless of their sexual behaviors, class, religious affiliation (or the lack thereof), or degree of adherence to tenets of respectability.

That focus on prevention and education is where our attention should remain when examining Duke's *Cover*. While the film does not participate in some of the most reprehensible framings of down-low men as threats to black women and communities, it presents a dichotomous narrative of innocence and guilt that is designed to save certain women and exclude others. To make this compromise work, we have to be willing to disavow many members of the black community. This strategy is focused on those few black women who live their lives within the boundaries of respectability. This should worry us.

It is imperative that we not let down-low discourses wash over us by accepting what seems to be obvious claims that we want black women to be safe, we want to reduce the disproportionate number of black women contracting HIV, and we want to advocate for healthier families and communities. Calls for black Americans to take care of their communities and protect women and families form the basis of many black nationalist sensibilities that appear not only innocuous but as, in fact, the right thing to do.[16] I do not argue that these are undesirable or unworthy goals: quite the contrary. However, *how* we achieve these goals and the precise ways by which we go about doing so matter.

On the surface, the discourse about the down low is about men and the harm they can do to women. However, when we consider the ways that women are characterized in these narratives, it is clear that we should be attentive to how these narratives, in and of themselves, harm black women. Married, middle-class black women ensconced in black respectability are certainly deserving of our sympathy and protection, but so are the many women who have made different choices, as they trouble the simplistic analysis of most down-low discourses. Women who do not confine themselves to respectability make it more difficult for those who construct this discourse to blame men on the down low for the high rate of HIV/AIDS among black women. In this logic, if the women's gendered and/or sexual choices are suspect, how can we blame down-low men entirely for black women's disproportionate presence in the epidemic? Monica's treatment in *Cover* parallels the ways down-low discourses make certain black women disappear. Women who cannot be easily incorporated in the frameworks down-low discourses construct pose a threat to a simplistic narrative whose goal is to assign clear, polarizing labels of innocence and guilt. These erasures and miscategorizations should haunt us all.

Finally, we must consider what happens in an epidemic when we ascribe labels of innocent or guilty, victim or culprit. Constructing HIV as a sexually transmitted virus requires us to think about sex, sexuality, and identity in fluid ways. The facile, oversimplistic labels of the discourses that are currently available have little relationship to the more fluid range of behaviors in which many people engage. Imposing a very strict standard of sexual conduct on black women, as many down-low discourses do, makes it more difficult to have discussions about sexuality, sexual pleasure, and sexual health in all our relationships—married, committed, or not—along a spectrum of sexualities. After more than three decades of this epidemic, we can and must do better than this. Silencing, erasing, and policing black women's bodies in support of commonsense black nationalisms that advocate respectability as a strategy for protection from down-low men not only restrict black women's choices about sexual behavior, but also constitute an ineffectual response to the HIV/AIDS epidemic. But this strategy also reduces and trivializes the entire issue of race, gender, and sexuality for black women and men. We need inclusive conversations and frameworks that center on the needs and desires of black women, breaking the culturally enforced silence and making ourselves fully visible.

NOTES

1. Keith Boykin, *Beyond the Down Low: Sex, Lies, and Denial in Black America* (New York: Carroll & Graf, 2005); David J. Malebranche, "Bisexually Active Black Men in the United States and HIV: Acknowledging More than the 'Down Low,'" *Archives of Sexual Behavior* 37, no. 5 (2008): 810–816; Gregorio Millet, David Malebranche, Byron Mason, and Pilgrim Spikes, "Focusing 'Down Low': Bisexual Black Men, HIV Risk and Heterosexual Transmission," *Journal of the National Medical Association* 97, no. 5 (2005): 810–816.

2. Cathy Cohen, *Boundaries of Blackness: AIDS and the Breakdown of Black Politics* (Chicago: University of Chicago Press, 1999); Paula Treichler, *How to Have Theory in an Epidemic: Cultural Chronicles of AIDS* (Durham, N.C.: Duke University Press, 1999).

3. Carlos Ulises Decena, "Profiles, Compulsory Disclosure and Ethical Sexual Citizenship," *Sexualities* 11, no.4 (2008): 397–413.

4. Malebranche, "Bisexually Active Black Men," 810–816.

5. See ibid.; and Linda Valleroy et al., "HIV Prevalence and Associated Risks in Young Men Who Have Sex with Men," *Journal of the American Medical Association* 284, no. 2 (2000): 198–204.

6. "Myth: HIV/AIDS Rate among Black Women Traced to 'Down Low' Black Men," *NPR*, October 16, 2009, http://www.npr.org/templates/story/story.php?storyId=114237523.

7. Cohen, *Boundaries of Blackness*; Cindy Patton, *Last Served? Gendering the HIV Pandemic* (London: Taylor & Francis, 1994).

8. Evelynn Hammonds, "Missing Persons: African American Women, AIDS and the History of Disease," *Radical America* 20, no. 6 (1986): 7–32; Evelynn Hammonds, "AIDS the Secret, Silent, Suffering Shame," in *Still Brave: The Evolution of Black Women's Studies*, ed. Frances Smith Foster, Beverly Guy-Sheftall, and Stanlie M. James (New York: Feminist Press, 2009), 268–280.

9. Treichler, *How to Have Theory in an Epidemic.*

10. See Hammonds, "Missing Persons."

11. Nikol Alexander-Floyd, *Gender, Race, and Nationalism in Contemporary Black Politics* (Basingstoke: Palgrave Macmillan, 2007); Patricia Hill Collins, *From Black Power to Hip Hop: Racism, Nationalism, and Feminism* (Philadelphia: Temple University Press 2006); Wahneema Lubiano, "Black Nationalism and Black Common Sense: Policing

Ourselves and Others," in *The House That Race Built: Original Essays by Toni Morrison, Angela Y. Davis, Cornel West, and Others on Black American Politics in America Today,* ed. Wahneema Lubiano, 232-252 (New York: Vintage Books, 1998).

12. Darlene Clark Hine, "Rape and the Inner Lives of Black Women in the Middle West," *Signs: Journal of Women and Culture and Society* 14, no. 4 (1989): 912–920; Candice Jenkins, *Private Lives, Proper Relations: Regulating Black Intimacy* (Minneapolis: University of Minnesota Press, 2007); Evelyn Brooks Higginbotham, *Righteous Discontent: The Women's Movement in the Black Baptist Church, 1880–1920* (Cambridge, Mass.: Harvard University Press, 1993).

13. Decena, "Profiles, Compulsory Disclosure and Ethical Sexual Citizenship."

14. Jenkins, *Private Lives, Proper Relations.*

15. Lisa B. Thompson, *Beyond the Black Lady: Sexuality and the New African American Middle Class* (Chicago: University of Illinois Press, 2009).

16. Lubiano, "Black Nationalism and Black Common Sense"; Alexander-Floyd, *Gender, Race, and Nationalism in Contemporary Black Politics*; Collins, *From Black Power to Hip Hop.*

Afterword

Being Present, Facing Forward

Joanne M. Braxton

It has been said that every ending holds a new beginning, so as I approach the afterword of *Black Female Sexualities,* I look back to the beginnings of black feminist criticism in works like Toni Cade Bambara's *The Black Woman* (1970) and the early writings of Audre Lorde, Barbara Christian, Alice Walker and others. I also look forward not only to the panorama of works covered in this volume but to the prophetic imagining of what will shape the discourse of black female sexualities in the twenty-first century and beyond. Simultaneously, I look back to my own entry into public view some time ago, one that was "brave and brisk and bright," as Gwendolyn Brooks wrote in her introduction to my first collection of poems.[1] And I pause to reflect because reflection is often denied to us as we struggle to get ahead in our publish-or-perish world. In moments of reflection, mindfulness, intentionality, and indeed self-determination are born.

I reflect not only on the beginnings of black feminist criticism or my own beginnings but also on the words of lesbian poet and activist Audre Lorde in her introduction to the anthology *Wild Women in the Whirlwind: The Contemporary Renaissance in Afra-American Literature.* Lorde wrote:

> Black women who are our inheritors will need to know why so many of these facts about their Black woman's history are hard to come by. They will need to know that hatred destroys by silence, by trivialization, by the pretense that nothing we have to say is worth anything simply because we are saying it. And of course there is the other side of that erasure so cleverly practiced against Black women and our words by those establishments that presume hierarchy over us: the arrogant assumption that anyone else knows better than we do which of our words should survive.[2]

Lorde named these fallacies of silencing and erasure and pronounced the diverse "spectrum of Black women's words and lives" as a "bulwark" against them.

We who are the inheritors of the Afra-American aesthetic and the tradition of Angelina Grimké, Gwendolyn Brooks, Barbara Christian, June Jordan, and Audre Lorde are still creating it; we have learned the authority of our own voices, our own bodies, and our own movement. The writers represented in *Black Female Sexualities* speak bravely, with brisk bright words that name and deconstruct the dehumanizing hierarchies and fallacies that would presume and delineate our otherness as we continue the Black woman's struggle for humanity, wholeness, and joy—and extend it into the future for those who become our inheritors. And we want more for them than struggle and perhaps even more than knowledge: we want the inner assurance that comes with self-naming and self-definition, as well as the fullest measure of human sustainability, resiliency, and joy.[3] So this is my starting point as I begin to shape these words of summation, the words that come after but look forward—the hope that this book will present a framework for intellectual activism and resiliency-based organizing not only for our time but for future generations of black women.

HEALING

In January 2012, I went to see Dee Rees's film *Pariah*. Moved by the depth of the film and its toughness, I was drawn in by an authenticity that goes all the way to the bone. I mark the observation of that authenticity and its needfulness as a through line that extends all the way back to Belinda's "The Cruelty of Men Whose Faces Were Like the Moon" through Audre Lorde and Ntozake Shange to the women in this volume and on to some seventh-generation future black woman—who has yet to be born—and everything that she will give birth to, create, invent, or imagine.

For the many who have found their coming-of-age story to be mingled with their coming-out story, *Pariah* is indeed a liberation narrative. And not for simple reasons either. The intellectual and spiritual resources of the Afra-American aesthetic are not easily found by the young black women who need them the most. Rees's producer, Nekesia Cooper, had attended the historically white university where I teach and I wondered why she had not taken any classes from me. But there was something in the élan of the film, in its very infectious grittiness and the way each character seemed to speak for so many others, and something about the very communal spirit of the film that reminded me of the early read-through of Ntozake Shange's *For Colored Girls Who Have Considered Suicide When the Rainbow Is Enuf* at the African American Cultural Center at Yale, back when Ntozake's sister Bisa was a student there and their cousin Khalid (Eric Lum) was director of the Center. This was the same place where many of us attended The Black Church at Yale and the spirit was one of ingathering.

People came in not only to testify but also to witness, and not only to witness but also to testify.

In all of the early productions of *For Colored Girls Who Have Considered Suicide When the Rainbow Is Enuf*, when the piece reached its crescendo in the final poem, "A Laying on of Hands," there was some healing going on. So it is no surprise to me that when I visited the official Web site of *Pariah*, the first thing that met my eyes was "Dee Rees Wants Your Story," and I felt welcome. The cast and crew also tell their stories, and one, Pernell Walker, who plays Laura in the film, reflects on the importance of the influence of Shange's original choreopoem: "What also struck me about [Shange's] play is how empowering it was for me to learn about a play created by a woman of color and which had an all female cast who were each expressing their own human needs in unique, dynamic and ethnically diverse choreopoems."[4] One of the gifts of Zake's genius in these early productions of *For Colored Girls Who Have Considered Suicide When the Rainbow Is Enuf* was the very particularity of the piece and the way it assumed diverse voices and yet shone through as something uniquely black and female, while aesthetically powerful and universal. It was a universal story told through a unique and particular point of view; and it was authentic ritual drama, drama that does the work of healing.

So whenever I teach *For Colored Girls Who Have Considered Suicide When the Rainbow Is Enuf*, I teach the whole title because I have known too many colored girls who have killed themselves because their lives had taken them to the place where nothing was enough. But as Alyson Williams sang at the homegoing service of Dr. Maya Angelou, "God put a rainbow in the clouds" for those times when it feels like the sun will never shine again.[5] The colored girl who lives to find the rainbow is not a colored girl or any other kind of girl anymore. She is a woman, full, and she has earned the right to name her own experience. She has earned the right to say yes to struggle and simultaneously to say yes to life. This is why Ntozake Shange's play tells the black woman that god is within herself, and that this god is to be loved "fiercely." So whenever I teach the written play and I want to show a clip, it never occurs to me to use any version other than the one made by Shange herself, the early film where she opens the piece by sitting at her typewriter with her hair in two braids while writing the words, "And this is for Colored Girls Who Have Considered Suicide When the Rainbow Is Enuf." Not only the title but also the dramaturgy is important. The audience needs the implied subtitle "Written by Herself," a postmodern late-capitalist gloss on the liberation trope of the slave narrative, and only when the author is in control of her/his/their narrative does authorial freedom truly reign.

Subsequent film productions of Shange's choreopoem lack this initial framing and authenticating structure. In these productions, a multitude of black female voices is present, but the original authorial intent becomes obfuscated and the deep-rooted healing impulse flies away and waits to be reborn in *Pariah*. Part of the through line is healing, too, along with self-authentication and a deep-rooted autobiographical need to tell one's own story in one's own words, to "tell it like it is" and not as defined by someone else's—anyone else's—stereotype. The problem is that stereotypes sell, and they can be massaged and manipulated so that the majority—however that majority is defined—feels good. And even black folks can fall into the embrace of the stereotype so that young black girls have been sent home even from black schools with negative comments about their natural hair and the internalized message that "ain't nothing black pretty." But stories heal, especially stories like *Pariah*, an aesthetic laying on of hands.

Reflecting on what kind of course I would have had to offer at the College of William and Mary for Nekesia Cooper to find and take it, I created "Identity and Sexuality in African American Literature" and engaged the students in the topics and themes addressed in this book. This course became the container or lens through which I continued conversations with my co-editor and the authors of the essays in *Black Female Sexualities*. I was looking for the next Nekesia Cooper. The class watched films and read not only black feminist writers, theorists, and critics but also the gender-bending works of men like James Baldwin, Rudolph Byrd, Essex Hemphill, Marlon Riggs, E. Patrick Johnson, and Matt Richardson. It was Baldwin who wrote prophetically long ago, "There is a man in every woman and a woman in every man. . . . Love between a man and a woman, or love between any two human beings, would not be possible did we not have the spiritual resources of both sexes. . . . The human being, in general does not like being intimidated by what he/she finds in the mirror."[6] Even today these words represent a truth-telling that many do not wish to hear.

Whoever we are, we black women have *earned* the right to tell our own stories. In reading the manuscripts that would become this book together with the assigned readings for "Identity and Sexuality," I learned from my students as well as other sources. Ari Pak taught me "an approach used for imagining the futures" borrowed from "a regional queer liberation organization, Southerners on New Ground (SONG)."[7] SONG's approach "starts with the centering of those most marginalized. . . . This visioning process serves to create an imagined reality where people are not only surviving but thriving."[8] "Black female sexuality began its queering trajectory the day black women started telling their stories," wrote Brittany Harrington. "As black women claim the power to tell their own stories and reclaim ownership over their sexual expression, this queering will continue . . . with a velocity that cannot be stopped."[9] These brave new voices, voices like those of the women whose words are represented in this volume, will not be stopped. They will not be destroyed by silence, hatred, trivialization, erasure, or pretense. In such a time as this, a time when young black women are increasingly challenged by the myth of a postracial society, these voices fall on our ears like a laying on of hands.

Many middle-class black folk are still policing the social respectability of young black people when they might be opening the paths to responsible social and personal transformation and joy—not just for themselves but for whole communities of people, female, male, and those in between, who they may not be able to see as being like themselves. *Black Female Sexualities* asks the reader to pause and reflect on the possibilities for humanity, wholeness, and the costs of not living into that vision as a possible future. Let the healing begin.

NOTES

1. Gwendolyn Brooks, "Introduction," in Jodi Braxton, *Sometimes I Think of Maryland* (Bronx, N.Y.: Sunbury Press, 1977), i.

2. Audre Lorde, "Foreword," in *Wild Women in the Whirlwind: Afra-American Culture and the Contemporary Literary Renaissance*, ed. Joanne M. Braxton and Andrée Nicola McLaughlin (New Brunswick, N.J.: Rutgers University Press, 1989), xiii.

3. These goals exemplify the purpose of The Joanne M. Braxton Institute for Human Sustainability, Resiliency and Joy, a not-for-profit corporation. See http://braxton -institute.org.

4. Peter Bowen, "Dee Rees Wants Your Story," Focus Features, November 17, 2011, http:// www.focusfeatures.com/pariah/news?bid=dee_rees_wants_your_story.

5. Gospel hymn by Kenneth Fulkerson, program, "A Celebration of Rising 'Joy'! The Homegoing of Dr. Maya Angelou," Wait Chapel, Wake Forest University, Winston-Salem, North Carolina, June 7, 2014.

6. James Baldwin, "Freaks and the American Ideal of Manhood," in *Collected Essays* (New York: Library of America, 1998), 814.

7. "Vision, Mission, & History," Southerners on New Ground (SONG): Building a Political Home across Race, Class, Gender, Culture, & Sexuality, http://southernersonnewground .org/about/vision-mission-history/.

8. Ari Pak, "Envisioning Futures of Black Female Sexualities," unpublished essay in author's possession; quoted by permission.

9. Brittney Harrington, "A New Generation of Black Women: Popular Entertainers," unpublished essay in author's possession, quoted by permission.

Bibliography

Abbot, Elizabeth. *Haiti: The Duvaliers and Their Legacy.* New York: Simon and Schuster, 1991.

Abdur-Rahman. *Against the Closet: Black Political Longing and the Erotics of Race.* Durham, N.C.: Duke University Press, 2012.

Alberta Hunter: My Castle's Rockin'. DVD. Dir. Stuart Goldman. New York: V.I.E.W. Video, 1992.

Allen, Jafari. "Blackness, Sexuality, and Transnational Desire: Initial Notes toward a New Research Agenda." In *Black Sexualities: Probing Powers, Passions, Practices, and Policies,* edited by Juan Battle and Sandra L. Barnes, 82–96. New Brunswick, N.J.: Rutgers University Press, 2010.

Alexander, Brian. "Marriage Eludes High-Achieving Black Women." *MSNBC,* August 13, 2009. http://www.msnbc.msn.com/id/32379727/ns/health-sexual_health/t/marriage-eludes -high-achieving-Black-women/. Accessed November 4, 2009.

Alexander, Bryant Keith. "Embracing the Teachable Moment: The Black Gay Body in the Classroom as Embodied Text." In *Black Queer Studies: A Critical Anthology,* edited by E. Patrick Johnson and Mae G. Henderson, 249–265. Durham, N.C.: Duke University Press, 2005.

Alexander-Floyd, Nikol G. *Gender, Race, and Nationalism in Contemporary Black Politics.* New York: Palgrave Macmillan, 2007.

Althusser, Louis. *Lenin and Philosophy and Other Essays.* New York: Monthly Review Press, 1971.

Anderson, Arnold E., and Andy Hay. "Racial and Socioeconomic Influences in Anorexia Nervosa and Bulimia." *International Journal of Eating Disorders* 4, no. 4 (1985): 479–487.

Anderson, Benedict. *Imagined Communities: Reflections on the Origin and Spread of Nationalism.* London: Verso, 1983.

Arnesen, Eric. "Willard Townsend: Black Workers, Civil Rights, and the Labor Movement." In *Portraits of African American Life Since 1865,* edited by Nina Mjagkij, 147–163. Wilmington, Del.: Scholarly Resources, 2003.

Arnheim, Rudolph. *The Power of the Center: A Study of Composition in the Visual Arts.* Berkeley and Los Angeles: University of California Press, 1988.

"'Awkward Black Girl' Garners Laughs." *NPR,* September 1, 2011. http://www.npr.org/ 2011/09/01/140113809/awkward-Black-girl-garners-laughs. Accessed September 7, 2012.

"'Awkward Black Girl' Web Hit." *CNN,* October 8, 2011. http://www.cnn.com/video/#/ video/living/2011/10/08/whitfield-issa-rae-interview.cnn. Accessed July 22, 2012.

Azoulay, Ariella. *The Civil Contract of Photography*. New York: Zone Books, 2008.

Bailey, Cameron. "Virtual Skin: Articulating Race in Cyberspace." In *Immersed in Technology: Art and Virtual Environments*, edited by Mary Anne Moser and Douglas MacLeod, 29–49. Cambridge: MIT Press, 1996.

Baldwin, James. "Freaks and the American Ideal of Manhood." In *James Baldwin: Collected Essays*, edited by Toni Morrison, 814–829. New York: Library of America, 1998.

Beauboeuf-Lafontant, Tamara. "Strong and Large Black Women? Exploring Relationships between Deviant Womanhood and Weight." *Gender and Society* 17, no. 1 (2003): 111–121.

Bell, Beverly. *Walking on Fire: Haitian Women's Stories of Survival and Resistance*. Ithaca, N.Y.: Cornell University Press, 2001.

Bell, Roseann P., Bettye J. Parker, and Beverly Guy-Sheftall, eds. *Sturdy Black Bridges: Visions of Black Women in Literature*. New York: Anchor, 1979.

Bellegarde-Smith, Patrick. *Haiti: The Breached Citadel*. Boulder: Westview, 1990.

Bhabha, Homi. *The Location of Culture*. New York: Routledge, 1994.

Blackman, Marci. *Po Man's Child*. San Francisco: Manic D Press, 1999.

Bordo, Susan. *Unbearable Weight: Feminism, Western Culture, and the Body*. Berkeley: University of California Press, 2003.

Boykin, Keith. *Beyond the Down Low: Sex, Lies, and Denial in Black America*. New York: Carroll and Graf Publishers, 2005.

Bowen, Peter. "Dee Rees Wants Your Story." Focus Features, November 17, 2011. http://www.focusfeatures.com/pariah/news?bid=dee_rees_wants_your_story.

Braxton, Joanne M. *Black Women Writing Autobiography: A Tradition within a Tradition*. Philadelphia, Pa.: Temple University Press, 1989.

Braxton, Joanne M., and Andrée Nicola McLaughlin, eds. *Wild Women in the Whirlwind: Afra-American Culture and the Contemporary Literary Renaissance*. New Brunswick, N.J.: Rutgers University Press, 1989.

Briggs, Laura. *Reproducing Empire: Race, Sex, Science, and U.S. Imperialism in Puerto Rico*. Berkeley: University of California Press, 2002.

Brown, Caroline. *The Black Female Body in American Literature and Art: Performing Identity*. Hoboken: Taylor and Francis, 2011.

Brown, Kimberly Juanita. "Black Rapture: Sally Hemings, Chica Da Silva, and the Slave Body of Sexual Supremacy." *Women's Studies Quarterly* 35, nos. 1–2 (2007): 45–66.

Browning, Christopher, Tama Leventhal, and Jeanne Brooks-Gunn. "Neighborhood Context and Racial Differences in Early Adolescent Sexual Activity." *Demography* 41, no. 4 (2004): 697–720.

Brueckner, Hannah and Natalie Nitsche. "Opting Out of the Family? Social Change in Racial Equality in Family Formations Patterns and Marriage Outcomes among Highly Educated Women." Paper presented at the annual meeting of the American Sociological Association, San Francisco, California, August 8, 2009.

Burns-Ardolino, Wendy. "Pedagogy of the Big Butt: Classification, Racialization, Sexualization, and Exoticization." In *Florida without Borders: Women at the Intersections of the Local and Global*, edited by Sharon Masters, Judy Hayden and Kim Vaz, 161–168. Newcastle upon Tyne, UK: Cambridge Scholars Publishing, 2008.

Butler, Judith. *Bodies that Matter*. New York: Routledge, 1993.

Butler, Octavia E. *Fledgling*. New York: Warner, 2005.

Cadet, Jean-Robert. *Restavec: From Haitian Slave Child to Middle-Class American*. Austin: University of Texas Press, 1998.

Campos, Paul, Abigail Saguy, Paul Ernsberger, Eric Oliver, and Glenn Gaesser. "The Epidemiology of Overweight and Obesity: Public Health Crisis or Moral Panic?" *International Journal of Epidemiology* 35, no. 1 (2006): 55–60.

Candelario, Ginetta. "Voices from Hispanolia: A *Meridians* Roundtable with Edwidge Danticat, Loida Marita Pérez, Myriam J. A. Chancy, and Nelly Rosario." *Meridians: Feminism, Race, Transnationalism* 5, no. 1 (2004): 69–91.

Carby, Hazel V. *Reconstructing Womanhood: The Emergence of the Afro-American Woman Novelist.* New York: Oxford University Press, 1987.

———. "Policing the Black Woman's Body in an Urban Context." *Critical Inquiry* 18, no. 4 (1992): 738–755.

Carpenter, Laura. "From Girls into Women: Scripts for Sexuality and Romance in *Seventeen* Magazine, 1974–1994." *The Journal of Sex Research* 35, no. 2 (1998): 158–168.

Cavanagh, Shannon E. "The Sexual Debut of Girls in Early Adolescence: The Intersection of Race, Pubertal Timing, and Friendship Group Characteristics." *Journal of Research on Adolescence* 14, no. 3 (2004): 285–312.

Centers for Disease Control and Prevention. "CDC HIV/AIDS Fact Sheet: HIV/AIDS among Women." Revised August 2008. http://www.cdc.gov/hiv/topics/women/resources/factsheets/pdf/women.pdf. Accessed May 21, 2014.

Chancy, Myriam J. A. *Framing Silence: Revolutionary Novels by Haitian Women.* New Brunswick: Rutgers University Press, 1997.

———. *Searching for Safe Spaces: Afro-Caribbean Women Writers in Exile.* Philadelphia, Pa.: Temple University Press, 1997.

Charles, Carolle. "Gender and Politics in Contemporary Haiti: The Duvalierist State, Transnationalism, and the Emergence of a New Feminism (1980–1990)." *Feminist Studies* 21, no. 1 (1994): 135–164.

———. "Popular Imageries of Gender and Sexuality: Poor and Working-Class Haitian Women's Discourses on the Use of Their Bodies." In *The Culture of Gender and Sexuality in the Caribbean,* edited by Linden Lewis, 169–189. Gainesville: University Press of Florida, 2003.

Christian, Aymar Jean. "The Web as Television Reimagined? Online Networks and the Pursuit of Legacy Media." *Journal of Communication Inquiry* 36, no. 4 (2012): 340-356.

Clarke, Cheryl. "The Failure to Transform: Homophobia in the Black Community." In *Home Girls: A Black Feminist Anthology,* edited by Barbara Smith, 197–208. New York: Kitchen Table: Women of Color Press, 1983.

Cleveland, Darrell. *A Long Way to Go: Conversations about Race by African American Faculty and Graduate Students.* New York: Peter Lang Publishing, 2004.

Cohen, Cathy J. *Boundaries of Blackness: AIDS and the Breakdown of Black Politics.* Chicago: University of Chicago Press, 1999.

———. "Deviance as Resistance: A New Research Agenda for the Study of Black Politics." *Du Bois Review* 1, no. 1 (2004): 27–45.

Collins, Patricia Hill. *Black Sexual Politics: African Americans, Gender, and the New Racism.* New York: Routledge, 2004.

———. *Black Feminist Thought: Knowledge, Consciousness, and the Politics of Empowerment.* London: Routledge, 1990.

———. *From Black Power to Hip Hop: Racism, Nationalism, and Feminism.* Philadelphia: Temple University Press, 2006.

———. "Learning from the Outsider Within: Sociological Significance of Black Feminist Thought." In *The Feminist Standpoint Theory Reader,* edited by Sandra Harding, 103–126. New York: Routledge, 2004.

Collins, Patricia Hill, and M. Andersen. *Race, Class, and Gender: An Anthology.* Florence: Wadsworth Publishing, 2006.

Conway, Danielle. "Being All Things to All People: Expectations of and Demands on Women of Color in the Legal Academy." In *From Oppression to Grace: Women of Color and Their Dilemmas within the Academy,* edited by T. R. Berry and Nathalie Mizell, 21–30. Sterling, Va.: Stylus Publishing, 2006.

Cooke, Marvel. "Alberta Hunter Is No Cinderella, But Her Story Is Just About as Romantic." *New York Amsterdam News,* November 5, 1938.

Cover. Directed by Bill Duke. DVD. Beverly Hills, Calif.: 20th Century Fox Home Entertainment, 2007.

Crenshaw, Kimberlé. "Mapping the Margins: Intersectionality, Identity Politics, and Violence against Women of Color." *Stanford Law Review* 43 (1991): 1241–1299.

———. "Demarginalizing the Intersection of Race and Sex: A Black Feminist Critique of Antidiscrimination Doctrine, Feminist Theory and Antiracist Politics." *University of Chicago Legal Forum* (1989): 139–168.

Daniels, Cora. *Ghetto Nation.* New York: Doubleday Broadway Publishing Group, 2007.

Danticat, Edwidge. *Breath, Eyes, Memory.* New York: Vintage, 1998.

———. "We Are Ugly, but We Are Here." *The Caribbean Writer* 10 (1996): 137–141.

Davis, Angela Y. *Blues Legacies and Black Feminism: Gertrude "Ma" Rainey, Bessie Smith, and Billie Holiday.* New York: Vintage Books, 1984.

Decena, Carlos Ulises. "Profiles, Compulsory Disclosure and Ethical Sexual Citizenship in the Contemporary USA." *Sexualities* 11, no. 4 (2008): 397–413.

Delgado, Richard, and Jean Stefancic, eds. *The Derrick Bell Reader.* New York: New York University Press, 2005.

Dill, Bonnie Thornton, and Ruth Enid Zambrana. *Emerging Intersections: Race, Class, and Gender in Theory, Policy, and Practice.* Piscataway, N.J.: Rutgers University Press, 2009.

Di Mauro, Diane, and Carole Joffe. "The Religious Right and the Reshaping of Sexual Policy: An Examination of Reproductive Rights and Sexuality Education." *Sexuality Research & Social Policy* 4, no. 1 (2007): 67–92.

Drew, Emily M. "Pretending to be 'Post-Racial': The Spectacularization of Race in Reality TV's *Survivor.*" *Television & New Media* 12, no. 4 (2011): 326–346.

Dr. Dre. *The Chronic.* CD. Death Row Records. 1992.

Dubey, Madhu. *Signs and Cities: Black Literary Postmodernism.* Chicago: University of Chicago Press, 2003.

Du Bois, W. E. B. *The Souls of Black Folk.* Chicago: McClurg, 1903.

Ducille, Ann. "Blues Notes on Black Sexuality: Sex and the Texts of Jessie Fauset and Nella Larsen." *Journal of the History of Sexuality* 3, no. 3 (1993): 418–444.

Dupuy, Alex. *Haiti in the World Economy: Class, Race, and Underdevelopment since 1700.* Boulder, Co.: Westview, 1989.

Duvivier, Sandra C. "My Body Is My Piece of Land': Female Sexuality, Family, and Capital in Caribbean Texts." *Callaloo* 31, no. 4 (2008): 1104–1121.

———. "(Re)Writing Haiti and Its 'Brave Women' into Existence: Edwidge Danticat and the Concept of *Métissage.*" *MaComère* 6 (2004): 49–56.

Elkins, James. *The Object Stares Back: On the Nature of Seeing.* New York: Mariner Books, 2007.

Eng, Joyce. "Ratings: *Scandal* Shoots to New Highs." *TV Guide,* December 7, 2012. http://www.tvguide.com/News/Ratings-Scandal-Highs-1057354.aspx. Accessed December 9, 2012.

English, Daylanne. *Unnatural Selections: Eugenics in American Modernism and the Harlem Renaissance.* Chapel Hill: University of North Carolina Press, 2004.

Espiritu, Yen L. "Race, Class, and Gender in Asian America." In *Making More Waves: New Writing by Asian American Women,* edited by E. Kim, L. Villanueva, and Asian American Women United of California, 135–141. Boston: Beacon Press, 1997.

Esposito, Jennifer. "What Does Race Have to Do with Ugly Betty? An Analysis of Privilege and Postracial(?) Representations on a Television Sitcom." *Television & New Media* 10, no. 6 (2009): 521–535.

Eugenios, Jillian. "Chatting up Shine Louise Houston." *Curve,* September 20, 2011, http://www.curvemag.com/Curve-Magazine/Web-Articles-2011/Chatting-up-Shine-Louise-Houston/. Accessed March 5, 2012.

Faderman, Lillian. *Odd Girls and Twilight Lovers: A History of Lesbian Life in Twentieth-Century America.* New York: Columbia University Press, 1991.

Farmer, Paul. *The Uses of Haiti.* Monroe, Me.: Common Courage Press, 2003.

Feimster, Crystal. "Ladies and Lynching: The Gendered Discourse of Mob Violence in the New South, 1880–1930." PhD diss., Princeton University, 2000.

———. *Southern Horrors: Women and the Politics of Rape and Lynching*. Cambridge, Mass.: Harvard University Press, 2009.

Fine, Michelle, and Sara I. McClelland. "The Politics of Teen Women's Sexuality: Public Policy and the Adolescent Female Body." *Emory Law Journal* 56 (2007): 993-1038.

Flores, Julia, and Silvia Garcia. "Latina *Testimonios*: A Reflexive, Critical Analysis of a 'Latina Space' at a Predominantly White Campus." *Race, Ethnicity & Education* 12, no. 2 (2009): 155–172.

Flynn, Kristin J., and Marian Fitzgibbon. "Body Images and Obesity Risk among Black Females: A Review of the Literature." *Annals of Behavioral Medicine* 20, no. 1 (1998): 13–24.

Foster, Patricia, ed. *Minding the Body: Women Writers on Body and Soul*. New York: Doubleday, 1994.

Foucault, Michel. *The History of Sexuality, Volume 1: An Introduction*. New York: Random House, 1978.

Francis, Donette. "'Silences Too Horrific to Disturb': Writing Sexual Histories in Edwidge Danticat's *Breath, Eyes, Memory*." *Research in African Literatures* 35, no. 2 (2004): 75–90.

Franco, Judith. "'The More You Look, the Less You Really Know': The Redemption of White Masculinity in Contemporary American and French Cinema." *Cinema Journal* 47, no. 3 (2008): 29–47.

Frisby, Cynthia M. "Does Race Matter? Effects of Idealized Images on African American Women's Perceptions of Body Esteem." *Journal of Black Studies* 34, no. 3 (2004): 323-347.

Future. *Astronaut Status*. Digital Recording. A-1 Recordings/Freebandz. 2012.

Gamson, Joshua, and Dawne Moon. "The Sociology of Sexualities: Queer and Beyond." *Annual Review of Sociology* 30 (2004): 47–64.

Garn, Stanley M., and Joan A. Haskell. "Fat Changes during Adolescence." *Science* 129, no. 3363 (1959): 1615–1616.

Geronimus, Arline T. "Teenage Childbearing and Personal Responsibility: An Alternative View." *Political Science Quarterly* 112, no. 3 (1997): 405–430.

Giddings, Paula. *Ida, a Sword among Lions: Ida B. Wells and the Campaign against Lynching*. New York: Harper Collins, 2008.

Gilbert, Lynn, and Gaylen Moore. "Alberta Hunter." In *Particular Passions: Talks with Women Who Have Shaped Our Times*, 245–253. New York: Clarkson N. Potter, 1981.

Gilman, Sander. "Black Bodies, White Bodies: Toward an Iconography of Female Sexuality in Nineteenth Century Art, Medicine, and Literature." In *Race, Writing, and Difference*, edited by Henry Louis Gates, Jr., 223–261. Chicago: University of Chicago Press, 1986.

Gilmore, Glenda Elizabeth. *Gender and Jim Crow: Women and the Politics of White Supremacy in North Carolina, 1896–1920*. Chapel Hill: University of North Carolina Press, 1996.

Glymph, Thavolia. *Out of the House of Bondage: The Transformation of the Plantation Household*. Cambridge: Cambridge University Press, 2008.

Gomez, Jewelle. "But Some of Us Are Brave Lesbians: The Absence of Black Lesbian Fiction." In *Black Queer Studies: A Critical Anthology*, edited by E. Patrick Johnson and Mae G. Henderson, 289–297. Durham, N.C.: Duke University Press, 2005.

Griffin, Hollis. "Never, Sometimes, Always: The Multiple Temporalities of 'Post-Race' Discourse in Convergence Television Narrative." *Popular Communication* 9, no. 4 (2011): 235–250.

Halberstam, Judith. *Female Masculinity*. Durham, N.C.: Duke University Press, 1998.

Hammonds, Evelynn. "AIDS: The Secret, Silent, Suffering Shame." In *Still Brave: The Evolution of Black Women's Studies*, edited by Stanlie M. James, Frances Smith Foster, and Beverly Guy-Sheftall, 268–280. New York: The Feminist Press at the City University of New York, 2009.

———. "Black (W)holes and the Geometry and Black Female Sexuality." In *African American Literary Theory*, edited by Winston Napier, 482–497. New York: New York University Press, 2000.

———. "Missing Persons: African American Women, AIDS and the History of Disease." *Radical America* 20, no. 6 (1986): 7–32.

———. "Toward a Genealogy of Black Female Sexuality: The Problematic of Silence." In *Feminist Genealogies, Colonial Legacies, Democratic Futures*, edited by M. Jacqui Alexander and Chandra Talpade Mohanty. New York: Routledge, 1997.

Harrington, Brittney. "A New Generation of Black Women: Popular Entertainers." Unpublished essay, College of William and Mary, 2013.

Harris, Laura Alexandra. "Queer Black Feminism: The Pleasure Principle." *Feminist Review* 54 (1996): 3–30.

Harris, Laura, and Elizabeth Crocker, eds. *Femme: Feminists, Lesbians and Bad Girls*. New York: Routledge, 1997.

Harris-Perry, Melissa V. *Sister Citizen: Shame, Stereotypes, and Black Women in America*. New Haven: Yale University Press, 2011.

Harper, Phillip Brian. "The Evidence of Felt Intuition: Minority Experience, Everyday Life, and Critical Speculative Knowledge." *GLQ: A Journal of Lesbian and Gay Studies* 6, no. 4 (2000): 641–657.

Hartman, Saidiya V. *Scenes of Subjection: Terror, Slavery, and Self-Making in Nineteenth-Century America*. New York: Oxford University Press, 1997.

Harvey, Steve. *Act Like a Lady, Think Like a Man: What Men Really Think about Love, Relationships, Intimacy, and Commitment*. New York: Harper Collins, 2009.

Haworth-Hoeppner, Susan. "The Critical Shapes of Body Image: The Role of Culture and Family in the Production of Eating Disorders." *Journal of Marriage and the Family* 62, no. 1 (2000): 212–227.

Henderson, Mae G. "What It Means to Teach the Other When the Other Is the Self." *Callaloo* 17, no. 2 (1994): 432–438.

Henry J. Kaiser Family Foundation. "HIV/AIDS Policy Fact Sheet: African Americans and HIV/AIDS." February 2006. www.kff.org.

Hesse, Barnor. "Racialized Modernity: An Analytics of White Mythologies." *Ethnic and Racial Studies* 30, no. 4 (2007): 643–663.

Higginbotham, Evelyn Brooks. *Righteous Discontent: The Women's Movement in the Black Baptist Church, 1880–1920*. Cambridge: Harvard University Press, 1993.

Hine, Darlene Clark. "Rape and the Inner Lives of Black Women in the Middle West: Preliminary Thoughts on the Culture of Dissemblance." *Signs: Journal of Women and Culture and Society* 14, no. 4 (1989): 912–920. Reprinted in *Unequal Sisters: A Multicultural Reader in U.S. Women's History*, 2nd ed., edited by Vicki L. Ruiz and Ellen Carol Dubois. New York: Routledge, 1994.

Holland, Sharon. "Death in Black and White: A Reading of Marc Forster's *Monster's Ball*." *Signs* 31, no. 3 (2006): 785–813.

hooks, bell. *Black Looks: Race and Representation*. Boston: South End Press, 1992.

———. "The Oppositional Gaze: Black Female Spectators." In *The Feminism and Visual Culture Reader*, edited by Amelia Jones. London: Routledge, 2003.

———. *Teaching to Transgress: Education as the Practice of Freedom*. New York: Routledge, 1994.

Hope, Clover. "That Awkward Moment When . . . 'Awkward Black Girl' Blows Up." *Vibe*, April 17, 2012. http://www.vibe.com/article/awkward-moment-when-awkward-Black -girl-blows. Accessed July 22, 2012.

Hunter, Alberta. *Downhearted Blues: Live at the Cookery*. CD. Stuart Goldman Productions. 2001.

Hunter, Marcus Anthony, Marissa Guerrero, and Cathy J. Cohen. "Black Youth Sexuality: Established Paradigms and New Approaches." In *Black Sexualities: Probing Powers,*

Passions, Practices, and Policies, edited by Juan Battles and Sandra Barnes, 377–400. New Brunswick, N.J.: Rutgers University Press, 2010.

Hurbon, Laennec. "Vodou: A Faith for Individual, Family, and Community from Dieu Dans le Vaudou Haitien." *Callaloo* 15, no. 3 (1992): 787–796.

Hurston, Zora Neale. *Sweat.* Edited by Cheryl Wall. New Brunswick, N.J.: Rutgers University Press, 1997.

———. *Their Eyes Were Watching God.* New York: Harper Collins, 1937.

Izrael, Jimi. *The Denzel Principle: Why Black Women Can't Find Good Men.* New York: St. Martin's Press, 2010.

Jenkins, Candice M. *Private Lives, Proper Relations: Regulating Black Intimacy.* Minneapolis: University of Minnesota Press, 2007.

Johnson, Eric. "Nightline Face-Off: Why Can't a Successful Black Woman Find a Man?" *ABC News,* April 21, 2010. http://abcnews.go.com/Nightline/FaceOff/nightline-Black-women-single-marriage/story?id=10424979. Accessed May 7, 2010.

Jones, Charisse, and Kumea Shorter-Gooden. *Shifting: The Double Lives of Black Women in America.* New York: HarperCollins, 2003.

Jones, Joy. "Marriage Is for White People." *The Washington Post,* March 26, 2006. http://www.washingtonpost.com/wpdyn/content/article/2006/03/25/AR2006032500029.html. Accessed November 4, 2009.

Kaplan, Elaine Bell. *Not Our Kind of Girl: Unraveling Myths of Black Teenage Motherhood.* Berkeley: University of California Press, 1997.

King, Emily. *A Century of Movie Posters: From Silent to Art House.* Hauppauge, N.Y.: Barron's Educational Series, 2003.

King, J. L. *On the Down Low: A Journey into the Lives of "Straight" Black Men Who Sleep with Men.* New York: Broadway Books, 2004.

Kitwana, Bakari. *The Hip Hop Generation: Young Blacks and the Crisis in African American Culture.* New York: Basic Civitas, 2002.

Knowles, Beyoncé. *Beyoncé.* Sony. 2013.

Kwan, Samantha. "Framing the Fat Body: Contested Meanings between Government, Activists, and Industry." *Sociological Inquiry* 79, no. 1 (2009): 25–50.

Laine, Tarja. "'It's the Sense of Touch': Skin in the Making of Cinematic Consciousness." *Discourse* 29, no. 1 (2007): 35–48.

Lee, Helen Elaine. *The Serpent's Gift.* New York: Scribner/Simon and Schuster, 1994.

Lester, Toni. "Race, Sexuality and the Question of Multiple, Marginalized Identities in U.S. and European Discrimination Law." In *Gender Nonconformity, Race, and Sexuality: Charting the Connections,* edited by Toni Lester, 84–101. Madison: University of Wisconsin Press, 2003.

Levy, Ariel. *Female Chauvinist Pigs: Women and the Rise of Raunch Culture.* New York: Free Press, 2005.

Lewis, Linden, ed. *The Culture of Gender and Sexuality in the Caribbean.* Gainesville: University Press of Florida, 2003.

Lewis, Mel Michelle. "Pedagogy and the Sista' Professor: Teaching Black Queer Feminist Studies." In *Sexualities in Education: A Reader,* edited by Erica Meiners and Therese Quinn, 33–40. New York: Peter Lang, 2012.

Logan, Shirley Wilson. *"We Are Coming": The Persuasive Discourse of Nineteenth-Century Black Women.* Carbondale: Southern Illinois University Press, 1999.

Lorde, Audre. "Foreword." In *Wild Women in the Whirlwind: Afra-American Culture and the Contemporary Literary Renaissance,* edited by Joanne M. Braxton and N. McLaughlin, xi–xiii. New Brunswick, N.J.: Rutgers University Press, 1989.

———. *Sister Outsider: Essays and Speeches.* Trumansburg, N.Y.: Crossing Press, 1984.

Lovejoy, Meg. "Disturbances in the Social Body: Differences in Body Image and Eating Problems among African American and White Women." *Gender and Society* 15, no. 2 (2001): 239–261.

Lowenthal, Ira P. "Labor, Sexuality and the Conjugal Contract in Rural Haiti." In *Haiti—Today and Tomorrow: An Interdisciplinary Study,* edited by Charles R. Foster and Albert Valdman, 15–33. Lanham, Md.: University Press of America, 1984.

Lubiano, Wahneema. "Black Nationalism and Black Common Sense: Policing Ourselves and Others." In *The House That Race Built,* edited by Wahneema Lubiano, 232–252. New York: Vintage Books, 1998.

Luke, Nancy. "Age and Economic Asymmetries in the Sexual Relationships of Adolescent Girls in Sub-Saharan Africa." *Studies in Family Planning* 34, no. 2 (2003): 67–86.

Lundahl, Mets. "History as an Obstacle to Change: The Case of Haiti." *Journal of Interamerican Studies and World Affairs* 31, nos. 1–2 (1989): 1–21.

Malebranche, David J. "Bisexually Active Black Men in the United States and HIV: Acknowledging More than the 'Down Low.'" *Archives of Sexual Behavior* 37, no. 5 (2008): 810–816.

Maraj, Onika T. *Pink Friday.* CD. Cash Money Records/Motown Records. 2010.

———. *Pink Friday: Roman Reloaded.* MP3. Cash Money Records. 2011.

Mask, Mia. "Monster's Ball." *Film Quarterly* 58 (2004): 44–55.

McBride, Dwight A. *Why I Hate Abercrombie & Fitch: Essays on Race and Sexuality.* New York: New York University Press, 2005.

McClintock, Anne. *Imperial Leather: Race, Gender, and Sexuality in the Colonial Contest.* New York: Routledge University Press, 1995.

McCollough, Antia. "The Awkward Black Girl Lands ABC Show." *Amsterdam News.* October 22, 2012. http://www.amsterdamnews.com/testing/the-awkward-Black-girl-lands-abc-show/article_efd08824–1c65–11e2–8bde-0019bb2963f4.html. Accessed October 31, 2012.

McGuire, Danielle L. *At the Dark End of the Street: Black Women, Rape, and Resistance—A New History of the Civil Rights Movement from Rosa Parks to the Rise of Black Power.* New York: Alfred A. Knopf, 2010.

Mehta, Brinda. "Re-Creating Ayida-wèdo: Feminizing the Serpent in Lilas Desquiron's *Les Chemins De Loco-Miroir.*" *Callaloo* 25, no. 2 (2002): 654–670.

Melancon, Trimiko C. "Toward an Aesthetic of Transgression: Ann Allen Shockley's *Loving Her* and the Politics and Same-Gender Loving." *African American Review* 42, nos. 3–4 (2008): 643–657.

Meschke, Laurie L., Suzanne Bartholomae, and Shannon R. Zentall. "Adolescent Sexuality and Parent-Adolescent Processes: Promoting Healthy Teen Choices." *Family Relations* 49, no. 2 (2000): 143–154.

Milkie, Melissa. "Social Comparisons, Reflected Appraisals, and Mass Media: The Impact of Pervasive Beauty Images on Black and White Girls' Self-Concepts." *Social Psychology Quarterly* 62, no. 2 (1999): 190–210.

Millet, Gregorio, David Malebranche, Byron Mason, and Pilgrim Spikes. "Focusing 'Down Low': Bisexual Black Men, HIV Risk and Heterosexual Transmission." *Journal of the National Medical Association* 97, 7 Supplement (2005): 52S–59S.

Miller-Young, Mireille. "Hip Hop Honeys and Da Hustlaz: Black Sexualities in the New Hip-Hop Pornography." *Meridians: Feminism, Race, Transnationalism* 8, no. 1 (2008): 261–292.

Mills, Charles. *Blackness Visible: Essays on Philosophy and Race.* Ithaca, N.Y.: Cornell University Press, 1998.

———. *The Racial Contract.* Ithaca, N.Y.: Cornell University Press, 1997.

Mitchell, W. J. T. *What Do Pictures Want? The Lives and Loves of Images.* Chicago: University of Chicago Press, 2006.

Moore, Mignon R. *Invisible Families: Gay Identities, Relationships, and Motherhood among Black Women.* Berkeley: University of California Press, 2011.

Moore, Mignon, and P. Lindsay Chase-Lansdale. "Sexual Intercourse and Pregnancy among African American Girls in High-Poverty Neighborhoods: The Role of Family and Perceived Community Environment." *Journal of Marriage and the Family* 63, no. 4 (2001): 1146–1157.

Morgan, Jennifer L. *Laboring Women: Reproduction and Gender in New World Slavery.* Philadelphia: University of Pennsylvania Press, 2004.

Morrison, Toni. *Playing in the Dark: Whiteness and the Literary Imagination.* New York: Vintage Books, 1993.

Moynihan, Daniel Patrick. *The Negro Family: The Case for National Action.* Washington D.C.: Office of Policy Planning and Research, United States Department of Labor, 1965.

Mumford, Kevin. *Interzones: Black/White Sex Districts in Chicago and New York in the Early Twentieth Century.* New York: Columbia University Press, 1997.

National Public Radio. "Myth: HIV/AIDS Rate among Black Women Traced to 'Down Low' Black Men." *NPR*, October 16, 2009. http://www.npr.org/templates/story/story.php ?storyId=114237523.

Nestle, Joan, Riki Wilchins, and Clare Howell. *GenderQueer: Voices from Beyond the Sexual Binary.* New York: Alyson Books, 2002.

Nicholls, David. "Haiti: The Rise and Fall of Duvalierism." *Third World Quarterly* 8, no. 4 (1986): 1239–1252.

———. *Haiti in Caribbean Context: Ethnicity, Economy and Revolt.* New York: St. Martin's, 1985.

Olney, James. "'I Was Born': Slave Narratives, Their Status as Autobiography and as Literature." *Callaloo* 20 (Winter 1984): 46–73.

Ordover, Nancy. *American Eugenics: Race, Queer Anatomy, and the Science of Nationalism.* Minneapolis: University of Minnesota Press, 2003.

Pak, Ari. "Envisioning Futures of Black Female Sexualities." 2013. Unpublished essay in author's possession.

Parker, Sheila, Mimi Nichter, Mark Nichter, Nancy Vuckovic, Colette Sims, and Cheryl Ritenbaugh. "Body Image and Weight Concerns among African American and White Adolescent Females: Differences that Make a Difference." *Human Organization* 54 (1995): 103–114.

Patton, Cindy. *Last Served? Gendering the HIV Pandemic.* London: Taylor & Francis, 1994.

Paris Is Burning. Directed by Jennie Livingston. New York: Miramax, 2005.

Parks, Suzan-Lori. *Getting Mother's Body.* New York: Random House, 2003.

Pascoe, Peggy. "Miscegenation Law, Court Cases, and Ideologies of 'Race' in Twentieth-Century America." *Journal of American History* 83, no. 1 (1996): 44–69.

Passel, Jeffrey S., Wendy Wang, and Paul Taylor. "Marrying Out: One in Seven New U.S. Marriages Is Interracial or Interethnic." *Pew Research & Social Demographic Trends,* June 4, 2010. http://pewresearch.org/pubs/1616/american-marriage-interracial -interethnic. Accessed July 3, 2001.

Peck, Jamie. "Interview with Issa Rae, Creator and Star of *The Misadventures of Awkward Black Girl.*" August 15, 2012. http://crushable.com/entertainment/interview-issa-rae-the -misadventures-of-awkward-Black-girl-414/. Accessed September 7, 2012.

Perry, Imani. *Prophets of the Hood: Politics and Poetics in Hip Hop.* Durham, N.C.: Duke University Press, 2004.

Phelan, Peggy. *Unmarked: The Politics of Performance.* New York: Routledge Press, 1993.

Phillips, Lynn M. *Flirting with Danger: Young Women's Reflections on Sexuality and Domination.* New York: New York University Press, 2000.

Racine, Marie M. B., and Kathy Ogle. *Like the Dew that Waters the Grass: Words from Haitian Women.* Washington: EPICA, 1999.

Rae, Issa. "Black Folk Don't Like to Be Told They're Not Black." *Huffington Post,* August 4, 2011. http://www.huffingtonpost.com/issa-rae/Black-folk-dont-movie_b_912660.html. Accessed August 13, 2012.

———. "How Awkward Black Girl Raised over $44,000 through Kickstarter." *Huffington Post*. August 10, 2011. http://www.huffingtonpost.com/issa-rae/kickstarter-awkward -Black-girl_b_922966.html. Accessed August 12, 2012.

———. "How to Write a Wildly Successful Web Series." *Huffington Post*. September 15, 2011. http://www.huffingtonpost.com/issa-rae/how-to-write-a-wildly-suc_b_964048.html. Accessed July 19, 2012.

Rainwater, Lee, and William Yancey. *The Moynihan Report and the Politics of Controversy.* Boston: Massachusetts Institute of Technology Press, 1967.

Renda, Mary A. *Taking Haiti: Military Occupation and the Culture of U.S. Imperialism, 1915–1940.* Chapel Hill: University of North Carolina Press, 2001.

"Restavèk Campaign." National Coalition for Haitian Rights, May 1, 2007. http://www.nchr .org/nchr/hrp/restavek/overview.htm.

Rhode, Deborah, and Annette Lawson. *The Politics of Pregnancy: Adolescent Sexuality and Public Policy.* New Haven, Conn.: Yale University Press, 1993.

Rhodes, Gary D. "The Origin and Development of the American Moving Picture Poster." *Film History* 19, no. 3 (1997): 228–246.

Robinson, Eugene. *Disintegration: The Splintering of Black America.* New York: Doubleday, 2010.

Rose, Tricia. *The Hip Hop Wars: What We Talk about When We Talk about Hip Hop and Why It Matters.* New York: Basic Civitas, 2008.

Ross, Rick. *Rich Forever.* Digital Recording. Maybach Music Group, Def Jam, and Warner Bros. Records. 2012.

Rothblum, Esther, and Sondra Solovay, eds. *The Fat Studies Reader.* New York: New York University Press, 2009.

Rothman, Lily. "Issa Rae of *Awkward Black Girl* on the Future of the Web Series." *Time*, July 10, 2012. http://entertainment.time.com/2012/07/10/issa-rae-of-awkward-Black -girl-on-the-future-of-the-web-series/. Accessed August 13, 2012.

Rowe, Aimee Carrillo. "Feeling in the Dark: Empathy, Whiteness, and Miscege-Nation in *Monster's Ball*." *Hypatia* 22, no. 2 (2007): 122–142.

Rowell, Charles. "An Interview with Helen Elaine Lee." *Callaloo* 23 (2000): 139–150.

Sapphire. *Push.* New York: Vintage Books, 1996.

Saguy, Abigail C., and Kevin Riley. "Weighing Both Sides: Morality, Mortality, and Framing Contests over Obesity." *Journal of Health Politics, Policy and Law* 30, no. 5 (2005): 869–921.

Sarlio-Lähteenkorva, Sirpa. "Weight Loss and Quality of Life among Obese People." *Social Indicators Research* 54, no. 3 (2001): 329–354.

Schafer, Markus H., and Kenneth F. Ferraro. "The Stigma of Obesity: Does Perceived Weight Discrimination Affect Identity and Physical Health?" *Social Psychology Quarterly* 74, no. 1 (2011): 76–97.

Schecter, Patricia. *Ida B. Wells-Barnett and American Reform, 1880–1930.* Chapel Hill: University of North Carolina Press, 2001.

Schwarz, A. B. Christa. *Gay Voices of the Harlem Renaissance.* Bloomington: Indiana University Press, 2003.

Scott, Jill. *Experience: Jill Scott 826+.* CD. Hidden Beach Recordings. 2001.

Scott, Michelle R. "Alberta Hunter: 'She Had the World in a Jug, with the Stopper in Her Hand.'" In *Tennessee Women: Their Lives and Times*, edited by Sarah Wilkerson Freeman and Beverly G. Bond, 99–101. Athens: University of Georgia Press, 2009.

———. *Blues Empress in Black Chattanooga: Bessie Smith and the Emerging Urban South.* Urbana: University of Illinois Press, 2008.

Sharpley-Whiting, T. Denean. *Pimp's Up, Ho's Down: Hip Hop's Hold on Young Women.* New York: New York University Press, 2008.

Shaw, Andrea Elizabeth. *The Embodiment of Disobedience: Fat Black Women's Unruly Political Bodies.* Lanham, Md.: Lexington Books, 2006.

Shaw, Stephanie J. *What a Woman Ought to Be and to Do: Black Professional Women Workers during the Jim Crow Era.* Chicago: University of Chicago Press, 1996.

Simon, William, and John H. Gagnon. "Sexual Scripts: Permanence and Change." *Archives of Sexual Behavior* 15, no. 2 (1986): 97–120.

Simpson, George Eaton. "The Vodun Service in Northern Haiti." *American Anthropologist* 42, no. 2, part 1 (1940): 236–254.

Somerville, Siobhan B. *Queering the Color Line: Race and the Invention of Homosexuality in American Culture.* Durham, N.C.: Duke University Press, 2000.

Solorzano, Daniel, Miguel Ceja, and Tara Yosso. "Critical Race Theory, Racial Microaggressions, and Campus Racial Climate: The Experiences of African American College Students." *Journal of Negro Education* 69, nos. 1–2 (2000): 60–73.

Souljah, Sister. *No Disrespect.* New York: Vintage Books, 1994.

———. *The Coldest Winter Ever.* New York: Pocket Star Books, 1999.

Southgate, Martha. *Third Girl from the Left.* New York: Houghton Mifflin, 2005.

Southerners on New Ground (SONG). "Vision, Mission and History." http:// southernersonnewground.org/about/vision-mission-history/.

Spillers, Hortense. "Interstices: A Small Drama of Words." In *Pleasure and Danger: Exploring Female Sexuality,* edited by Carole S. Vance, 73–100.London: Pandora, 1992.

Springer, Kimberly. "Divas, Evil Black Bitches, and Bitter Black Women: African American Women in Post-Feminist and Post-Civil Rights Popular Culture." In *Interrogating Post-Feminism: Gender and the Politics of Popular Culture,* edited by Yvonne Tasker and Diane Negra, 249–276. Durham, N.C.: Duke University Press, 2007.

Springer, Sarah. "'Scandal' Updates Image of Black Women on Network Television." *CNN,* March 25 2012. http://inamerica.blogs.cnn.com/2012/05/25/scandal-updates-image-of -Black-women-on-network-television/. Accessed June 8, 2012.

Springer, Sarah, and Sarah Edwards. "'Awkward Black Girl' Creator Issa Rae Responds to Racism." *CNN,* April 24, 2012. http://inamerica.blogs.cnn.com/2012/04/24/awkward -Black-girl-creator-issa-rae-responds-to-racism. Accessed July 22, 2012.

Stallings, L. H. *Mutha' Is Half a Word: Intersections of Folklore, Vernacular, Myth, and Queerness in Black Female Culture.* Columbus: Ohio State University Press, 2007.

Stephens, Dionne P., and Layli D. Phillips. "Freaks, Gold Diggers, Divas, and Dykes: The Sociohistorical Development of Adolescent African American Women's Sexual Scripts." *Sexuality and Culture: An Interdisciplinary Quarterly* 7, no. 1 (2003): 287–299.

Suvin, Darko. "Estrangement and Cognition." In *Speculations on Speculation: Theories of Science Fiction,* edited by James Gunn and Matthew Candelaria, 23–35. Toronto: Scarecrow Press, 2005.

Taylor, Frank C., and Gerald Cook. *Alberta Hunter: A Celebration in Blues.* New York: McGraw-Hill, 1987.

Thompson, Becky Wangsgaard. "'A Way Outa No Way': Eating Problems among African-American, Latina, and White Women." *Gender and Society* 6 (December 1992): 546–561.

Thompson, Lisa B. *Beyond the Black Lady: Sexuality and the New African American Middle Class.* Chicago: University of Illinois Press, 2007.

Thorpe, Rochella. "'A House Where Queers Go': African American Lesbian Nightlife in Detroit, 1940–1975." In *Inventing Lesbian Cultures in America,* edited by Ellen Lewin, 40–61. Boston: Beacon Press, 1996.

Three 6 Mafia. *Most Known Hits.* CD. Sony. 2005.

Tolman Deborah L. *Dilemmas of Desire: Teenage Girls Talk about Sexuality.* Cambridge: Harvard University Press, 2005.

Treichler, Paula A. *How to Have Theory in an Epidemic: Cultural Chronicles of AIDS.* Durham, N.C.: Duke University Press, 1999.

Trouillot, Michel-Rolph. *Haiti, State against Nation: The Origins and Legacy of Duvalierism.* New York: Monthly Review, 1990.

"Turkey Scraps Virginity Tests." *BBC News,* February 28, 2002. http://news.bbc.co .uk/2/hi/europe/1845784.stm.

Upchurch, Dawn M., William Mason, Yasamin Kusunoki, and Maria Johnson Kriechbaum. "Social and Behavioral Determinants of Self-Reported STD among Adolescents." *Perspectives on Sexual and Reproductive Health* 36, no. 6 (2004): 276-87.

"V Exclusive: Vibe Gets to Know the Creator of YouTube's Hit 'Awkward Black Girl.'" *Vibe,* August 4, 2011. http://www.vibe.com/article/v-exclusive-vibe-gets-know-creator -youtubes-hit-awkward-Black-girl. Accessed July 22, 2012.

Valleroy, Linda A., et al. "HIV Prevalence and Associated Risks in Young Men Who Have Sex with Men." *Journal of the American Medical Association* 284, no. 2 (2000): 198–204.

Vinovskis, Maris. An *"Epidemic" of Adolescent Pregnancy? Some Historical and Policy Considerations.* New York: Oxford University Press, 1988.

Wanzo, Rebecca. *The Suffering Will Not Be Televised: African American Women and Sentimental Political Storytelling.* Albany: State University of New York Press, 2009.

Watkins, S. Craig. *Hip Hop Matters: Politics, Pop Culture, and the Struggle for the Soul of a Movement.* Boston: Beacon Press, 2005.

Waugh, Debra Riggin. "Delicious, Forbidden: An Interview with Shay Youngblood." *Lambda Book Report* 6, no. 2 (1997): 1, 6–7.

Weaver, Joshua R. "7 Must-Watch Black Web Series." *The Root,* August 9, 2012. http:// www.theroot.com/articles/culture/2012/08/best_black_web_series_the_roots_favorites .html. Accessed September 1, 2012.

Webb, Tammy T., E. Joan Looby, and Regina Fults-McMurtery. "African American Men's Perceptions of Body Figure Attractiveness: An Acculturation Study." *Journal of Black Studies* 34, no. 3 (2004): 370–385.

West, Cornel. *Race Matters.* New York: Vintage Books, 1994.

White, Deborah G. *Too Heavy a Load: Black Women in Defense of Themselves, 1894–1994.* New York: W.W. Norton, 1999.

White, Renée. T. *Putting Risk in Perspective: Black Teenage Lives in the Era of AIDS.* Lanham, Md.: Rowman and Littlefield, 1999.

Wilderson, Frank B. III. *Red, White & Black: Cinema and the Structure of U.S. Antagonisms.* Durham, N.C.: Duke University Press, 2010.

Witt, Doris. "What (N)ever Happened to Aunt Jemima: Eating Disorders, Fetal Rights, and Black Female Appetite in Contemporary American Culture." In *Skin Deep, Spirit Strong: The Black Female Body in American Culture,* edited by Kimberly Wallace-Sanders, 239–262. Ann Arbor: University of Michigan Press, 2002.

Wright, David. "Streetwise Urban Fiction." *Library Journal* 131, no. 12 (2006): 42–45.

Wright, Laura. "Casting the Bones of Willa Mae Beede: Passing and Performativity in Suzan-Lori Parks's *Getting Mother's Body.*" *Tulsa Studies in Women's Literature* 30, no. 1 (2011): 141–157.

Yancey, Antronette K., Joanne Leslie, and Emily K. Abel. "Obesity at the Crossroads: Feminist and Public Health Perspectives." *Signs* 31, no. 2 (2006): 425–443.

Youngblood, Shay. *Soul Kiss.* New York: Riverhead, 1997.

Zéphir, Flore. *Haitian Immigrants in Black America: A Sociological and Sociolinguistic Portrait.* Westport, Conn.: Bergin & Garvey, 1996.

Contributors

JOANNE "JODI" BRAXTON, author of *Sometimes I Think of Maryland*, is a mother, poet, playwright, scholar, university professor, ordained campus minister, and founder of the Braxton Institute. She has been a fellow at the Wellesley Center for Research on Women and the W. E.B. Du Bois Institute and a senior Fulbright professor in Europe. Braxton edited *The Collected Poetry of Paul Laurence Dunbar* and a series of biographies of women of color writers. Her own poems have appeared in *Black Box, Black World, Callaloo, Caprice, Chrysalis, Cordite Review, Daesin, Journal of Black Poetry, Redstart,* and *Sunbury* and as broadsides from the Furious Flower Poetry Center and the Folger Shakespeare Library. Braxton's book *Black Women Writing Autobiography* is a foundational text for the field. She is Frances L. and Edwin L. Cummings professor at the college of William and Mary. Joanne Braxton is currently at work on a memoir.

KIMBERLY JUANITA BROWN, a PhD graduate of Yale University, is an assistant professor in the Department of English at Northeastern University. Her book, *The Repeating Body: Slavery's Visual Resonance in the Contemporary,* examines the gendered manifestations of slavery's memory and is forthcoming from Duke University Press. She is an interdisciplinary scholar working at the intersection of feminist theory, literature, and visual culture studies (particularly photography). Her scholarship has been supported by research grants from the Andrew Mellon and Woodrow Wilson Foundations and the Ruth Landes Memorial Research Fund. She has also held fellowships and visiting appointments at Rice University and Brown University's Pembroke Center for Teaching and Research on Women. Her next project explores the visuality of indifference in documentary photographs in the *New York Times.*

ERIN D. CHAPMAN, a graduate of the doctoral program in African American Studies and History at Yale University, is a professor at George Washington University.

She is the author of *Prove It on Me: New Negroes, Sex, and Popular Culture in the 1920s* (Oxford University Press, 2012). Her research has been supported by the Ford Foundation, the Mellon Foundation, and the American Association of University Women. She is currently working on a second book entitled *Making Freedom Real: Gender and Emancipation in the African American Imaginary, 1865–1965*.

ARIANE CRUZ is an assistant professor in the Department of Women's Studies at The Pennsylvania State University. She holds a doctorate from the University of California, Berkeley in African Diaspora Studies with a designated emphasis in women, gender, and sexuality. Her teaching at Penn State includes classes on feminist visual culture, racialized sexuality, and representations of race, gender, and sexuality. Her research interests include images of black female sexuality, black visuality, and pornography. She is currently working on a manuscript exploring black women, BDSM, and pornography. Her recent publications appear in *Camera Obscura, The Feminist Porn Book: The Politics of Producing Pleasure* (The Feminist Press at CUNY), *Hypatia*, and *Women & Performance*. Other publications are forthcoming in *Feminist Studies* and *Pornography: Contemporary Perspectives* (Rowman & Littlefield).

SANDRA C. DUVIVIER is an assistant professor of English at Bronx Community College, where she teaches courses in African American and Caribbean literature, critical race studies, gender and sexuality studies, and writing. She is currently working on her book *Beyond Nation, Beyond Diaspora: Mapping Transnational Black American Women's Literature*. Her articles have appeared in *Callaloo, JENdA, The Journal of African American History*, and *MaComère*, and she has published essays in *A House Divided: The Antebellum Slavery Debates in America, 1776–1785* and *Pearl Cleage and Free Womanhood: Essays on Her Prose Works*.

K. T. EWING is a doctoral candidate in the history department at the University of Memphis. She is a member of the Association for the Study of African American Life and History, Southern Association for Women Historians, and the American Historical Association. Her research interests include African American history, women and gender studies, and the influence of blues culture in American society. Currently she is working on a dissertation about the life of Alberta Hunter, a twentieth-century blues and cabaret singer from Memphis, Tennessee.

JOHANNA X. K. GARVEY is an associate professor of English at Fairfield University, where she was founding co-director of Women's Studies and Black Studies, and is chair of the English Department. Her areas of expertise include literature of the African Diaspora, especially in the United States and the Caribbean; gender and sexuality studies; and global women's literature in a cultural studies framework. She has published articles in *Callaloo, The Journal of Commonwealth and Postcolonial Literature,* and *Textual Practice* and has published essays in *Emerging Perspectives on Maryse Condé, Black Imagination and the Middle Passage,* and *Black Liberation in the Americas.* She is currently working on three books: *The Sides of the Sea: Caribbean Women Writing Diaspora,* a book on Black women writers and New York City, and a book-length study of Afro-Caribbean author Dionne Brand.

MELISSA HARRIS-PERRY is Presidential Chair of Politics and International Affairs at Wake Forest University. She is also founding director of the Anna Julia Cooper Project in Gender, Race and Politics in the South. She hosts MSNBC's *Melissa Harris-Perry.* She is the author of *Barbershops, Bibles and BET: Everyday Talk and Black Political Thought* and *Sister Citizen: Shame, Stereotypes and Black Women in America.* Harris-Perry writes monthly columns for both *The Nation* and *Essence* magazine.

ESTHER L. JONES is the E. Franklin Frazier Professor of African American Literature, Theory, and Culture and assistant professor of English at Clark University in Worcester, Massachusetts. Her research areas include Black female subject formation, Black women's literatures and feminisms, and black women and popular culture. She is the author of "On the Real: Agency, Abuse, and the Politics of Sexualized Violence in Rihanna's 'Russian Roulette'" (*African American Review,* forthcoming) and "What's My Name? Reading Rihanna's Autobiographical Acts" in the edited collection *Rihanna: Bad Girl, Done Best* (2012). Her current book project, *Telling: Black Women Narrate the Sexual Self,* explores black women's coming-of-age narratives within the matrix of reproductive health, sexuality, and motherhood.

MEL MICHELLE LEWIS is an assistant professor of Women, Gender, and Sexuality Studies and affiliate faculty in Africana Studies at Goucher College in Baltimore, Maryland. Dr. Lewis also serves on the Governing Council of the National Women's Studies Association as the Lesbian Caucus chair. Her research focuses on Black queer feminist women, pedagogy as performance, and feminist inquiries at the intersections of race, gender, and sexuality. Her publications include "Pedagogy and the Sista' Professor: Teaching Black Queer Feminist Studies" in *Sexualities in Education: A Reader* (Peter Lang), and "Body of Knowledge: Black Queer Feminist Pedagogy, Praxis, and Embodied Text" (*Journal of Lesbian Studies*).

MAHALIAH AYANA LITTLE is a 2013 graduate of Spelman College. As a United Negro College Fund/Mellon Mays Undergraduate Fellow, she has conducted scholarly research at Emory University and the University of California, Los Angeles. She has presented at the Southeastern Regional Mellon Mays Undergraduate

Fellow Conference at the University of Texas, San Antonio; the Summer Humanities Institute at Emory University; and the Summer Programs for Undergraduate Research Conference at UCLA. She is interested in contemporary African American studies and gender inquiries, especially how media and popular culture intersect to mold the minds of twenty-first-century Black youth. She plans to enter a doctoral program in African American and/or Gender Studies in the fall of 2014.

TRIMIKO MELANCON is an assistant professor of English, African American Studies, and Women's Studies at Loyola University New Orleans. She has been a Woodrow Wilson Career Enhancement Fellow, an Andrew W. Mellon Fellow, a Frederick Douglass Teaching Fellow, and a J. William Fulbright Scholar of American Literature and American Studies in Berlin, Germany. She was the inaugural visiting scholar and fellow at Emory University's James Weldon Johnson Institute for Advanced Interdisciplinary Studies and the inaugural postdoctoral fellow at the Anna Julia Cooper Project on Gender, Race, and Politics in the South at Tulane University. Her book *Unbought and Unbossed: Transgressive Black Women, Sexuality, and Representation* examines representations of black women in the American literary and cultural imagination through the politics and tropes of sexuality. Her scholarship has also appeared in *African American Review, Callaloo, Reconstruction*, and the *Journal of Popular Culture*, among other venues.

COURTNEY J. PATTERSON is a doctoral candidate in the Department of African American Studies at Northwestern University. She holds a bachelor's degree in Afro-American Studies from the University of Pennsylvania and a master's degree in African American Studies from Northwestern. Her dissertation, "Fat Chance, Slim Chance: Identity, Culture, and a Politic of Fatness," studies fat black women and the political construction of body size through lenses of popular culture, fashion, and sexuality to understand how their sociocultural experiences may frame, define, and regulate their identity. Her research interests include Black women's sociopolitical histories and realities; fat studies; race, class, and gender; sexuality; cultural sociology; medical sociology; and HIV/AIDS. She is author of "Plus Size Black and Latino Women: The Implications of Body Shape and Size for Apparel Design," in *Designing Apparel for Consumers: The Impact of Body Shape and Size* (2014), and is second author of "Precious: Black Women, Neighborhood HIV/AIDS Risk, and Institutional Buffers" in the *Du Bois Review*.

CHERISE A. POLLARD, PH.D., is an associate professor of English at West Chester University of Pennsylvania and the director of the African and African American Literature Minor. A NEH Fellow who participated in the Summer Institute in Contemporary African American Literature, Pollard has published several articles on contemporary black women poets and writers. Her critical essays have appeared in edited anthologies (*New Thoughts on the Black Arts Movement, Reclaiming Home, Remembering Motherhood, Rewriting History: African American and Afro-Caribbean Women's Literature in the Twentieth Century*) and peer-reviewed journals (*FORECAAST (Forum for European Contributions to African American Studies)* and *The Langston Hughes Review*). She has also published reader's guides for two of Barbara Chase-Riboud's novels, *Sally Hemings* and *The President's Daughter*. A Cave Canem Fellow, Pollard has published multiple poems in a variety of journals and anthologies, including *5 AM, African American Review, PoemMemoirStory, Affilia: The Journal of Women in Social Work,* and *The Healing Muse.*

AYANA K. WEEKLEY is an assistant professor in Women's and Gender Studies at Grand Valley State University in Michigan. Her research and teaching interests include race, gender, and the HIV/AIDS epidemic; black feminist studies; and black sexualities. Her current manuscript, *Now That's a Good Girl: Discourses of African American Women, HIV/AIDS, and Respectability,* draws upon black feminist theory, black queer studies, and HIV/AIDS cultural studies to examine discursive representations of African American women and the HIV/AIDS epidemic. She is the author of "Don't We All Want the Same Things? Race, Feminist Theory, and the Feminist Classroom," which appears in *Transformations: The Journal of Inclusive Scholarship and Pedagogy,* and she presents regularly at the National Women's Studies Association.

Index

ABC News Nightly, 79–80

Abdur-Rahman, Aliyyah, 26n19

ABG. See Misadventures of Awkward Black Girl, The (ABG) (web series)

abortion, 68n15, 138; in *Getting Mother's Body,* 161, 162. *See also* pregnancy

abstinence-only education, 51–52

Academy Awards, 13, 157n17, 157n22

adolescent sexuality, 28; black female precocity stereotypes about, 59–61, 62; coming out and, 192; family-state management of, 60–61, 63, 65–68, 68nn13, 15; in *Fledgling,* 57, 63–65; of Precious Jones, 36–37, 117, 119–121, 123; pregnancy and, 34, 36, 59–61, 63–65, 117, 119–120, 123; research on, 31–32, 34–37, 38, 39n21, 51–52; during slavery, 30–31; in *Soul Kiss,* 167–168; Tolman on, 34–37, 51–52. *See also* sexuality; teenage pregnancy

Afra-American aesthetic, 192

African American Cultural Center (Yale), 192–193

African Americans. *See under* blacks

African American teenage girls. *See* black female teenagers

African identity, 43; of Professor Deborah, 47

Afro-Diaspora dance traditions, ix

age: Dr. Mariposa and, 43; identity intersections with, 38. *See also* adolescent sexuality

agency: of black women characters in rape fantasy films, 142–143; of Haitian women, 129–130, 134, 135, 139; in *Third Girl from the Left,* 174

AIDS. *See* HIV/AIDS

Alberta Hunter Papers, 107

Alexander, Bryant Keith, 45

Alexander, M. Jacqui, 4

Anatomy of a Murder (film), 14

Anderson, Marian, 108

Angelou, Maya, 193

Arnheim, Rudolph, 20

asexuality, 52

assimilationism, 100

Atlanta University Center (AUC), 90

aunt figures: in *Getting Mother's Body,* 161–162; in *Po Man's Child,* 170–172, 174, 176; in *Soul Kiss,* 167, 169, 176. *See also* families; mothers/motherhood

authenticated black female sexuality on *ABG,* 6, 7, 74, 76–81, 83

authenticity, 2, 193–194; of masculinity, 92; of *Pariah,* 192; in urban fiction, 113, 114, 125nn1, 2; visibility and, 162

awkward epithet, 74, 75–77, 83, 85n16. *See also Misadventures of Awkward Black Girl, The (ABG)* (web series)

Azoulay, Ariella, 143, 156n9

Baartman, Saartjie (Hottentot Venus), vii–viii, xi

baby fat, 27, 28

baby f(ph)at, 29–30. *See also* body size; f(ph)at black female teenagers

215

CPSIA information can be obtained at www.ICGtesting.com
Printed in the USA
BVOW07s1431150115

383357BV00001B/7/P